Marketing Strategies *for* Nurse Managers

A Guide for Developing and Implementing a Nursing Marketing Plan

Vi Kunkle, RN, MSN

Faculty, Nursing Administration Masters Program
Bradley University
Peoria, Illinois

Clinical Instructor
College of Nursing
University of Illinois at Chicago
Chicago, Illinois

AN ASPEN PUBLICATION®
Aspen Publishers, Inc.
Rockville, Maryland
1990

Library of Congress Cataloging-in-Publication Data

Kunkle, Vi.
Marketing strategies for nurse managers: a guide for
developing and implementing a nursing marketing plan/ by Vi Kunkle.
p. cm.
Includes bibliographical references.
ISBN: 0-8342-0110-0
1. Nursing services--Marketing. I. Title.
RT86.7.K86   1989   362.1'73'0688--dc20   89-17683
CIP

Editorial Services: Mary Beth Roesser
Lisa J. McCullough

Library of Congress Catalog Card Number: 89-17683
ISBN: 0-8342-0110-0

Printed in the United States of America

1 2 3 4 5

This book is dedicated to my wonderful children, Christy and Julie Kunkle, and to my parents, who are always there for me.

Table of Contents

Special Note

Every effort has been made to ensure the accuracy of calculation in the tables, figures, and exhibits of this book. However, some inconsistencies exist because of rounding of numbers and using multiple reference sources that present the data in different ways.

Foreword

Vi Kunkle's book *Marketing Strategies for Nurse Managers* makes a very important contribution not only to nursing but to the health care field as a whole. The book responds to two increasingly clear facts about the competitive health care marketplace.

1. Success comes to organizations who know how to build volume across their multiple businesses.
2. Line managers make marketing.

SUCCESS COMES TO THOSE WHO KNOW HOW TO BUILD VOLUME ACROSS THEIR MULTIPLE BUSINESS LINES

Hospital leaders are realizing that under the umbrella *Hospital,* there are in fact many distinct businesses. The surgery business is distinct from the psychiatry service business, which is distinct from the emergency service business, etc. Each is distinct because it has different customers that make choices in distinctive ways. It follows that the more the individual businesses flourish, the more the hospital as a whole will flourish. Hospitals need leaders at the helms of each of the business lines who are capable marketing managers.

The likely candidates for the role of "growing the businesses" are nursing managers already in place.

In the past, nursing managers were responsible for clinical care, period. In recent years, their role has been expanded to include financial management. In the new competitive era, nursing managers will take on a third important responsibility. With this third role, nursing managers will become general managers. Not only will they be responsible for the quality of the product and for controlling expenses, they will also be responsible for satisfying customers and building volume.

LINE MANAGERS MAKE MARKETING

When one studies successful services all around the country, one usually finds at the helm of the service a market-oriented line manager. Most often, these line managers come from a clinical background, either nursing, physical therapy, pharmacy, etc. This should not come as any surprise. Clinicians have had the opportunity to know the health care business inside and out. They are used to working in collaboration with physicians, and they are in touch on a day-to-day basis with the needs of patients. In fact, with more formal training, clinical managers make excellent candidates for marketing positions.

To say that every line manager is a marketer is not a euphemism. It is not like saying every employee is a marketer. Marketing is more than smile training. It is a set of skills, not a type of motivation.

Vi Kunkle's book lays out the concepts and skills that nursing managers will need to seize the opportunities before them. It brims with a subdued excitement at the vision of the possibilities for nursing. She does not make marketing one more responsibility to be piled on an already heavy plate. She presents marketing as an integrating mind set and cluster of skills that will make current burdens lighter. With these skills, the nursing profession will become more important and powerful than ever.

Terrence J. Rynne
President
Rynne Marketing Group
Evanston, IL

Foreword

As the context of the delivery of health care services undergoes rapid evolution, nursing must continually redefine itself. In the past decade, the acute care segment of the health care industry has accommodated significant changes in the environment: the payment for services has declined and the sources of patients have shifted; new technology has been introduced for both diagnosis and treatment; and shortages have appeared in the supply of adequately trained manpower in some areas. The result has been a marked intensification in competition among health care providers for patients. In response, planners and marketing executives have worked to reposition their institutions to a more customer oriented view.

Nursing has, to varying degrees, kept pace with these changes. It is the message of this book that nursing must play a key role in administration as a member of the health care management team. This book provides a much needed introduction to the art and practice of marketing from the point of view of nursing management. In particular, it makes nursing administrators, practitioners, and educators aware of

- the context of physician and patient satisfaction in their own daily professional lives
- the role of the market positioning of services in relationship to other providers
- the research tools that are available to identify and measure sources of satisfaction and other factors influencing care choices
- the promotional vehicles that have proven both effective and acceptable in the health care field

Since nursing, along with medicine, is basic to the provision of health care, it will also be at the center of developing the innovations in health care delivery and clinical practice that will be the hallmarks of the 90s.

Tomorrow's nursing professionals need to acquire the awareness and the technical skills that will permit them to forge alliances with the medical staff and administration, particularly the planning and marketing departments. An understanding of the role of marketing and of strategic thinking in nursing is crucial to the success of tomorrow's nursing manager.

J. Christopher Newman
Assistant Vice President
Corporate Planning and Market Research
Rush-Presbyterian-St. Luke's Medical Center
Chicago, Illinois

Preface

Marketing is a method of management that is not unlike the nursing process. Nurses are experts in the inductive process of gathering data, analyzing data, formulating a diagnosis, developing and implementing a plan, and then monitoring the results. Marketing is a similar process. This book was written specifically for nurse administrators, directors, nurse managers, nurse educators, home health directors, staff development managers, product line managers, special project nurses, and clinical specialists. The principles presented here are applicable to nurses in other settings such as consultants, clinic managers, and nurses in private practice.

It is anticipated that this book will be used in the following capacities:

1. method of organizing processes and systems in the nursing organization, maximizing staff participation in these processes
2. business approach to planning and organizing activities in nursing
3. customer-oriented conceptual framework that actually drives departmental goals and objectives
4. stimulus for the development and implementation of innovative and competitive programs
5. guide to the development of nursing marketing plans
6. reference for students interested in marketing in nursing

Last, this book was developed to add to the literature available on nursing marketing. Additionally, the book has historical value. The discussions of the nursing supply problems, economy, and social conditions influencing nursing are documentaries of what is as the year 1990 approaches.

Acknowledgments

Many thanks go to Gary Kaatz, Peter MacDonald, and Diane Biondi for helping me along the way.

Introduction

The market-based planning model as an approach to decision making has evolved in hospitals with the increased emphasis on operating hospitals as a business. The model, which is borrowed from industry and big business, is effective in competitive environments and conditions of oversupply. The application of the marketing model to nursing is appropriate because nursing is the largest department in hospitals and because nursing interfaces more directly and more frequently with the customers of the hospital.

The same basic model is appropriately applied to nursing education and to change strategies in an organization. Specific benefits of using market-based planning include

- augmentation of the organization's strategic plan
- integration of decentralized departments
- increased morale, productivity, and teamwork in the department
- provision of a united nursing effort
- facilitation of innovation
- facilitation of customer satisfaction
- facilitation of appropriate program dissolution
- provision of a driving force for nursing objectives, budgets, and the use of human resources

Although marketing strategies in services have been used for more than 20 years, it is only in the last decade that a defined marketing function has been integrated into hospital organizational structure. Further, it has been only most recently that the marketing function has appeared in nursing organizational structure. Although many articles appear in the literature on the application of marketing to nursing, the focus is application to certain programs. A research base is needed to determine the long-range applicability of the marketing model to the organization of nursing in health care institutions. Complete application involves use of the model to drive the nursing processes and function, integration of the marketing function in the organizational structure, and reorganization based on identified consumer demand for services and the organization's capability to meet the demand.

The capacity and the versatility of nursing to adapt and change in response to the environment are affirmed in the stormy history of the profession. The effective use of the marketing model will produce a change in the response of nursing to prevailing economic and social conditions. Likewise, the change in nursing's response will improve the status, image, and identity of the profession as well as further the efforts to become colleagues with business and professional counterparts.

Although this book includes topics in health care marketing, it is specifically about marketing in nursing. Chapter 1 provides the groundwork by describing the conditions that brought about the evolution of marketing in service firms, specifically hospitals. Further, it examines regulatory influences that make marketing in hospitals different than in pure, market-driven firms. The chapter concludes with a discussion of how the nurse functions as a microlevel marketing agent for the hospital.

In Chapter 2, *marketing* is defined as a basic model applicable to services. The foundation of the marketing plan is presented as the mission, and because clients, customers, or consumers are the foci of all marketing efforts, a discussion of buyer behavior is included.

Since competitive positioning in the marketplace is crucial to any marketing plan, considerable space is devoted to this topic in Chapter 3. Additionally, an ongoing marketing program for nursing is presented as a mechanism to improve the image and perceptions of nursing in the mind of nursing's three primary customers: patients, nurses, and physicians.

The market-based planning process is outlined in Chapter 4, focusing heavily on the use of environmental assessments to determine market demand and organizational capability to meet the demand. The data from the environmental assessments and the analysis of strengths, weaknesses, opportunities, and threats (SWOTS) are combined to produce a profile that can be compared to obtaining a nursing diagnosis.

Chapter 5 discusses how the marketing objectives are developed and how the marketing plan is used for promotion. Monitoring is presented as a method of controlling outcomes.

The nurse manager is at the critical juncture between the nursing strategic plan and those who will carry it out. Chapter 6 discusses the role of the nurse manager as a facilitator of this process. The chapter also discusses marketing at the nursing unit level.

The business plan is presented in detail as a method of organizing and presenting the nursing department strategic plan for approval. Based on the justifications, cost benefits, and marketing strategy presented in the business plan, marketing objectives are approved. Chapter 7 presents product lines and elements of the business plan.

Because the shortage of nurses is one of the most critical marketing problems for hospitals today, Chapter 8 departs somewhat from the nursing department marketing plan to discuss why marketing objectives to recruit nurses are not successful. The chapter explores nurse supply issues from both a service and an education perspective. With economics being the major determinant in the supply of nurses, the chapter concludes with a discussion from a marketing prospective of how nursing education can survive the losses.

Marketing principles are increasingly being applied to programs for social change. Chapter 9 briefly touches on this concept, using the modification of employee behavior as an example.

Appendix A shows a business plan for a new nursing unit, and Appendix B shows a business plan for a home care program. The purpose of presenting both is to show how the elements of the business plan are adapted to fit a specific situation.

Today, the extent to which marketing is developed in nursing ranges from the use of marketing to promote programs to the establishment of nursing marketing positions. Although the nursing literature abounds with articles on marketing programs, future writings on marketing in nursing could include research on the effectiveness of product lines and their relation to marketing in nursing as well as the qualifications and effectiveness of nursing marketing positions. A good research base on marketing in nursing is needed. It is anticipated that this book will be an initial contribution to that base.

Chapter 1

Marketing: An Alternative Approach to Decision Making

The use of planning, organizing, leading or directing, and controlling or evaluating as a management decision-making process has not changed dramatically throughout the years. However, the approach to the process of decision making is in a state of dynamic change. Marketing presents one such evolutionary and alternative approach. With marketing firmly established in the organizational structures of most hospitals today, it cannot be called new. Rather, marketing has evolved as an alternative approach to the management functions of planning, organizing, leading, and evaluating. The primary difference between marketing and more traditional methods, such as management by objectives, is the emphasis on consumer, or customer, research in the market-based model. The literature, however, is noncommittal on narrowing the definition of *marketing* as an appraoch. In fact, there is considerable controversy about the definition of *marketing*, not only in management but in the marketing field.

MARKETING—WHAT IS IT?

Since the 1970s, hospitals have increasingly integrated marketing into management functions. Whether or not it is commonly understood, the term *marketing* is both commonly and frequently used in health care today. The question is: What is marketing? Is it a philosophy, a concept, a management tool, a theory, or a discipline? Even experts are unable to come to a consensus. McCarthy stated that "marketing graduates would be hard pressed to give a precise definition of marketing."[1] Others are more venturesome. Rynne defined *marketing* as an "approach,"[2] Keith as a "business function,"[3] Arnold, Capella, and Sumrall as a "philosophy,"[4] and Camunas as an "applied science."[5] A comprehensive definition was given by Kotler who defined marketing as "the analysis, planning, implemen-

1

tation, and control of carefully formulated programs to bring about voluntary exchanges of values with target markets for the purpose of achieving organizational objectives."[6] Kotler then defined *marketing* as the management of programs designed to facilitate exchanges with customers to the benefit of the organization. Accepting marketing as the management of programs then, Cooper and Robinson provided further insight by defining health care marketing management as "a process of understanding the needs and wants of a target market. Its purpose is to provide a viewpoint from which to integrate the analysis, planning, implementation and control of the health care delivery system."[7]

Thus, *marketing* is the integrated management of programs or services designed according to a philosophy in which the driving force is the matching of customer needs and wants with the capabilities of the organization to achieve organizational objectives (exchanges of values). More simply, *marketing* is a management process and a philosophical, integrated approach that managers use for decision making in order to fulfill the mission of the organization.

Integration, which is essential in understanding the concept of marketing, is the coordination of the various departments or segments in the health care agency to the extent that each department contributes to the whole. It is, in fact, impossible for a marketing department to design and implement a marketing plan in isolation. The marketing process is dynamic and participative. It involves a commitment of the entire management team and cooperation from every employee in the organization.

MARKETING—WHAT IT IS NOT

In defining *marketing,* it is helpful to discuss what marketing is not. Two common misnomers are the labeling of marketing as public relations (PR) or selling. Marketing is neither. PR involves promoting positive identities and name awareness, and selling, in the most literal sense, is convincing a target population that they should buy certain goods and services.

Marketing Is Not Public Relations

Before marketing departments, positions, and functions were developed and integrated into hospital organizational structures, hospitals relied on PR departments. PR was responsible for what little contact the hospital had with the media. When marketing concepts were first introduced in hospitals, marketing functions were (erroneously or not) relegated to the

PR department. Some PR departments accepted the challenge and developed marketing as a PR domain. However, as marketing became more sophisticated and mature in hospitals, PR became a separate but related function. Most PR departments evolved into a broader communication department, with PR as one aspect of the department.

Today, PR departments are charged with the responsibility of identifying and monitoring changes in the attitudes of the many clients, or publics, of hospitals. Other responsibilities include maintaining a top-of-mind name awareness of the hospital in the mind of the key publics as well as supporting and promoting the objectives of the hospital, including the marketing objectives.

Marketing Is Not Selling

Selling is often confused or used synonymously with *marketing*. However, there are vast differences. Marketing focuses on four basic processes:

1. research into the needs and wants of the targeted market
2. identification of customer/provider exchanges
3. assessment of the organization's ability to provide the needed service
4. development of the marketing objectives

Selling consists of methods used to convince a selected population that they need the goods or services of the seller. Selling becomes less necessary with customer research–based marketing. However, sales forces do exist in both service and product firms as one of the options in the marketing mix, which is discussed further in Chapter 5.

A more clear differentiation is made by examining the marketing mentality versus the selling mentality. The philosophy of a selling mentality is that services and products are sold, not bought; thus, if the buyers are dissatisfied, there are always more buyers in the market. In other words, with the selling mentality, programs are developed and sold without marketing research. Some historical disasters are fine examples of the selling approach: the Ford Edsel, the "new" Coke, and the nation's railway system. All, of course, were failures that reflected selling mentalities rather than marketing mentalities. In other words, the products were developed and sold without regard to market demand. Figure 1-1 compares planning mentalities. Product mentalities judge quality by colleague approval, selling mentalities by number of sales, and marketing mentalities by customer satisfaction. Additionally, a critical indicator of customer satisfaction is

	KEYSTONE OF PRODUCT DESIGN	ATTITUDE TOWARD CUSTOMER	TEST OF QUALITY
PRODUCT MENTALITY	Expert Knowledge	Needs to be Educated	Colleague Approval
SELLING MENTALITY	Pizzaz	Needs to be Sold	Number of Sales
MARKETING MENTALITY	Customer's Needs and Wants	Needs to be Satisfied	Customer Satisfaction

Figure 1-1 Comparison of Planning Mentalities. *Source:* Reprinted with permission from "How to Implement a Powerful Marketing Tool" by Terrence J. Rynne, © 1982.

repeat business. A customer returning to a hospital suggests that the first visit was satisfactory.

A common activity after a service or program fails is to educate the consumer better concerning the value of the program. Conversely, a marketing mentality assumes that:

- The customer is capable of articulating needs and wants.
- Marketing research into customer needs and wants drives programs and services.
- All departmental activities are integrated in the health care system to focus on the targeted market and research-based objectives.
- Continuous research and monitoring define and direct changes in services and programs.

Marketing provides a mechanism to know the customer so well that the product or service sells itself. Hence, marketing makes selling easier. A good marketing plan is the foundation of strategic decision making.

MARKETING SERVICES VERSUS PRODUCTS

Product firms develop and market tangible products that are bought and used by customers. The customer has something in hand to represent the purchase. Hospitals, nursing service agencies, nursing consultants, and academic institutions are all services without tangible products. For example, nursing is a service that delivers the intangible product *health care.* Does the tangibility of a product make a difference in terms of marketing? Without tangible products, can marketing principles from product firms be applied? Clearly, there are differences between marketing services and products. Responsive nurse managers are aware of these as the marketing plan is developed and implemented. Some of the more significant differences are as follows:

- *Services are intangible and cannot be touched.*[8] Tangibility in product firms represents what has been purchased. In nursing, the simple act of giving a customer something such as a card, sheet of information, or list of resources helps resolve the issue. One hospital emergency department gives discharging patients the small Addressograph stamp to bring with them if they ever need to return. This simple act not only provides tangibility to the services but links patients to the hospital via an inexpensive plastic card. Patients actually return with the card in hand.

- *Services are less standardized than products.*[9] As a result, there is less control over price, delivery, and results. Service agencies cannot be sure that the intangible product is being consistently delivered in an appropriate way. Specifically, nursing cannot be sure that the manner in which a nurse delivers care is consistent with management's philosophy.
- *Services are often more individualized than products.* Therefore, prices vary accordingly. For example, an average but not absolute estimate for the price of an appendectomy can be given.
- *Services are simultaneously produced and consumed.*[10] For example, health care is sold, then the service is performed and consumed at the same time, and then the customer is billed. The billing time is a critical period since the customer has no tangible goods to represent the purchase.
- *Services are perishable.*[11] Products last and can be stored for the future by the customer and the product firm. Empty beds and vacant student classrooms mean loss of revenue.
- *Services call customers clients, and the purchase relationship is called a client relationship.*[12] In health care, the customers cannot be called patients categorically since the customers encompass patients, physicians, nurses, employers, accrediting bodies, and insurance agents, to name a few.
- *With services, the traditional buyer/seller relationship does not exist.* Buyers must conform to a set of rules. For example, physicians cannot admit patients to hospitals without complying with rules such as obtaining privileges, providing information to admitting, and waiting to be scheduled in the operating room (exclusive of emergencies).
- *Services distinguish the place of sales as access or distribution of services.* In contrast, product markets consider the place of sales as the entire production to distribution process that affects the price and promotion of the product. In services, the health care provider's location and easy access will determine the marketability of the service. Providing easy access is difficult in large teaching facilities. Because these hospitals are both labor intensive and equipment intensive, moving services to provide better access becomes a problem.

These differences affect strategy. For example, in the product lines, customers buy the product, take it home, use it, and are either satisfied and keep the product or are dissatisfied and return the product. In health care, dissatisfaction cannot be monitored by return of the product. Therefore, responsive health care managers establish a method for both monitoring customer satisfaction and responding to the changing needs of the customer.

Because the service is performed and consumed simultaneously, the patient consumer uses up the product, health care, and returns home without tangible assets representing the health care dollars spent. If no mechanism exists for monitoring satisfaction while the patient is in the hospital, negative feedback will occur when the first bill for services is received. Unhappy patients will scrutinize the charges and determine that the charge exceeds the benefit gained. Nursing can reverse the reaction by developing systems to monitor the patient's perception of care continuously. Monitoring strategies are discussed in more detail in Chapter 3.

Nursing and the admitting department cooperate to provide efficient and uncomplicated patient admissions. A long wait in admitting or on the unit sets a negative tone for the patient's admission. Although many nursing units are architecturally designed to facilitate nurse and physician efficiency, the design is often at the expense of easy patient access to the nurse. Again, nursing can design systems to provide better patient access to the primary nurse. For example, if the nurses' notes are placed at the patient's bedside, the patient will have easier and more frequent access to the primary nurse. Decentralized bedside linen supplies, medicines, supplies, and equipment accomplish the same purpose.

Unlike product firms, service firms rely on employees to interface with the customers to produce, deliver, and market the product *health care*. Therefore, the human resource becomes the most valuable asset of the hospital or health care provider. Extensive investments in employee satisfaction, training, evaluation, attitude surveys, reward packages, and recognition are justified because satisfied employees are critical to the success of the service or program.

Additionally, nursing adds tangibility to care with discharge instructions and teaching materials. A marketing package for nursing is provided in more detail in Chapter 3.

In order to appreciate fully how marketing evolved in health care, it is necessary to understand the influencing economic and governmental forces. The remainder of this chapter provides an overview of the significant events leading to the fierce competition among hospitals and the increasing emphasis on operating like big businesses. Regulation and deregulation are discussed because reimbursement to hospitals is becoming more and more regulated and this variable is the most significant in marketing strategies. Characteristics of regulated markets are discussed to show that hospitals do indeed resemble regulated markets and, therefore, must compete more on services than on price.

Likewise, survival strategies are discussed because the result affects the way in which nursing is integrated into the total organization. Additionally, survival strategies can be applied effectively in the nursing organization. The last part of this chapter outlines the critical role of the staff nurse in marketing. Similarities between the marketing process and the nursing process are presented to emphasize the fact that nursing is already skilled in the marketing process.

WHY MARKETING IN HOSPITALS?

Marketing is not new in hospitals. It has evolved into a major hospital operation from an earlier, modest, and token existence in hospital PR departments. Increased government regulation and other economic forces in the early and mid-1970s (approximately ten years after Medicare) shifted the focus of hospitals from a social to a business orientation. Health care as a basic human right versus health care as a luxury became a prominent issue. Finally, in the early 1980s, diagnosis-related groups (DRGs) as well as other technological, biological, biochemical, and social factors contributed to declining patient days in hospitals, decreasing consumer utilization of health care. Consequently, the shrinking total available market of health care consumers led to fierce competition among health care providers.

Marketing assumes competition and oversupply. The competition is for clients, and the oversupply is in hospital beds, physicians, and vacant registered nurse (RN) positions. In the absence of competition, marketing is unnecessary and is, in fact, too expensive to justify. Marketing evolved in hospitals out of the need to survive in a more competitive marketplace.

In response to the competition and oversupply of the early 1980s, hospitals and health care providers swiftly borrowed from and capitalized on the solid marketing experiences of firms in business to produce goods. However, in contrast to profit-making firms, health care providers are operating in a more regulated economic environment in which the price of services is not closely aligned with the cost of providing the services. Therefore, marketing in health care cannnot be viewed apart from its economic (or noneconomic) environment.

THE ECONOMIC ENVIRONMENT

Hospitals entered the 1980s with optimism. Occupancy was stable, and the RN shortage of the 1970s had abated. The foreboding signs of the economic discord yet to come were there but went unheeded (and perhaps even unnoticed) at first. Some of these signs were:

- In 1972, the government established professional standard review organizations (PSROs) to review the appropriateness of hospital lengths of stay of Medicare recipients.[13] This marked the beginning of organized government intervention in health care practice patterns.
- In 1972, the National Health Planning and Resource Development Act established health system agencies (HSAs) and the certificate of need (CON) process for expenditures of $150 thousand or more.[14] The act regulated where and when hospital beds, services, and technology would be added.
- The Health Maintenance Organization (HMO) Act of 1973 authorized $375 million in grants, loans, and contracts to develop and operate HMOs and prepaid health plans.[15] This regulation was designed to place a cap on health care expenditures.
- In 1977, the government sponsored the "voluntary effort" of cost containment for hospitals.[16] Some hospitals participated by freezing wages and position vacancies. The voluntary effort failed because beds were still filled and the cost associated with full occupancy did not decrease.
- In order to qualify for government funding, medical schools were required to increase enrollment. Consequently, the number of physicians increased 50 percent from 1965 to 1980.[17] The plan was to increase the supply, thus lowering demand and fees.
- Industrial downsizing occurred in the late 1970s and 1980s because of "declining world market shares, growing import penetration, mediocre growth rates, overregulation, shrinking capital, and down right economic stagnation."[18] Out of the downsizing came a loss of insurance benefits and population out-migration, resulting in an increasing market share of self-pay, charity care, and public aid for hospitals.

By April 1983, DRGs were a reality under Public Law 98-21, the government's prospective payment system for Medicare recipients. Hospitals were to be reimbursed not for cost, but by a fixed sum per DRG as determined by the federal government. DRGs and major layoffs in industry, with subsequent population out-migration from the North to the South and Southwest, resulted in dramatic declines in hospital occupancy across the nation. Hospitals were caught off guard even though the signs were evident, and reorganization came too late. Table 1-1 lists some of the forces in the 1980s that resulted in the reorganization of health care.

Table 1-1 Summary of External Forces in the 1980s: Impact and Consequences to Health Care Providers

Forces	Impact	Consequences
Declining birthrate	Decrease in market share in pediatrics and obstetrics	Increased competition
Decreased infant mortality rate	Increase in chronic, ventilator-dependent, and pediatric population	Increase in uncompensated care
Increased life expectancy	Increase in number of people 65 and older	Increase in fixed revenues from Medicare
DRGs	Decrease in ALOS Decrease in occupancy	Competition Vertical integration
Reimbursement favoring outpatient and ambulatory care	Decrease in patient days	Competition for inpatients
Increased HMO enrollment	Decrease in patient days	Competition for inpatients and physicians
Increase in PPOs	Ensured volume	Fixed revenues
Industrial downsizing	Population out-migration Loss of total market	Competition for patients
Advances in technology	Decrease in patient days Regulation by CON	Competition for technology and patients
Increased medical school enrollment	Physician surplus	Competition among physicians
Increase in career options for women	Nurse shortage	Competition for nurses
Increased consumer sovereignty	Consumers choosing among options for health care	Marketing integrated into health care structures

Major population changes included a declining birthrate, decreased infant mortality, an increased life span, and out-migration because of industrial downsizing.[19] Other forces in the 1980s affecting the health care industry were the increasing enrollment in HMOs, DRGs, outpatient versus inpatient reimbursement for selected procedures, increasing technological developments, physician surpluses, a more informed consumer, preferred provider organizations (PPOs), and increased career options for women, leading to a shortage of nurses.[20-23] In summary, the consequences to hospitals were

- decreased occupancy rates
- decreased patient days
- increased percentage of Medicare patients

- increased proportion of noncompensated care
- decreased length of stay
- increased patient acuity, requiring more professional care (RN)
- decreased supply of nurses
- increased consumer sovereignty
- increased proportion of fixed revenues from PPOs, HMOs, and Medicare reimbursement

Competition created a favorable environment for health care marketing strategies. However, because of increased government regulation and an increased proportion of fixed revenues, competition among hospitals is more characteristic of competition in regulated markets. Traditionally, these markets compete on nonprice, noneconomic factors such as service and amenities. Some of these characteristics are discussed here.

CHARACTERISTICS OF REGULATED MARKETS

Performance under regulatory conditions has characteristic attributes such as price setting, barriers to entry, decreased consumer sovereignty, price inelasticity of demand, cross subsidization, and competition in noneconomic areas. These attributes, which describe some hospital environments, affect marketing strategy.

Price Setting

In regulatory environments, prices are fixed and do not reflect the cost of providing the service or the supply and demand for the service. In contrast, prices in free markets are based on the cost of producing the product and fluctuate according to the supply and demand for the product. In hospitals, governmental and other contractual agreements regulate what care is reimbursed, regardless of the cost. Therefore, prices are fixed, and increased revenues are achieved primarily through increased volume. Consequently, a marketing strategy will not be based on competitive pricing but on additional or better services with special amenities.

Barriers to Entry

It is extremely difficult for new firms to enter a regulated market. Some of the barriers to entering hospital markets are licensure regulations, CONs,

HSAs, community planning boards, and other hospitals, to name a few. From 1977 to 1982, the number of hospitals in the United States decreased by 5,881.[24] In a totally free market, there are many sellers and many buyers, with many new firms entering the market. With hospitals today, the buyers are already in the business and the purchases are smaller hospitals by larger ones.

Decreased Consumer Sovereignty

Consumer sovereignty is the degree to which product or service information is easily obtained by the consumer. In regulated markets, it is difficult for consumers to obtain information about the price and quality of services. For example, prices or fees such as the total cost of an appendectomy or cardiovascular surgery are difficult to obtain. The consumer must expend considerable time and effort uncovering these costs; thus, it is difficult to compare competing costs of a hospitalization.

Inelasticity of Demand

Price elasticity of demand means that when prices rise, consumption decreases and when prices decrease, consumption increases, which is characteristic of free markets. Additionally, when consumption increases and supply decreases, prices rise. Conversely, when consumption decreases and oversupply exists, prices decrease. In contrast, and under similar conditions, hospitals exhibit a price inelasticity of demand characteristic of regulated markets. For example, neither vacant nor full beds necessarily translate into changed room rates. In other words, the price may be the same regardless of the demand.

Cross Subsidization

Consistent with regulated markets, wide profit margins exist with some hospital services but not with others. There are several reasons for this, but primarily, prices are raised in profit-making sections in order to subsidize nonprofit sections to pay for care that is reimbursed at or below cost (e.g., cardiovascular surgery, which is age specific to middle-aged men with private insurance, and stroke programs, which are age specific to persons primarily 65 and over with Medicare reimbursement based on the DRG; low-profile ancillary services such as laboratory and radiology and the high-profile room rates). In a 1984 study of selected prices for hospital services in Illinois, a range of prices was shown to exist for the gastrointestinal X-ray in Health System Agency Area 5 from $44 in one hospital to $144 in another, a variation of 227 percent.[25] On the other hand, the semiprivate room rates, a more consumer-visible charge, had a reported range from $125 to $190, a variation of only 52 percent.[26] Clearly, competitive pricing does not occur. The implication here is that price cannot always be used as a marketing strategy.

Competition in Noneconomic Areas

The last characteristic of regulated markets is competition in noneconomic areas. This indeed occurs in hospital marketing strategies. Rather than price, competition is based on the attractiveness of the facility, convenience, service, and other amenities.

SURVIVAL STRATEGIES

Market share is defined as the percentage of the total market that a hospital can claim.[27] Market share is calculated as follows:

$$\text{Market share} = \frac{\text{Patient days}}{\text{Total available patient days}} \times 100$$

Strategies for replacing lost revenue from declining market share include vertical integration, horizontal integration, expansion of present services, and diversification.

Vertical Integration

Vertical integration means moving into related businesses. For example, a hospital buys a nursing home, thus entering the long-term care business, or establishes a durable medical equipment or home care service. With vertical integration, hospitals present strong competition to long-established free-standing agencies in the same market. Because of declining patient days, hospitals not only have the staff and other resources to enter these related markets, but the staff is also already trained in high technology and the diagnostic and therapeutic services are sophisticated. The capability to offer such "high tech" services as chemotherapy and intravenous therapy in the home as part of a home care program is a definite marketing vantage point. Additionally, hospitals have other resources to allow easy entry into these markets such as billing, medical records, administration, purchasing, social services, and stores.

On the other hand, hospitals are at a disadvantage in vertical integration because they must learn how to manage the related businesses. The rules for operating home care, long-term care, and durable medical equipment services are quite different than the rules for operating hospitals. In spite of the abundance of available and sophisticated resources, hospitals cannot manage these related businesses without hiring expert managers in the field or investing time and money in training in-house managers to become experts. Even when this is done, methods to evaluate the effectiveness of these experts must be learned. Consequently, profitability in these markets may take several years.

Nursing services are needed in most vertical integration strategies. Nursing, however, initiates its own vertical integration strategies. For example, nursing can offer a speakers' bureau on community education topics for a small fee or nurse certification classes for a fee. Other examples are clinical preceptor programs for nurses from other hospitals, physical examinations for companies, cardiopulmonary resuscitation (CPR) certification for the public, diagnostic testing and blood pressure clinics for the public, and refresher nurse courses. Not only do such programs bring in revenues for nursing, but they maintain name awareness for the hospital and the nursing department in the mind of nurses, the community, and other hospitals. This promotes a positive image of nursing while positioning the nursing department strategically in the mind of its customers.

Horizontal Integration

Horizontal integration means moving, literally, into satellite or feeder sites that offer a range of services such as outpatient testing, outpatient rehabilitation, ambulatory, and emergency services, to name a few. Horizontal integration addresses the problems of access and distribution of health care services, or the "place" of the service that affects the marketability of the service. Large teaching medical centers most often use the competitive strategy of horizontal integration because size and location in inner cities often create the perception of inaccessibility.

A common approach to horizontal integration is the hospital and physician joint venture. In the joint venture, a hospital agrees to finance the satellite practice and in return the physician uses the services of the hospital for inpatient and outpatient services. This ensures the hospital a steady flow of patients from a primary care physician and provides a referral base for the hospital's specialty physicians. The primary care physician benefits since exorbitant start-up costs are financed by the hospital.

Physicians have negotiated elaborate and comprehensive joint ventures with hospitals covering relocation, start up, free or shared office leasing, all or part of malpractice insurance, and other smaller amenities such as free and easy access parking at the hospital and paid dues to various associations and clubs. In fact, these joint ventures have become so lucrative that hospitals are paying premium prices for retiring physicians' practices to replace them with joint practice ventures. In the past, retiring physicians quietly and professionally turned their practices over to younger colleagues. Today's physician recognizes that his or her practice is worth a premium. The salient outcome of all of this is the transformation of the physician, a professional, into the physician, a shrewd, professional businessperson.

With some exceptions, the primary care physician is the most valuable to the hospital's market share of patients. The reason is that the primary physician is not only the admitting physician but is the physician who feeds the specialty physicians. Exceptions to this are obstetricians and pediatricians, who are often selected directly by the patient. Therefore, joint practice ventures or other joint financial arrangements also occur with these specialty physicians. Maintaining a market share in obstetrics is important because the obstetrics services feed the pediatric services in hospitals. Primary care physicians, not surgeons, are often the targeted physician market segment of hospitals. Most other specialties are generated by referrals from primary care physicians.

Nursing, in the allocation of scarce resources, ensures nursing support to primary care physicians in their role as gatekeepers of the census and market share of the hospital. In order for the primary joint venture to be successful, nursing services must be marketable in the area. Issues such as adequate staff, staff level of expertise, staff attitudes, adequate support staff, and availability of supplies and equipment must be addressed.

Nursing plans horizontal integration as target markets are defined in the marketing plan. One obvious market is the market for RNs since, historically, shortages have occurred in cyclical patterns. A horizontal integration strategy designed to ensure supply while maintaining a market share of nurses is a joint venture with an academic institution that graduates nurses. An example is a shared faculty/staff position in which a qualified nurse functions both as hospital staff and faculty of the academic institution. This program is discussed in more detail in Chapter 3. Each institution shares the salary and benefits of the nurse. The exchange process defines the benefits to the hospital as a mechanism to recruit new graduates. The benefits to the academic institution are the availability of a clinically expert faculty member and a consistent clinical practicum site for students. Such an arrangement in students' senior year can become a part of students' academic education and nursing units' orientation. In this way, horizontal integration occurs by the moving and merging of the feeder site (the academic institution) into the nursing department, and vice versa, to ensure a continuing supply of nurses and maintain a market share.

Expansion of Present Services

Another competitive strategy by hospitals is simply to expand their present services to include nontraditional markets. For example, the hospital laundry can serve area motels for a fee. Another example is the hospital laboratory serving other hospitals, physicians' offices, and clinics. Still another example is the hospital's employee health service performing employment examinations for companies and employers in the community. These strategies not only replace revenues lost from declining patient days but decrease staffhours per activity in the laboratory, laundry, and employee health service. Additionally, such strategies help offset the indirect overhead and fixed indirect costs of the hospital.

In these expansion modes, hospitals compete with free-standing businesses in the same service area. This means that hospitals must be able to compete on price, and therein lies the problem. Because of the history of cost shifting to ancillary services, the price of these services is often not competitive. In order to be competitive, the hospital would have to establish a lower charge to the nontraditional markets or lower the charge to its primary clients. The dual fee structure would not be acceptable to third-party payers, and because hospital costs are built into the ancillary fee structures, lowering the charge to primary customers would not be possible.

A common solution for hospitals is to establish a separate, for-profit organization for the nontraditional, expansion, and vertical integration services. Organized as such, these services do not share the indirect and direct overhead costs of the hospital and can, therefore, compete in price with free-standing agencies.

An example of expansion of present services in nursing is the expansion of a nursing consultation service, such as rehabilitation nurse consultation, to nursing homes. On a fee-for-service arrangement, the nursing department bills the nursing home for the services of the consulting nurse.

Diversification

Diversification means moving into nonrelated businesses. Examples include entering the computer software business or audiovisual production business. Hospitals buy into these nonrelated businesses or enter them because of marketable expertise developed in departments or services in the process of delivering service to the primary hospital markets, e.g., computer programing skills learned as a result of a hospital computer programing experience. In this example, the hospital diversifies, forming a computer programing business for other firms for a fee.

Another example is the purchase and management of a hotel. Usually, the diversification becomes a spin-off business with the purpose of providing a source of income that will offset losses in other sections of the hospital.

If the diversification is not developed as a separate business, the inherent danger is that its cost will merely drive up the cost per patient day or per activity beyond the boundaries of what is reimbursed. The critical aspect of diversification needing examination is the relation of the new business to the mission. The critical questions are: What is our business? What should our business be?

Diversification in nursing is carefully weighed by considering the mission of the nursing department. First, it is unlikely that the nursing department will be creating a spin-off, non-health-related business. Second, if the diversification is not in line with the mission, it is likely to create an additional workload, driving up nursing costs and reducing profit margins.

The emphasis now is on the consumer as a purchaser and user of the product *health care*. Consequently, management efforts are shifting from decision making based on institutional needs to decision making based on customer research and careful matching of customer needs with the capabilities of the organization. In market-based management, customer wants and needs are best identified by those closest to the customer. This requires a participative process, with the manager being the knowledgeable facilitator. The management style, therefore, is participative.

Nursing, more than any other department, is closer longer to the primary customers of the hospital: the patients, physicians, and RNs. Therefore, nursing is in a position to design, develop, implement, and market service programs effectively. Additionally, because of the competitive environment, the marketing model is an appropriate nursing management tool in developing and implementing objectives designed to meet customer needs.

THE ROLE OF THE NURSE IN MARKETING

The product of the hospital and health care providers is health care. Nursing produces and delivers this health care. The outcome and purpose of patient care are patient compliance with the health care regimen and a resulting physical and mental state called *health,* restored at least to the previous level. In the process of producing and delivering health care, nursing is simultaneously selling an image of both nursing and the health care provider to the patient. Nursing is at the critical juncture in the health care system where hospital and nursing philosophy and goals are carried out. Chapter 2 discusses in more detail nursing's role both as a customer of and a powerful marketing force for the hospital. An overview is provided here.

The Nurse As a Microlevel Marketing Agent

Nursing, by definition, is the primary interface between the hospital and its customers. Nursing evaluates the health status of patients, coordinates the activities of other departments, develops a treatment plan consistent with the medical treatment plan, implements the plan, and monitors the patient's progress throughout the entire hospitalization. This is no small task. Because hospitalized patients are too ill to coordinate their own plan of care, nurses also act on behalf of patients, representing patients to physicians and other professional disciplines. Figure 1-2 shows the relationship of nursing to ancillary and professional services. Nursing, with support systems, coordinates the therapies of other departments, monitoring and assessing the patient's progress with the therapies. In short, the nurse is the manager of the patient's health care plan. Although nurses at the bedside are key figures in microlevel marketing, nursing at the organizational level works in close collaboration with the planning, marketing, and communications departments of the hospital.

Via the nursing process, the nurse utilizes the marketing model as a microlevel marketing agent in the health care system. Figure 1-3 shows the relation of the nursing process to the market-based planning model. Both the marketing model and the nursing process employ research-based decision making. Research occurs at two points in each process: the assessment and the monitoring and evaluation of implementation strategies. Implementation is carried out in both processes by the planners or their designees. Nursing has used the nursing process to identify problems and set objectives for decades. Not only are nurses in the best position to be marketing agents for the hospital, they inherently possess the skills required.

The image being marketed by nurses at the microlevel depends entirely on their attitudes and job satisfaction.

> Nurses who are "burned out" because of chronic understaffing, inadequate support from administration and support services, lack of autonomy to make decisions and plan care, or lack of recog-

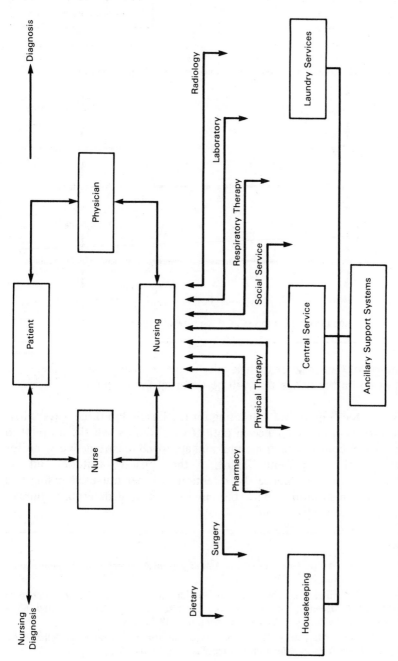

Figure 1-2 Relation of Nursing to Professional and Ancillary Services

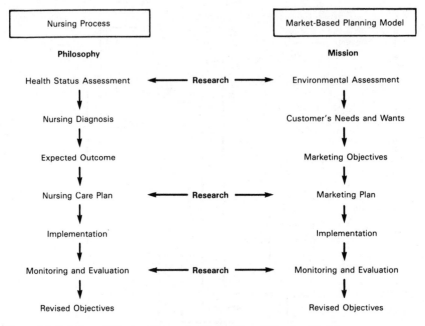

Figure 1-3 Relation of Nursing Process to Market-Based Planning Model

nition of their role or their loyalty to the company are not likely to present the image that will best market the hospital.[28]

The nurse does microlevel marketing for the hospital in three ways. First, in the provision of excellence in patient care, nurses sell the hospital to physicians. Second, by their manner and approach to care delivery, nurses sell the hospital to patients. Third, by their positive attitudes and job satisfaction, nurses influence the retention of other nurses. Nursing and hospital administration provide the environment that determines nurses' attitudes and job satisfaction.

NOTES

1. E. Jerome McCarthy, *Basic Marketing: A Management Approach,* 6th ed. (Homewood, Ill.: Richard D. Irwin, Inc., 1978), 4.

2. Terrence J. Rynne, "The Third Stage of Hospital Marketing," in *Strategic Planning in Health Care Management,* ed. William A. Flexner, Eric M. Berkowitz, and Montague Brown (Rockville, Md., Aspen Publishers, Inc., 1981), 258.

3. Jon G. Keith, "Marketing Health Care: What the Recent Literature Is Telling Us," *Hospital & Health Services Administration* (special issue, 1981): 67.

4. Danny R. Arnold, Louis M. Capella, and Delia A. Sumrall, "Hospital Challenge: Using Change Theory and Process To Adopt and Implement the Marketing Concept," *Journal of Health Care Management* 7, no. 2 (June 1987): 15.

5. Caroline Camunas, "Using Public Relations To Market Nursing Service," *Journal of Nursing Administration* 16, no. 10 (October 1986): 26.

6. Phillip Kotler, *Marketing for Non-Profit Organizations* (Englewood Cliffs, N.J.: Prentice-Hall, Inc., 1982), 6.

7. Phillip D. Cooper and Larry M. Robinson, *Health Care Marketing Management* (Rockville, Md.: Aspen Publishers, Inc., 1982), 1–2.

8. Thomas C. Kinnear and Kenneth L. Bernhardt, *Principles of Marketing* (Glenview, Ill: Scott, Foresman & Co., 1983), 655.

9. Kotler, 9.

10. Kinnear and Bernhardt, 655.

11. Kotler, 9.

12. Kinnear and Bernhardt, 658.

13. Paul J. Feldstein, *Health Care Economics,* 2d ed. (New York, N.Y.: John Wiley & Sons, Inc., 1983), 308–309.

14. Roxane B. Spitzer, "Health Legislation: Impact on Nursing Service Delivery," in *DRGs: The Reorganization of Health Care,* ed. Leah Curtin and Caroline Zurlage (Chicago, Ill: 5-N Publications, Inc., 1984), 14.

15. John R. Coleman, Elizabeth C. Dayani, and Elsie Simms, "Reorganization of Health Service Delivery: Emerging Systems," in *DRGs: The Reorganization of Health Care,* ed. Leah Curtin and Caroline Zurlage (Chicago, Ill.: 5-N Publications, Inc., 1984), 14.

16. Spitzer, 53.

17. Feldstein, 314.

18. John Naisbitt, *Megatrends* (New York, N.Y.: Warner Books, Inc., 1984).

19. H. Steven Lieber and Lauri Rustand, *Illinois Hospitals: A Decades' Perspective* (Naperville, Ill.: Illinois Hospital Association, 1984), 42–43.

20. Lieber and Rustand, 52.

21. Ibid., 27.

22. Coleman, Dayani, and Simms, 22.

23. John Stullinsky, "The Ninth Annual Working Woman Salary Survey," *Working Woman,* January 1988, 60.

24. Lieber and Rustand, 1.

25. *A Report of Selected Prices at Illinois Hospitals* (Springfield, Ill.: Illinois Health Care Cost Containment Council, Health Service Area V, March 1985).

26. Ibid.

27. McCarthy, 481.

28. Rose D. Pheland, "Nursing: An Unrecognized Major Marketing Force for Hospitals," *Journal of Health Care Marketing* 7, no. 2 (June 1987): 48.

Chapter 2

The Basics

This chapter begins with a model for market-based planning and discusses a marketing plan as it relates to the more global concept of a strategic plan. The mission as the critical foundation of a marketing plan is also discussed, and the chapter concludes with a discussion of buyer behavior and exchange relationships.

MARKET-BASED PLANNING MODEL

If an organization is in need of change, there is strong competition in the marketplace, organizational performance is stagnant, and the environment is one of rapid growth, a marketing approach to planning may be used to achieve organizational objectives. A good marketing model facilitates the development of the marketing plan and communicates the desired approach to the management team responsible for setting and achieving organizational objectives. Exhibit 2-1 shows one model that can be used as a guide to the process of management by consumer needs.

In the mission statement, the business and customers are defined or confirmed, and the mission firmly sets the position or image the organization chooses to project. The environmental assessment defines the internal and external factors limiting and enhancing the organization's capabilities. Defining the market competition provides an in-depth view of the organization's position compared to that of the competition.

Analyzing strengths, weaknesses, opportunities, and threats (SWOTS) helps the organization match organizational strengths to market needs and wants for a strategic fit. From the SWOTS, a profile of the organization is developed. With the profile, key result areas and marketing objectives are developed.

Exhibit 2-1 Market-Based Model

     I. Mission Statement
    II. Environmental Assessment
        A. Internal
        B. External
   III. Implication of Environmental Assessment (SWOTS)
    IV. Organizational Strengths and Market Demand: The Strategic Fit
     V. Profile of the Organization
    VI. Marketing Objectives
   VII. Marketing Plan
        A. Segmenting the market
        B. Targeting the market
        C. Researching the market
        D. Analyzing and setting exchange relationships
        E. Designing the marketing mix
           1. Service
           2. Price
           3. Distribution and access
           4. Promotion
  VIII. Implementation
    IX. Evaluating the Results

Each objective has its own marketing plan. The marketing plan consists of segmenting and targeting the market, researching the market, analyzing exchange relationships, and designing the marketing mix. Designing the mix includes naming the product, program, or service; pricing; promoting; and determining how to deliver the product or service to the consumer.

A carefully designed system to monitor progress in achieving the marketing objectives makes evaluation easier. Because customer needs change rapidly, continuous evaluation facilitates changing the marketing plan accordingly.

STRATEGIC PLANNING AND MARKETING

The strategic plan incorporates the business plans of each department into one grand strategic plan. Figure 2-1 shows that the first step is the development of a hospital marketing plan that provides the initial direction to the various departments and ensures consistency. This figure shows the relation applied to the nursing department. As shown, the strategic plan is the overall operating plan of the department. Annually, each hospital department submits business plans, beginning with the consumer-oriented marketing plan. These business plans are the strategic plan of the depart-

Figure 2-1 Strategic Planning Sequence

ment, and together become the strategic plan of the hospital. The nursing strategic plan incorporates the business plan of each department or unit. It is important for each department to know the emphasis or foci of the hospital marketing plan in order to support, promote, and implement organizational goals. For example, if one of the hospital's marketing objectives is to increase revenue in the pediatric department, nursing (as well as other involved departments) must know the objective so that a nursing objective can be developed to support and augment the administrative objective. Almost every hospital objective will involve nursing. Likewise, marketing objectives developed by nursing are communicated to the unit staff since many of the objectives will be implemented at the unit level.

Market-based planning requires a top-down, bottom-up approach involving every employee in the organization. The participative process is crucial to achieving hospital objectives. Chapter 6 further discusses integration of the marketing function into the strategic planning process in nursing.

NURSING MISSION: A FOUNDATION

Just as the marketing plan is a foundation for the strategic plan, the nursing mission is the foundation for the marketing plan. Marketing experts differ on whether the mission is derived from the environmental assessment or vice versa. The concept presented here is that there is a basic mission of the nursing department, health care agency, or academic institution that does not change in response to customer needs. For example, the mission "to provide nursing care" would change only if there were no more patients. In starting with the mission, providers reaffirm and confirm basic and unchanging philosophies; then, customer needs and wants influence new and changing philosophies.

Figure 2-2 shows the flow of the nursing organization around consumer demand. The philosophy defines the basic beliefs of an organization. These beliefs are reflected in the mission, which states the reason for the existence of the organization. The theory of nursing practice evolves out of the organizational philosophy and defines a theoretical framework for carrying out the mission. The departmental objectives define how the organization will fulfill the mission. From these permanent goals and objectives, the nursing administration standards and organizational structure are established. Likewise, out of the standards of care, the care delivery system, performance standards, and productivity standards are set. Finally, the entire process is evaluated in the environmental assessment. From this assessment, annual goals and objectives and a business plan are developed.

This schema shows that the philosophy and mission is relatively stable, influencing and being influenced by customer needs and demands. In matching customer needs with organizational capabilities, the nursing department responds to these needs by providing that which is possible and that which is congruent with the nursing mission and the organizational culture. For example: marketing research into customer needs shows that a burn unit would be a viable program for the hospital to offer and that the mission and capabilities of the hospital would permit the development of the unit. However, the nurse manager presents the research to the medical and nursing staffs and administration and finds that there is no interest in developing the service. In this case, the organizational culture is the barrier, and the service cannot be implemented unless staff is hired

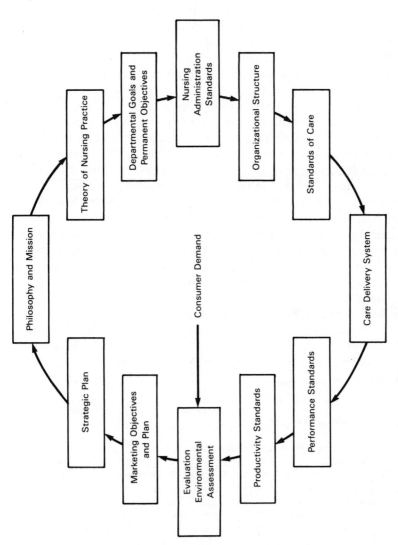

Figure 2-2 Influence of Consumer Demand on the Organization of Nursing

specifically to develop and implement the service. Even then, the low level of cooperation may jeopardize the success of the program.

In another example, a nurse manager finds that the hospital's obstetric service is losing a market share to another hospital that offers tubal ligation postdelivery. It is against the religious beliefs and mission of the hospital to provide this service. Therefore, the organization could provide the service, but the mission would not permit it.

Fulfilling the mission yet balancing the cost is yet another problem. A hospital may have a mission to serve the poor of the community. However, a disproportionate share of the poor will financially cripple the organization because it must at least meet costs in order to operate. Without charitable funding, such an organization must have other profit-making sections to offset the financial loss of serving the poor. Consequently, the mission of the hospital must be modified. McManis, president of McManis Associates, Inc., a management research and consulting firm, stated "the challenge facing religious hospitals is to survive in a competitive, local market-driven environment without compromising their mission."[1] Some hospitals may prefer nonexistence to compromising their mission.

Because the nursing mission drives all of the other functions and processes in nursing, it is developed in a scope broad enough to permit flexibility in planning services and programs. Hillestad and Berkowitz warned that narrow mission statements encourage "myopic thinking," preventing organizations from being responsive to potential growth.[2] Exhibit 2-2 is an example of a comprehensive mission statement.

Exhibit 2-2 Mission Statement

Rush Home Health Service exists to provide

skilled nursing and other therapeutic services to patients who reside within Cook, Dupage, Kane, or Will Counties, and who are patients of physicians affiliated with Rush–Presbyterian–St. Luke's Medical Center or its associated network hospitals; to contribute to the knowledge and skills which effect improvement in patient and health care services through the collaborative practice of community health nursing and other disciplines; to contribute to the Medical Center's system of coordinated and comprehensive care; to provide opportunities for education and research activities.

Source: Reprinted from Rush Home Health Service Articles of Organization with permission of Rush Home Health Service, 1988.

Contents of a Mission Statement

A good mission statement answers the following five questions:

1. Who are our customers?
2. What is our business?
3. What should our business be?
4. What is our position?
5. What should our position be?

The mission provides a sense of purpose and direction to the nursing department in developing the marketing plan. For example, the mission in Exhibit 2-2 defines the customers as patients in four counties, physicians at Rush Home Health Service, and students in education and research. The customers served are intentionally narrowed to the specific four-county area and the patients of Rush Presbyterian-St. Luke's Medical Center physicians. The business is home care and other services, education, and research. The positioning is "coordinated, comprehensive" care. The mission clearly defines the business, customers, and positioning.

Chapter 3 discusses positioning in detail from the perspective of becoming and remaining marketable. The rest of this chapter discusses customers, buyer behavior, and exchange relationships.

CUSTOMERS

Nursing has many customers. In hospitals, some of the customers include patients, physicians, nurses, third-party payers, accreditors, faculty, universities, other hospital departments, nursing homes, and nurses in physicians' offices. In home health agencies, customers are patients, physicians, discharge planners, third-party payers, social workers, community agencies, accreditors, and community vendors, to name a few. In academic institutions, some of the customers are graduate and high school students, parents, grant awarding agencies, teachers, accreditors, alumni, media staff, hospitals, and other faculty. However, in hospitals, patients, physicians, and nurses are major customers. Kotler defines a responsive organization as "one that makes every effort to sense and satisfy the needs and wants of its focal clients and publics."[3] Rynne further details that managers should "know their customers so well that they would not only know what the customers want but also know the customers' deeper needs."[4]

In hospitals, nursing interfaces with the major customers more than does any other department. It is essential that nurse managers develop marketing objectives to attract, retain, and maintain these focal clients. It is also essential that nurse managers recognize customers and respond to them appropriately. Responsive nurse managers learn about buyer behavior, exchange relationships, positioning, and developing a nursing marketing package not only to achieve hospital and nursing goals but to position the nursing department (and therefore the hospital) competitively in the community.

Buyer Behavior

Although third-party payers are the real, behind-the-scenes customers of hospitals, patients and physicians still influence which patients will patronize the hospital. By what criteria do physicians and consumers select one hospital over another? Kinnear[5] described the processes leading to consumer purchase as

1. problem arising
2. information seeking
3. evaluating alternatives
4. deciding to purchase
5. postpurchase evaluating

New automobile advertisements go unnoticed until the customer needs a new automobile. Then, all of a sudden, the advertisements seem to be everywhere, and the information search begins. The consumer carries out a similar process when selecting a physician or hospital. Figure 2-3 relates the process to selecting a hospital for elective surgery. The higher the cost, the more risk, and the more extensive information seeking and evaluating are before purchase. As shown, the consumer completes much of the information seeking by gathering perceptions: their own and those of friends, relatives, and social groups. Often, the consumer is evaluating the provider by reputation and word-of-mouth advertising. Therefore, perceived image and positioning are paramount to purchasing decisions. The implications here for nursing are that the development of a desired nursing image and identity, as well as proper positioning, will influence customer selection of a hospital. Responsive nurse managers cultivate a positive image in the mind of the customers.

In selecting a hospital, patients are able to evaluate hospitals objectively on such factors as scientific advances, technology, and specific services.

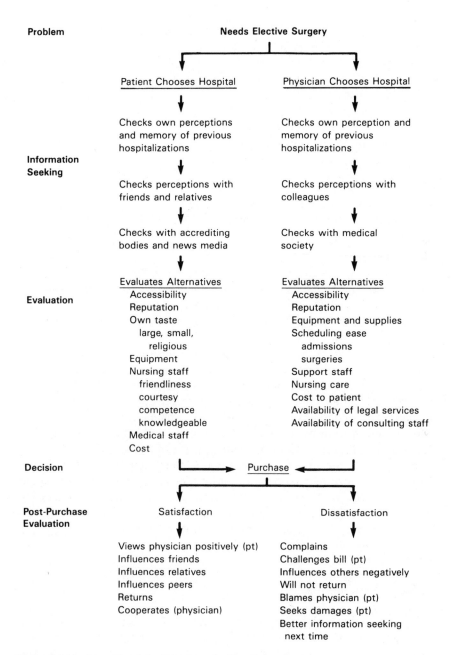

Figure 2-3 Decision Model for Selection of a Hospital

However, once admitted, their evaluation is based on subjective, affective qualities such as services, staff attentiveness, and "friendliness of the environment."[6] On the other hand, physicians choose hospitals for "the quality of nursing staff" and the "reputation of the hospital."[7] Other determining factors for physicians are

- accessibility of consultant physicians
- availability of special programs
- equipment
- medical libraries
- professional development programs
- whether malpractice insurance is paid or at reduced rates
- adequate parking (easy access)
- legal counsel[8]

In fact, nursing is the most important variable in determining customer satisfaction. Physicians are interested in the quality of nursing services not only from a humanitarian but also from a financial perspective. The patient who is satisfied with the hospital and nursing services is generally satisfied with the physician. If the patient selected the hospital, the postevaluation is likely to be more favorable than if the physician selected the hospital. Buyer behavior principles maintain that people will justify their choices to preserve the rationale of their judgment.[9] When the patient does not choose the hospital, nursing has more of a marketing challenge. The influence of word-of-mouth information seeking cannot be underestimated. One dissatisfied patient may produce a negative image of the hospital in the mind of many people, depending on the scope of the patient's private world.

Customer selection by perception, not necessarily realities, is the salient value factor involved. Marketing involves researching the values, setting up exchange relationships, and positioning the nursing department to reflect the appropriate image and identity to its customers.

Exchange Relationships

Kotler stated that the discipline of marketing is based on the concept of exchange.[10] Bagozzi postulated that exchange may be the "core phenomenon" in the study of marketing.[11] Economic exchange theory defines the exchange as an activity used to maximize profits and minimize losses. For every winner, there is a loser, and the cost of losing may be high.

Exchange behavior, a term commonly used in economics and social psychology, is defined here as giving something of value in order to receive something of equal or exceeding value. It is beyond the scope of this book to present exchange theory or discuss the various types of exchange relationships. However, it is appropriate to discuss the conditions of exchange and what is exchanged between nursing and major customers. Exchange requires

1. two or more parties
2. something of perceived value to each
3. freedom to communicate needs
4. freedom to reject the exchange

Figure 2-4 shows the exchange transaction and the outcome variables between nursing and nursing's major customers. In each situation, nursing gives something of value to the customer in exchange for something that is valued equally or more.

Nursing may purposely set up exchanges with customers by researching their values. For example: a brilliant endocrinologist practices at Hospital A and Hospital B. The nurse administrator of Hospital B wishes to capture more of the market share of the endocrine patient population. The strategy is to find out what the physician values and then set up the appropriate exchange. The exchange values are as follows for the physician:

1. specialized unit with specialized staff
2. nurse specialist to develop and coordinate the program
3. mechanism to consult with a pediatric endocrinologist
4. home care program

The nurse administrator values

1. higher occupancy on the medical unit (revenue)
2. new challenges for the medical nursing staff (job enrichment and productivity)
3. recognition from administration for achieving the hospital goal for increased patient days and revenue (reward and praise)

If the physician gives the hospital more endocrinology patients, the hospital will provide the items on the physician's value list. Likewise, if the hospital gives the physician the items on the physician's value list, the physician will bring in more patients and therefore provide the items on the nurse administrator's value list. There are two parties, each has something of

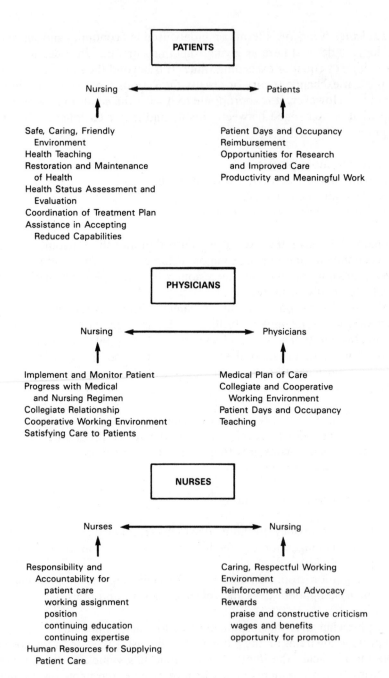

Figure 2-4 Exchange Transactions and Outcome Variables

value to give to the other, and both are free to communicate and reject the exchange. In the market-based model, the establishment of programs and services is based on researching customer values and setting up exchange relationships.

NOTES

1. "Is Religion a Competitive Edge?," *Hospitals* 61, no. 8 (April 1987): 60–61.

2. Steven G. Hillestad and Eric N. Berkowitz, *Health Care Marketing Plans: From Strategy to Action* (Homewood, Ill: Dow Jones–Irwin, 1984), 38.

3. Phillip Kotler, *Marketing for Non-Profit Organizations* (Englewood Cliffs, N.J.: Prentice-Hall, Inc., 1982), 62.

4. Terrence J. Rynne, "The Third Stage of Hospital Long-Range Planning: The Marketing Approach," in *Strategic Planning in Health Care Management,* ed. William A. Flexner, Eric N. Berkowitz, and Montague Brown (Rockville, Md.: Aspen Publishers, Inc., 1981), 258.

5. Thomas C. Kinnear and Kenneth L. Bernhardt, *Principles of Marketing* (Glenview, Ill.: Scott, Foresman & Co., 1983), 141.

6. "Satisfaction Surveys Found To Be Deceptive," *Hospitals* 61, no. 8 (April 1987): 53–54.

7. "Quality, Not Ads, Increase Physician Loyalty," *Hospitals* 61, no. 12 (June 1987): 56.

8. "Satisfaction Surveys Found To Be Deceptive," 53–54.

9. Ibid., 54.

10. Kotler, 37.

11. Richard P. Bagozzi, "Marketing As Exchange," *Journal of Marketing* 39 (1975): 32.

Positioning

As a part of the mission statement, *position* is defined as where and what the organization wants to be in the marketplace. Positioning is discussed here as the public part of the mission. For example, for what does the organization wish to be known in the mind of its customers? Positioning is concerned with marketability differentiation, identity, and image.

BEING OR BECOMING MARKETABLE

Often, organizations turn to marketing because of poor performance problems, loss of market share to the competition, and image problems. In order to market effectively, an organization must have something to market. Marketability is a measure of the organization's market attractiveness. For example: the physical facility is attractive and accessible, there is adequate staff, staff attitudes are good, and the organization is productive and cost-efficient. From a nursing perspective, the nursing department ensures marketability by providing a clean, safe, friendly environment for its customers. Additionally, careful attention is given to recruiting adequate staff, negotiating competitive employee benefits, and conducting employee orientation in customer relations. Good nursing management practices include maintaining the following:

- productive staff-to-patient ratio
- fair and professional employee relations program
- competitive employee wage
- comprehensive RN recruitment and retention program
- adequate employee orientation including hospitality programing or guest relations

- mechanism for obtaining customer satisfaction levels
- system to monitor the effectiveness of the above
- system for initiating change based on feedback

These and other activities are packaged into a nursing marketing program that is a part of routine nursing administration.

DIFFERENTIATION

Differentiation means defining what it is about the organization that is different from other organizations. From a nursing perspective, why should the target market patronize the organization over others? Does the nursing organization offer primary care at a competitive price? Are there more specialized programs available? Is the staff primarily RNs? Is the department small and friendly, large and "high tech," better at obstetrics, more prompt in service, or more innovative? In marketing terms, *differentiating* is claiming the special niche in the marketplace in comparison to the competition. Sometimes the niche is something special about the department that is already in place on a small scale.

For example: a community hospital nursing department developed a simple program for the diabetes patient. Based on the needs of the patient population, the program became a little more sophisticated each year until, finally, a diabetes nurse specialist was hired. In differentiating from others, the nursing department found that it was already recognized in the community for the diabetes program. With the help of the nurse specialist and an endocrinologist, the nursing department developed and promoted an efficient, cost-effective diabetes inpatient unit and outpatient program.

In order to claim a niche, the nursing department must practice three principles of marketing by knowing itself, its customers, and its competition well. *Positioning* is mental imaging of specialized strengths, developing or enhancing those strengths, and then setting customer perceptions accordingly.

Some nursing departments believe that professing a higher quality of care than the competition is a strength. However, the community believes that all hospitals are equal in the quality of care given to patients. Quality is, indeed, difficult to quantify to the community. After all, hospitals are all licensed by the state to operate, and most are accredited by the Joint Commission on Accreditation of Healthcare Organizations (Joint Commission). Furthermore, the way in which nursing professionals define *quality* is better not communicated. Consider promoting a medication error rate of less than 1 percent, a mortality rate of 5 percent, or a hospital-acquired infection rate of less than 1 percent. What can be communicated is more registered professional staff, more patient teaching programs, more specialized units, or more prompt service, to name a few.

IDENTITY AND IMAGE

Having both culture and a tradition of its own, each organization also has a unique image and identity in the community. This image may or may not be the image and identity the staff wishes to convey. Some organizations may capitalize on the image of *large, teaching, high tech,* and/or *charity.* Others may desire to shed these images. Often, the organization's perception of its image is not consistent with that of the community. Consulting firms exist solely to research organizational image and identity perceptions, both internally and externally, and make recommendations for strengthening or changing perceived images. The desired image is included in the mission statement and compared with actual perceptions during the environmental assessment.

Likewise, the nursing mission defines the image and identity desired in the mind of the targeted market. This image becomes the theme, or the "look," of the department, service, or program. In order to set perceptions, the look, theme, or logo is incorporated in all of the department's promotional communications. The following RN recruitment advertisements appeared in the *Chicago Tribune:*

- come grow with us (challenge and growth)
- a responsive, precision team (progressive, dynamic)
- the sign of good things in nursing (interpretation open)
- time for TLC (slower paced)
- a refreshing change (bring your "burned out" body to us)
- a job that waits for you (name your tune)
- putting people first (caring)
- teaching the way to recovery (education oriented)
- exceptional care in Chicago (we are the best)
- if you're one of the best (pride and prestige)
- we care for life (dedication)
- nursing: a professional privilege (nursing is special)
- large enough to help you grow, small enough to care (the best of both worlds)
- for excellence in nursing (sophisticated)[1]

Most of these themes are metaphorical representations of subjective qualities that the organizations are using to convey a certain look or image, i.e., literary symbols that conjure the desired picture of the organization.

In summary, nursing differentiates, develops an image, takes on a look, and communicates the identity in a promotional campaign that positions the department competitively in the marketplace. The marketing program for nursing addresses the issue of becoming marketable in the eyes and perceptions of the major customers of nursing.

MARKETING PROGRAM FOR NURSING

In order to become or remain marketable and retain competitive positioning in the marketplace, responsive nurse managers develop and implement an ongoing marketing and image package or program designed (1) to attract and maintain current customers, (2) to monitor the pulse of the primary customers, and (3) to plan change based on customer research. The concept of a marketing package means that there are systematic and well-established activities that can be grouped together and integrated into the routine administration of nursing. A few examples are given as a starting point.

Patients

Patients select a hospital by its reputation and technology and the preference of their physician. The criteria for a positive postevaluation of a hospital are subjective factors such as staff competence, skill, friendliness, courtesy, and availability of other amenities. The marketing package for patients attempts to approximate the patients' expectations (or demand) for service, amenities, and tangibility. A few routine marketing packages for patients are presented here.

Admission Programs

The patient's first contact with a hospital and hospital staff is during the admission process. Consequently, the efficiency or the inefficiency of the admission sets the tone for the entire hospitalization. Therefore, nursing and admitting collaborate cooperatively to ensure that the patient admission process is organized and as individualized as possible. Some programs for scheduled admissions are presented here.

Preadmission Registration Program. The preadmission registration ensures that patients do not wait long in the admitting department. Patients who are scheduled for admission are contacted at home prior to admission by an admission representative who obtains all of the required information. The admission sheet, identification tag, name plate, and room assignment are completed when the patient presents. Nursing contacts the patient at home to answer questions the patient may have about the nursing care and hospitalization in general. These activities not only facilitate a more efficient admission but impress upon the patient that the process is individualized and planned.

Admission Representative Program. On admission, a clerk is assigned to each patient. Patients who are not preregistered are taken directly to the room where the admission representative visits to obtain the required information. The admission representative also visits assigned patients several hours after admission to ask about the efficiency of the admission, welcome the patient to the hospital, and complete any final paper work.

Admission Diagnostic Testing Program. Laboratory and radiology services are located in the admission area. Admission laboratory and radiology tests are completed before patients are taken to the unit. Preoperative electrocardiograms are also completed. This provides better utilization of ancillary services and ensures that diagnostic testing results return to the units in a timely manner.

Admitting/Nursing Room Assignment Program. The admission representative and the unit primary nurse collaborate, assigning patients to rooms based on the patient's condition, diagnosis, expected acuity level, nurse assignment, compatibility with other patients, sex, and geographical configuration of the unit.

The extent of nursing involvement in the room assignment depends on (1) the care delivery system, (2) how nurses are assigned to patients in terms of patient acuity levels and nurse competencies, and (3) how patients are grouped geographically on the unit by disease or physician. A well-planned room assignment minimizes room transfers and facilitates improved nurse access to patients.

Escort/Room Orientation Program. If a room orientation program is not written and assigned to trained staff, it may not be given or may be given haphazardly. The nursing unit manager and staff work with admitting, training admitting escorts to complete the room orientation at the time the escort brings the patient to the room. Trained escorts are hired for minishifts covering peak admission hours. Escort duties include welcoming the patient and family to the hospital, escorting the patient (and family) to the assigned room by wheelchair, explaining the admission booklet (reinforcing visiting hours, use of telephone, and disposition of personal belongings), and room orientation. The orientation includes an explanation of the following:

- geographical layout of the unit
- location of family waiting areas
- physical facilities in the room
- manual controls such as television controls and the nurse call system
- scheduled mealtimes and special visiting hours

Some hospitals use closed-circuit television for the orientation; thus, the staff time involved in the orientation is limited to that necessary to provide a specific time for viewing and for answering questions the patient may have.

Admission Day Welcome Program. Since the admission day is special, special amenities are given. Some of these include

- validated parking for the family
- free-meal coupon for two, redeemable in the cafeteria
- first patient meal tray served with linen, china, and a carnation in a vase
- free newspaper and television guide book
- free admission kit containing a toothbrush, toothpaste, facial tissue, comb, lotion, and mouthwash

The amenities are as creative as the imagination and budgets permit.

Primary Nurse Program

For scheduled admissions, patients are assigned to nurses in advance of admission. The primary nurse is responsible for planning the care of the patient from admission to discharge. Depending on the care delivery system of the unit, the primary nurse may or may not be assigned to provide the physical care of the patient. In either case, the admission nurse completes the admission assessment, initiates the care plan, and gives the patient the business card of the primary nurse. At the first opportunity, the primary nurse visits the patient, completes the assessment and plan of care, and explains the care delivery system of the unit and role of the primary nurse.

A brochure describing the scope and function of the unit, the unit care delivery system, the on-duty dates and shifts of the primary nurse, and how to contact the nurse manager is given to the patient. Exhibit 3-1 shows an abbreviated sample.

Exhibit 3-1 Description of Unit Scope and Function for Patients

To the Patient:

Welcome to 5 East, Surgical Nursing Unit. 5 East is a 23-bed unit designed to provide nursing care to the postoperative patient. Your nurse manager is Jane Lawrence, MSN, (telephone extension #982), and your primary nurse is Susan Perchard, RN. The care delivery system on the unit is primary nursing. This means that one primary nurse assigned to you will be planning your nursing care with you from admission to discharge. Your primary nurse may not always provide your direct care but will always be in communication with other nurses involved in your care in order to ensure that your patient care needs are met. Primary nurse responsibilities include

- pain management
- wound care management
- diet progression
- activity progression
- discharge teaching
- after-care coordination

The average length of stay on the unit is three to seven days. However, the course of your hospitalization will depend on the type of surgery you have had as well as your response to treatment.

The unit is family oriented, and we wish to encourage visiting by your family during the hours of 1 PM and 8 PM. A discharge conference will be planned by your primary nurse for you and your family prior to discharge to discuss your posthospitalization needs. Also, your primary nurse will telephone you at home posthospitalization to discuss unanticipated issues arising during your first few hours at home.

You will have the opportunity to evaluate the nursing care on our unit before you are discharged. We encourage you to complete the questionnaire that will be given to you at that time.

Please feel free to express your needs and concerns to the unit nurse manager or your primary nurse. We hope to make your stay with us as comfortable as possible and facilitate your rapid recovery.

Sincerely,

The 5 East Nursing Staff

Frequent questioning of the patient by the primary nurse about the care allows nursing to resolve complaints quickly and before the patient takes up the problem with others outside nursing.

The primary nurse program is tailored to the needs of the patient and the availability of nursing staff. However, consistent key concepts include providing

- business cards of the primary nurse (tangibility)
- brochures describing the unit and the care delivery system (tangibility)
- assignment of a primary nurse to the patient from admission to discharge to plan the care and be the patient's advocate

From a marketing perspective, the primary nurse model provides an excellent mechanism to know the patient well. The primary nurse maintains frequent contact with the patient not only to know the patient well but to obtain continuous feedback on the satisfaction level of the patient.

Morning Wake-up Program

Dietary staff give patients morning coffee, tea, or juice and a newspaper prior to breakfast, setting a positive tone for the day. This morning wake-up nutrition also offsets the waiting time between the patient's awakening and the arrival of the breakfast tray.

Patient Teaching Programs

Teaching sheets and educational booklets provide additional tangibility for the patient and reinforce verbal instructions and teaching given by nurses. Free literature is available on many disease processes from various associations such as the American Heart Association and the Arthritis Foundation. Nursing develops formal and informal teaching programs for patients based on current literature, current practice, and collaboration with physicians and other departments. Medication teaching sheets, discharge instructions, and booklets are grouped by disease on each unit as resources. The teaching plan specifies which materials are to be given to each patient by disease category. See Appendix 3-A for a sample discharge instruction handout for emergency department patients. A consistent format for patient teaching plans is as follows:

1. disease process, etiology, course, symptoms, and prevention
2. medications, actions, and side effects
3. diagnostic testing

4. discharge instruction
   - activity
   - diet
   - medications and treatments
   - restrictions and limitations
   - symptoms of recurrence
   - follow-up care
   - community resources

This informational material is given to the patient by the primary nurse during hospitalization and verbally reinforced at the time of discharge.

Discharge Program

A written discharge program with policies and procedures along with assignments for responsibility ensures that the discharge process is efficient and thorough, promoting a high level of patient satisfaction. The following are included in the discharge program:

- discharge instruction sheets, booklets, and prescriptions
- patient satisfaction-with-care survey
- nonstop wheelchair transport to automobile by escort service
- special waiting area for discharged patients
- coffee and cookies in the discharge waiting area
- parking validation for driver
- follow-up telephone call from the nursing unit to express concern for a safe arrival home

Again, the written discharge instructions are tangible evidence representing the purchase of nursing care. The survey questionnaires are coded by unit, filled out by patients while in the discharge area, and dropped in a special box for the purpose. Volunteers return the questionnaires to units on a weekly basis so that immediate feedback concerning customer satisfaction levels can be obtained.

The timing of the discharge is important. The physician visit and discharge order, the giving of prescriptions, and the arrival of transport are coordinated to occur at a discharge time specified by the patient who must arrange transportation home. The special area designated for discharge waiting is close to the parking facility. This area is staffed with a clerk during peak discharge hours. Ideally, the escorted patient arrives at the discharge area just in time for the ride home. If he or she does not, family members picking up the patient call the unit from the discharge area and wait there briefly until the patient arrives. This prevents the driver from having to navigate through the hospital and facilitates a speedy discharge.

Nurses

Marketing programs for nurses center on three areas:

1. recognition
2. recruitment
3. image

Nursing literature proliferates with articles about the role of nurses as both emissaries for and customers of the hospital.[2,3] In actuality, all hospital employees are both emissaries and customers. However, nurses are unique marketing agents and customers because of the duration and frequency of their contact with patients and the problems present in recruiting and retaining qualified nurses.

Presently, nursing is experiencing a shortage unlike any other in history. This time, the problem is one of supply, originating in the academic institutions that graduate nurses. Nursing student enrollment declined from 251,000 in 1983 to 218,000 in 1985.[4] Furthermore, a classic article on the nursing shortage reported that "between 1970 and 1980, the number of women enrolled in law school increased from 7,000 to 42,000" and that "women enrollment [in medicine] increased from 9 percent in 1969 to 28 percent in 1979."[5] Other conclusions made in this report were:

- Nurses' incomes have not increased with vacancy rates according to normal supply and demand factors.
- Nurses' incomes have not kept pace with that of teachers and other predominately women-filled positions.
- Nurses' income averages nationally that of secretaries.
- Effects of inadequate wages are more part-time nurses, increased employment in nursing agencies, the use of nurses for duties of other departments, decreasing nursing school enrollment, falling qualifications of nursing school applicants, dissatisfaction, high turnover, and attempts at collective bargaining.[6]

The nursing supply problem is discussed in more detail in Chapter 9.

Nursing marketing is concerned with the supply of nurses because nurses are the producers of the product, health care, and because they are the sales force representing the hospital to the patients. The satisfied nurse will deliver care in a positive manner, reflecting favorably on the image of the hospital. Because nursing is the largest hospital department and because nurses interface directly and frequently with the customers of the hospital, they are the hospital's most valuable resource. Furthermore, the inability to attract nurses is largely due to service-end problems, one of which is a low wage relative to the responsibility.

Various recruitment gimmicks for attracting nurses exist in the marketplace. Some examples are

- $1,000 bonuses every six months for working the night shift
- full-time pay for 12-hour weekend tours of duty
- free vacation trips
- added vacation days for night and evening duty
- $2,000 bonuses for recruiting a nurse

These are all short-term solutions that are given in times of shortages and taken away in times of adequate supply. Consequently, the weekend bonuses, shift differentials, and added vacation days cannot be used when calculating the real income of nurses. Further, none of these solutions represents a milestone in resolving the cyclical shortage problems. Only solid compensation and benefit programs combined with fair employment practices and meaningful recognition will result in long-term solutions to the nursing shortage.

Responsive nurse managers maintain a constant vigil on the supply and demand for nurses, articulating the needs of nursing to those in positions influencing the recruitment and retention of nurses. Otherwise, substitution for nurses will continue during times of shortages, modifying the role of nurses and preventing salaries from reflecting supply, demand, and the relative worth of the position. Already, in 1988, plans for substitution are underway with the recent American Medical Association's proposal for registered care technologists (RCTs). These RCTs would be prepared for basic (nine months) and advanced (18 months) training. Such a proposal would only lower the standard of care given to patients and reduce the potential market for RNs. Additonally, the proposal would further reduce the attractiveness of that market because of suppression of salaries, resulting from the availability of low-cost substitutes. The following programs can be used in the practice setting to attract nurses in the shrinking total market.

Recruitment, Retention, and Recognition Programs

In order to market and attract nurses effectively, an organization must have marketable programs. Effective recruitment requires that recognition and retention programs be in place. Basic retention programs include the following.

Adequate Salary and Benefit Packages. Responsive nurse managers compare the organization's RN salary and benefits with those of other professional groups in the organization and to other hospitals in the area. Specifically, in-house RN salaries are compared with those of physical therapists, occupational therapists, dietary staff, paramedics, and social workers. Does equity exist among professional salaries according to the degree of job demand, consequences of error, frequency and duration of contact with patients, and education and orientation required for the job? Does the benefit package allow enough paid time for rest and renewal? Does the benefit package include adequate tuition reimbursement, allowing nurses to grow in the profession and become better nurses?

Flexible Scheduling. Because nursing is required 24 hours a day, seven days a week, creative and flexible scheduling is both possible and necessary. Responsive nurse managers create competitive flexible staffing options for nurses to fill according to their individual needs.

Positive, Caring, Professional Working Environment. Even the best salary and benefit package will not compensate for a poor working environment. Porter-O'Grady[7] defined five categories of individual needs that must be met in the work environment:

1. respect
2. trust
3. appropriate information
4. human and material support
5. meaningful rewards, both economic and personal

Clinical Ladders Program. The implementation of clinical ladders for nurses accomplishes four major goals for nursing:

1. improved care to patients
2. growth and recognition for nurses
3. performance evaluation on objective criteria
4. effective recruitment strategy

Clinical ladders are treated here as a basic recognition and retention program since the concept is no longer the exception but a commonplace employment program.

Continuing Education. Because of rapid changes in technology and practice trends, continuing education for nurses is essential. Four paid education days per nurse annually is a competitive retention strategy. More days are added with longevity.

Nurse managers analyze nurse turnover, determining the average length of employment in order to structure major benefits to begin at the critical turnover point. For example, if the average length of stay for RNs is 18 months, wage increases, ladder progression, number of paid continuing education days, and number of vacation days are accelerated at that point. First, a professional working environment is provided; then the benefit package is structured to accelerate at the critical point in employment. This strategy ensures that the nurse is recognized and rewarded for continued employment. Other innovative retention strategies include the following.

• *Nursing newsletter.* A nursing newsletter or journal provides recognition for nurses and exposes them to writing for professional publication. The Stanford University newsletter is a good example of how a simple newsletter can evolve into a professional journal, becoming a powerful nurse recognition and image strategy.[8]

• *Shared governance. Shared governance* is a participative management strategy designed to give nurses maximum input into nursing issues affecting them. Although this innovative approach has been adopted by many nursing administrations, an entire book is available on the topic written by Porter-O'Grady and Finnigan.[9] Even if this program cannot be implemented in full, specific concepts can be adapted such as staff nurse participation in nurse hiring, nursing standards policies and procedures, quality assurance, and marketing and recruitment activities.

• *Active recruitment and retention committee.* Even if the department has a recruitment nurse, satisfied staff nurses are more effective in recruiting other nurses. Suggested here is a formal recruitment committee, chaired by the recruitment nurse or a nurse manager, consisting of staff nurses from nursing units. Activities of this committee include

• attending recruitment fairs and expositions with the recruitment nurse
• planning in-house recruitment activities sponsored by units needing staff
• sponsoring and planning nurses' week activities
• sponsoring employee activities such as marathons, "pot luck" dinners, and ball and bowling leagues

- Selling nursing memorabilia such as t-shirts with the nursing department logo and theme, with proceeds going to nursing continuing education activities or other worthy causes identified by the nursing department
- identifying unit recruitment and retention problems
- brainstorming recruitment strategies
- planning recognition activities (e.g., management/staff nurse teas and celebrations to honor staff for excellence in predefined areas, appreciation events for units displaying teamwork and cooperation during periods of high census and low staffing, nurse-of-the-month and nurse-of-the-year activities)
- sponsoring nurse mentor programs for new nurses
- developing unit recruitment activities
- sponsoring summer internships for student nurses
- identifying the need for a refresher nurse course
- planning burnout prevention programs such as paired rotation in and out of high-stress areas

Professional Image Programs

"In order to accept and love another, one must first be accepted and loved."[10] Nurse managers cannot provide a caring, professional, trusting, and respectful working environment for nurses until they first receive trust and respect from the nurse administrator. In order to build a positive image for the nursing department, attention must first be given to the nurse manager. It begins with open communication, management development, professional and personal development, and team building.

Management Development. First, for the new manager, a management course is provided outside the hospital. The benefits gained will exceed the cost as the new manager begins to apply the learned management theory and human relations skills. Second, an in-house management course is given covering topics specific to the institution and position such as staffing, budgeting, and orientation to other department managers. Third, continuing management education is given either in-house or outside on specific clinical and management topics.

Personal and Professional Development. Topics for managers in personal development are money management, stress management, professional dress, group dynamics, personal goal setting, and assertiveness training. Nurse managers who are personally and professionally comfortable assist their staff in developing similar qualities.

Team Building. Individual success is often conditional on the failure of another. In fact, the manager selection process is a clear example. One nurse is selected as manager at the expense of several others who are not selected. Unfortunately, this phenomenon pervades many other management issues and events, setting up a malevolent environment encouraging scapegoating. The nurse manager reverses this process so that nursing has all winners and no losers.

Success is structured in such a way that it cannot be attained in isolation. The department of nursing stands out, not the individual unit. Team building is the conditional structuring of success to include every manager and every unit. As a simple and small-scale example, when one nurse manager presents an innovative nursing assignment sheet, the manager can be successful with implementation only after chairing a task force for revising the nursing assignment sheets for the entire department. The manager must lead, negotiate, share, and compromise with peers for the benefit of the entire department. Other team-building activities include nurse manager–chaired leadership meetings, retreats, and nursing administrative projects.

Nurse managers are limited in their capacity to manage the units by two things: (1) their own perceptions of their capabilities, and (2) the nurse administrator. The responsive nurse administrator builds the manager's image of self-competence and self-worth, providing the latitude for development and the support to ensure success. When managers feel good about themselves, they are capable of providing a caring, professional environment for their staff. Likewise, when staff nurses are satisfied with their work, patients will benefit. From this basic foundation, the nursing image is formed.

Image Building Programs for Nursing

After nursing defines its unique image or position in the nursing mission, all that remains to be done is the campaign. The campaign is a promotional plan to carry the image to the customers. A few programs to accomplish this follow:

Guest Relations Program. Employees need not be taught to be nice to customers. Rather, employees are taught customers' definition and perceptions of *nice, courteous,* and *caring.* Undoubtedly, nursing desires to deliver quality and satisfying care to the patient customers. To nursing, this may mean careful vigilance and monitoring of a patient's condition, precision implementation of the treatment regimen, and comprehensive documentation. Nursing can do all of these things and still have dissatisfied customers. In fact, patients assume that this quality of care exists at all hospitals equally. Patients equate satisfaction with care to "social courtesies" and other services.[11] A guest relations program for nursing employees assists nursing in delivering care to patients in a way that satisfies both the patient and employee.

Community Outreach Education Programs. As a professional opportunity to staff and as an image-building event for nursing, community outreach education can be designed and managed by the nursing development staff. Nursing has specialists capable of speaking on various topics such as breast self-examination, cancer detection for women, smoking cessation, risk factors in heart disease, and obesity and weight reduction, to name a few. Such programs create a positive image for nursing as well as high visibility in the community and top-of-mind name recognition for the hospital. Another community image builder is the offering of education to nursing home staffs. Some topics include quality assurance, infection control, intravenous therapy, and staffing. This contact will encourage nursing home staff to think of the hospital when their patients need hospitalization.

Joint Faculty/Staff Positions. Because nursing academic institutions are also customers of nursing and because these institutions are a part of the community from which patients are drawn, nursing can create a special bond, linking education to practice with joint faculty/staff positions. These positions are held by RNs with qualifying degrees who work half-time as faculty and half-time as hospital nursing staff. Salary and benefits are shared equally by both institutions. Some of the benefits of such a cooperative program are

- special recruitment opportunities for the nursing department
- high visibility and image projection in the community for the nursing department
- clinically expert faculty
- guaranteed clinical sites for the academic organization

Nursing utilizes the half-time staff in positions appropriate to the nurse's credentials and experience. For example, some may function as managers, clinical specialists, or staff nurses.

Marketing Committee. A marketing committee consisting of a representative from each unit, chaired by a nurse manager, provides high visibility for the nursing department as the members direct and implement internal marketing programs for nursing's major customers. Additionally, the committee is responsible for identifying problems with the marketability of the units or department.

Research Committee. By developing research-based practice innovation, nursing improves its image to physicians and other professionals. A research committee consisting of staff nurses, chaired by a nurse manager, identifies practice problems, researches similar problems in the literature, develops research innovations, conducts clinical trials, and implements the research-based innovations on the unit and housewide if appropriate. Participation on this committee provides recognition for nursing and improved practice to patients.

Nursing Grand Rounds. The establishment of unit nursing grand rounds enhances the professional image of nursing in the mind of physicians and other professionals, provides recognition for staff nurses, and improves the care given to patients.

Manager/Unit Award Program. The manager/unit award consists of a 5 percent bonus for the manager, a gold plaque of excellence for the unit with dates and names of unit employees, and a recognition tea or breakfast for unit staff with nursing management. The criteria for award include

- 100 percent compliance with the unit quality assurance standard
- 100 percent rating on the patient questionnaire survey
- 100 percent rating on the employee and physician questionnaire surveys

Awards are given each month. Since this is an ongoing program and not a one-time contest, all managers and staff are eligible for the award each month. Having all winners and no losers is a possibility. Criteria are developed by the nursing administration and tailored to the standards of excellence defined by each nursing department. The benefits include

- high visibility and positive image projection for the nursing department
- incentive for nursing to achieve excellence
- recognition for the manager and nursing staff

Management Breakfast. The management breakfast is a monthly event scheduled from 9 to 11 AM and is designed so that departmental managers can drop in, network with other managers, and leave. Sponsored by the nursing administration, this event provides high visibility for nursing and enhances the nursing image as being cooperative with other departments. Another benefit is that informal networking and problem resolution occur naturally among departments. The results are increased cooperation among departments, mutual respect, team-building behaviors, and more efficient patient care.

Management Retreat. This annual event is specifically for nursing management and is designed intentionally by the nurse administrator to recognize the need of management to reflect on where the nursing department has been and where it is going. The purpose of the retreat is to develop goals and objectives for the coming year. One or two days are set aside, and the agenda and program are as sophisticated or as simple as the nurse administrator desires or can afford. Keynote speakers are scheduled, or nursing plans, develops, and presents the agenda items. The management retreat is further discussed in Chapter 6 where it is treated as a forum for developing the nursing marketing objectives. Serendipitous benefits of the management retreat include

- professional image development
- team building
- networking and problem resolution
- recognition for managers

Physicians

Because physicians bring patients into the hospital, they are customers of nursing. However, the relationship is reciprocal. Nurses are customers of physicians, and the exchange relationship is one in which nursing needs physicians for patient referrals and physicians need nursing to deliver nursing care to their patients. The manner in which care is delivered can be a direct reflection of the physician's judgment in the mind of patients. Additionally, nursing can alter the efficiency of physicians by making hospital rounds organized or disorganized. On the other hand, physicians can produce nurse turnover by creating a tense working environment for nurses. In the ideal situation, both professionals collaborate, taking the time to discover how each can make the work place more efficient for the other. Chapter 4 discusses how to assess the needs and wants of the physician customer. Presented here are a few basic approaches used in marketing nursing to physicians.

Physician/Nursing Newsletters and Journals

A nursing section or column in the physicians' newsletter or journal keeps physicians updated on nursing news, increasing the visibility of nursing and improving communication between nursing and the medical staff.

Topic examples include

- new nursing consulting services
- physical changes scheduled to occur in units
- new accreditation requirements for nursing
- new nursing forms
- nursing research being conducted
- new nursing protocols

The nursing news column does not replace verbal communication and face-to-face collaboration with physicians on nursing issues affecting them but serves as an additional communication mechanism. As a reciprocal gesture, nursing may also invite the chief or president of the medical staff to provide an update on medical issues in a column or section of the nursing newsletter.

Nursing Representation on Physician Committees

Physicians make decisions in hospitals by committee and majority rule. Although nurses cannot be voting members, nurses can influence the vote. Nursing representation is now required on most physician/hospital committees by the Joint Commission. This positions nursing in the physician decision-making arena. Active involvement, however, occurs by working with the chairperson to become a regular part of the departmental agenda. In so doing, nursing educates, communicates, and influences. Benefits include high visibility for nursing, input into physician/patient care decisions, and better working relationships between the medical staff and nursing.

Nursing/Physician Joint Practice Committee

The joint practice committee is a standing committee of both the medical and nursing staffs, consisting of an equal number of physicians and nurses as voting members. The ideal number is five physicians and five nurses, three of whom are staff nurses. The purpose of the committee is to examine, discuss, collaborate, and come to a consensus on any issue affecting the way in which care is given. This committee is the most effective method of establishing a good working relationship with physicians. The decisions rendered in the committee are challenged by neither the medical staff nor nursing because of the composition and standing of the committee. Examples of agenda items are

- critical nurse staffing issues
- problems with support services that prevent nursing from carrying out the plan of care, such as delayed laboratory reporting, delayed medication delivery, and shortages or lack of adequate supplies
- problems and issues related to house staff affecting nursing's ability to provide care to patients
- inappropriate requests by specific physicians for nursing to perform medical practice procedures
- physician complaints with nursing's care delivery system, chart forms, or method of assignment of nursing staff
- new nursing procedures or systems expected to affect medical practice

Both nursing and the medical staff may place items on the agenda for discussion and recommendations. Recommendations from the committee go to the nursing and medical executive committees for approval. The nurse administrator will discover widespread acceptance of deferring practice problems to this committee. Physicians accept the committee's decisions because of its standing as a bona fide medical staff committee written into the professional staff bylaws and governed by majority rule. The benefits of the committee are high visibility for nursing, a more satisfied nursing and medical staff, improved relationships between nursing and medical staff, and improved patient care.

Physician Unit Representative Program

Another effective method of creating a good working relationship with the medical staff is the physician unit representation program. The chief of staff appoints a physician to each of the nursing units to act as a physician liaison and representative for mediconursing issues needing immediate attention. The purposes of the program are as follows:

- Provide crisis intervention between the medical and nursing staffs.
- Defer appropriate problems and issues to the joint practice committee.
- Resolve urgent problems in collaboration with unit nurse managers.

Consequently, critical problems are resolved before becoming magnified and unmanageable. Examples of appropriate problems and issues are

- serious nursing complaints with a physician, resident, or intern
- serious physician complaints with a nurse or nursing care
- serious patient complaints with a nurse or physician

To differentiate further, the joint practice committee collaborates on issues requiring extensive problem solving and research, and the physician representative and nurse manager collaborate on more critical problems requiring immediate resolution. All issues resolved by the liaison physician and nurse manager become agenda items for the joint practice committee. The benefits of the physician representative program are improved nurse/physician relationships and improved patient care.

Physicians' Week

During nurses' week, many physicians recognize nursing by funding some of the events or offering other kinds of participation. If they do not, they should be invited to become involved. Likewise, by proclaiming physicians' week recognizing physicians, nursing establishes a strong marketing strategy for one of its major customers. During physicians' week, nursing recognizes those wonderful collaborative physicians as a group. Activities include

- handmaiden day (today we carry your charts)
- rounds with coffee and cookies
- carnations for lapels
- contests with awards for the most supportive physician, the most courteous physician, and departmental physician of the year
- other promotional activities

Resident Orientation Program

What could be a better way for the nursing and medical staffs to begin on a positive note than for nursing to organize a formal resident orientation program for new house staff? Orientation includes

- unit protocols
- unit-specific orders for laboratory, radiology, and pharmacy
- introduction to key nursing staff

- explanation of unit layout
- standing orders of attending physicians

Resident orientation is written and scheduled annually with the arrival of the new house staff.

Office Nurse Hospitality Program

The unit staff of specialty physicians increase referrals to their units by reaching out to market services to the physicians' office nurses. The program includes

- mailing the nursing newsletter to office nurses
- meeting with office nurses in the office to explain various patient services
- inviting office nurses to in-house inservices and seminars
- making telephone calls to office nurses, updating them on unit changes between office meetings

The benefits are high visibility for nursing in the community, improved nurse/physician relationships, improved care to patients, and increased patient referrals.

MONITORING THE PULSE OF NURSING'S CUSTOMERS

One of the basic principles of marketing is that the provider must know the customers well in order to serve them well. In the environmental assessment, all aspects of customer behavior are researched in order to know customers well. The concept of monitoring the pulse of the customer is a strategy requiring continuous feedback concerning the perceptions of nursing care in the mind of its customers. Responsive nurse managers devise and implement ongoing systems for continuous feedback.

For hospital nursing departments, a common feedback system is the questionnaire. Presented here are sample tools for monitoring the perceptions of patients, nurses, and physicians.

Patients

Patients are the primary customers of the nursing department, and as such, their satisfaction with care is of paramount value to the providers.

With so many classifications of personnel coming in contact with patients, it is difficult to control and standardize approaches to patient care. One of the best methods of obtaining immediate feedback concerning patient perceptions of care is to simply ask patients about the care received.

Patient Questionnaires

A simple feedback tool for patients to use is the survey questionnaire. Appendix 3-B shows a sample satisfaction with care and information questionnaire for patients to complete anonymously at discharge. On discharge day, the nurse gives the unit-coded questionnaire to patients, who complete them in the discharge area and place them in a special box for the purpose. Volunteers collect the questionnaires and transport them to the unit as soon as possible. After the nurse manager reads the questionnaires, they are forwarded to the department responsible for summarizing them into monthly reports. The advantage of having patients complete the questionnaires at discharge rather than by mail is that the return rate is almost 100 percent, whereas the return rate by mail is much less. Also, dissatisfied patients are more likely to return the survey by mail, which tends to skew the results negatively.

Some of the benefits of the questionnaire are

- immediate patient satisfaction feedback for nursing units
- nurse awareness of patients' expectations for care
- patient awareness of the responsibilities of nursing

Responsive nurse managers call dissatisfied patients at home. One midwestern hospital arranges home visits to dissatisfied patients to obtain more information about what could have been done to avoid situations that resulted in dissatisfaction with care. The nursing patient questionnaire is incorporated in or is in addition to the hospital questionnaire.

Administrative Welcome Rounds

A positive and high-visibility program to determine the efficiency of the admission process is the administrative welcome rounds. In large hospitals, nurse administrators share the role of welcoming administrator with nursing directors. The program is a daily administrative welcome greeting to all patients admitted the night before. Obviously, the pediatric and normal newborn welcome is given to the parents and children if appropriate. The nurse administrator, accompanied by the manager or staff nurse, chats briefly with each patient admitted the night before, giving a welcome and leaving a business card for future use by the patient in contacting the nurse administrator. This program sets a positive tone for the admission and leaves the patient with an accessible person's name if problems should occur later. The nurse manager makes rounds daily for the same purpose. Organized in this way, the nursing administrator sees all patients in the house, keeping a pulse on patients' perceptions of care.

Postdischarge Follow Up

Primary nurses call the discharged patient within three days postdischarge to reinforce patient compliance with the treatment regimen, express concern about the patient's condition and health status after discharge, and inquire about satisfaction with care. The telephone call in and of itself is a powerful marketing strategy for nursing. It shows that the nursing organization cares about the customers.

Physicians

The responsive nurse manager keeps a constant pulse on the perceptions and attitudes of physicians. Small dissatisfactions become larger complaints, resulting in physician uprisings and threats to use another hospital. A physician questionnaire is developed and administered to physicians monthly to monitor perceptions. A more informal method is face-to-face discussions with physicians about items on the questionnaire. The feedback is used to assess physicians' satisfaction level, and immediate action is taken where appropriate. Appendix 3-C shows a sample questionnaire. The questionnaire is patient oriented and not nurse or physician oriented except for question 8. Using a patient-oriented questionnaire avoids the evaluation of nursing based on subjective criteria such as likes and dislikes of a particular unit, nurse manager, or nurse. Generally speaking, physician satisfaction with nursing care is quid pro quo satisfaction with the staff and unit management. Physicians can expect that nursing will do the following:

- maintain patient satisfaction with care
- provide care in a safe, friendly environment
- assess patient conditions and patient progress with treatment, keeping the physician informed
- maintain efficient nursing units so that physician rounds may be made in an organized manner

The comment section on the questionnaire allows physicians to write in other factors, which are considered for addition to the questionnaire. Anonymity is preserved during administration of the questionnaire.

Nurses

Responsive nurse managers continuously monitor not only the supply of nurses but nurse vacancy rates and the reasons for the vacancies. Analyzing the reasons for resignations requires an accurate monitoring system of the attitudes and beliefs of the resigning nurses and those who are still employed. Continuous feedback strategies for nurses include termination, or exit, interviews, an attitude questionnaire, and a nurse ombudsman program.

Termination, or Exit, Interview

The termination interview is used to determine why nurses leave the hospital. A systematic format is developed for the interview so that the data can be summarized and analyzed for patterns. Each nurse manager receives a monthly report of the termination data. Nurse administrators analyze the data for evidence of generalized problems or problems with a specific unit or issue.

Questionnaire

Most hospitals have employee attitude surveys that are administered annually. If one does not exist, responsive nurse managers devise and administer one just for nursing employees. Tools having a high degree of validity and reliability can be found in the nursing literature. Even if a questionnaire is administered housewide to employees annually, responsive nurse managers administer the survey more frequently in order to keep abreast of the major attitude and perception problems of nurses. The feedback tool can be a simple, self-devised instrument or a more sophisticated tool found in the nursing literature or purchased from a consultant. A sample questionnaire devised and used monthly by a nurse manager is included in Appendix 3-D.

In order to provide an environment in which self-assessment is the norm, nurse administrators devise a feedback questionnaire to be given to nurse managers that surveys their satisfaction with the nursing department. Satisfied managers produce satisfied RNs who produce satisfied patients. Appendix 3-E shows a sample feedback tool for managers to use to rate the nursing department and nursing administration.

Nursing Ombudsman

In order to implement the nursing ombudsman program, a position is created or responsibility added to another position. In some hospitals, a similar position is called patient advocate or patient representative with responsibilities for patient satisfaction. Often, this is not a nurse, and the position does not report to nursing. The nursing ombudsman is concerned with customer relations with and satisfaction levels of all of nursing's customers: patients, nurses, and physicians. The position is filled by an RN who reports to nursing. Responsibilities include

- visiting patients
- following up with orientees
- visiting physicians

The primary purpose of the follow ups and visits is to monitor attitudes and perceptions, keeping the nursing department informed of what is satisfying to customers as well as problems and dissatisfaction levels. The nurse ombudsman also monitors satisfaction with new employment policies, changes in orientation content, compliance and acceptance of new protocols, and acceptance of new staff. Additionally, the nurse ombudsman administers the physician and nurse surveys, summarizing the data for analysis by nursing administration.

ADMINISTRATION, COORDINATION, AND ANALYSIS OF SURVEYS

Each nursing department determines the survey designs, how often the surveys will be administered, how data will be tabulated and analyzed, and how coordination will occur so that the same physician or patient is not surveyed more than once during a survey period. For example, if a physician routinely makes patient visits on more than one unit, the questionnaire is structured so that each unit is represented and only one nurse manager approaches the physician with the questionnaire. The size, complexity, resources, and degree of decentralization are a few of the factors that will influence methods.

For example, a monthly survey of physicians in a small hospital may only irritate physicians. Therefore, a preferable method would be to meet informally with the physicians, discussing items on the questionnaire. Physicians could be assigned to nurse managers on the basis of who works more closely with them and who would care the most about their opinions. Patient questionnaires are given to discharging patients by the nurse manager or a designee, and employee surveys are administered monthly. Smaller hospitals may prefer to limit the number of items on the patient and employee surveys to reflect only major issues. This will reduce the amount of data needing tabulation. The nurse manager then assigns data tabulation to secretaries, clerks, or volunteers.

In a large hospital with more than 500 physicians on staff, the preferred method may be to survey a representative sampling of physicians, i.e., 150 to 200. Also, large hospitals may prefer to administer a written survey quarterly, using face-to-face discussions between quarters. The major thrust of the physician surveys is that physicians' attitudes are in some way monitored continuously. Structured, written survey questionnaires yield data that can be used as a baseline and trended from month to month, quarter to quarter, and year to year. Additionally, the structured questionnaire provides anonymity to physicians, which facilitates obtaining more realistic results. Minimally, physicians and employees are surveyed once a year, but patients are surveyed at discharge.

Large hospitals have more resources with which to tabulate the incoming data from the surveys. Among the options for data tabulation are using staff from the following departments:

- patient advocacy
- quality assurance
- public relations
- planning
- marketing research
- communication
- nursing quality assurance
- volunteer services
- nurse recruitment

The administration of surveys and tabulation of data for the employee surveys are often part of the duties and responsibilities of the nurse recruiter or the staff development department. The administration of surveys and tabulation of data for the physician and patient surveys fit in well with the duties and responsibilities of nursing quality assurance.

Ideally, the nursing management team designs the questionnaires and formulates a plan for implementation, data tabulation, and analysis. The specific means for accomplishing these must be individualized for each hospital according to available resources. Central coordination is necessary to avoid duplication and to integrate data into a profile of the nursing department as a whole. Computerized nursing departments have the capability to enter the data and obtain printouts by unit, department, specific item, and a host of other options that will assist in data analysis. In the absence of computerization, decentralization of data tabulation is a viable alternative. For example, each unit could be responsible for a portion of the data tabulation.

Analysis of the data is performed by the nursing management team or a committee appointed by the nursing management team. Results will be presented at quarterly planning meetings, which are further described in Chapter 6.

NOTES

1. *Chicago Tribune,* April 17, 1988, pp. B-26–B-28.

2. John C. Hafer and Carl Joiner, "Nurses As Image Emissaries: Are Role Conflicts Impinging on a Potential Asset for an Internal Marketing Strategy? " *Journal of Health Care Marketing* 4, no. 1 (June 1984): 45–49.

3. Rose D. Phelan, "Nursing: An Unrecognized Major Health Care Marketing Force for Hospitals," *Journal of Health Care Marketing* 7, no. 2 (June 1987): 45–49.

4. Sherry L. Shamansky, Lynne S. Schilling, and Troy L. Holbrook, "Determining the Market for Nurse Practitioner Services: The New Haven Experience," *Nursing Research* 34, no. 4 (August 1985): 70.

5. Linda M. Aiken, Robert J. Blendon, and David E. Rodgers, "The Nursing Shortage of Hospital Nurses: A New Prospective," *Annals of Internal Medicine* 95, no. 3 (1981): 370.

6. Ibid., 365–70.

7. Timothy Porter-O'Grady, *Creative Nursing Management* (Rockville, Md.: Aspen Publishers, Inc., 1986), 35.

8. J. DeJoseph and M. Swarts, "On the Scene: Professional Enrichment and Positive Image," *Nursing Administration Quarterly* 10, no. 1 (Fall 1985): 35–40.

9. Timothy Porter-O'Grady and Sharon Finnigan, *Shared Governance for Nurses: A Creative Approach to Professional Accountability* (Rockville, Md.: Aspen Publishers, Inc., 1984).

10. Fred Elwood, "Understanding Human Behavior," lecture at Bradley University, Peoria, Illinois, December 1981.

11. Lillian R. Erickson, "Patient Satisfaction: An Indicator of Quality? " *Nursing Management* 18, no. 7 (1987): 35.

Appendix 3-A

Discharge Instructions for the Patient with Burns

1. The following will help you prevent infection and heal your burn:

   • Wash your hands before changing bandages or dressings.
   • Change your dressing two times a day. If the old dressing sticks to your skin, soak it in cool, clear water.
   • Clean the burned area with mild soap and water.
   • Pat the area dry with a clean, dry cloth.
   • If your physician has given you any cream, ointment, or solution to apply to the burn, follow the instructions you have been given.
   • Apply a clean bandage.

2. Observe the burn for signs of infection.

   • excessive pain
   • increased redness or tenderness
   • pus
   • elevated temperature

3. Keep the area and dressing clean, dry, and in place.
4. Elevate the burn (if hand or foot) for the first 24 hours.
5. Take pain medication as directed by your physician.
6. Contact your physician or emergency department referral for follow-up care.

Special note: If your physician or the hospital emergency department used Silvadene (silver sulfadiazine) cream on your burn, a material will form on the surface of the burn that looks like pus but is harmless. This is called coagulum. Pus is usually associated with a bad odor and pain. Coagulum has practically no noticeable odor, and there is no increased pain associated with it.

Source: Reprinted from Emergency Room Discharge Instructions for Patients with permission of Rush Sheridan Road Hospital, Chicago, Illinois, 1988.

Patient Satisfaction with Care Questionnaire

Key: Strongly Disagree   Disagree   Agree   Strongly Agree
            1   2   3   4

Please fill in appropriate rating next to the item being rated.

Item	Rating
1. The admission procedure was organized and prompt.	
2. My primary nurse introduced herself (or himself) to me.	
3. I was oriented to the physical facility and to my room.	
4. I was introduced to my roommate.	
5. My pain medication was given promptly upon request.	
6. My primary nurse addressed my concerns.	
7. My primary nurse treated me as an individual.	
8. My nursing care was given in a warm, courteous manner.	
9. My primary nurse involved me in my plan of care.	
10. The nursing staff showed consideration and concern for my family.	
11. Procedures were explained to me before completion.	
12. The purpose of diagnostic tests was explained to me.	
13. I was informed about the length of stay in surgery.	
14. I received instructions about my medications.	
15. I received instructions about my illness.	
16. I received information about physical activity allowed posthospitalization.	
17. I was informed about signs and symptoms of recurrence.	
18. I was instructed on proper diet posthospitalization.	
19. I was given information on my follow-up appointment with my physician posthospitalization.	
20. I received written discharge instructions.	

Appendix 3-C

Physician Satisfaction with Care Questionnaire

Key: Strongly Disagree   Disagree   Agree   Strongly Agree
         1   2   3   4

Please place rating of item next to item.

Item	Rating
1. My patients receive their pain medication in a timely manner.	
2. My patients are satisfied with the physical care.	
3. My patients receive caring, personalized nursing care.	
4. My patients receive adequate patient teaching concerning	

    a. disease
    b. pain control
    c. medications
    d. treatment regimens
    e. life style changes
    f. activity
    g. diet
    h. follow up

5. My patients receive competent and skilled care.
6. My patients' diagnostic tests and treatment are scheduled in a timely manner.
7. My patients enjoy
    a. a clean environment
    b. a safe environment
    c. a therapeutic environment
    d. a friendly environment

8. I am able to make patient rounds efficiently.
Comments: _____
_____
_____
_____
_____

Appendix 3-D

Unit Survey

Job Title: _____   Work Shift: _____

Please use the following scale to rate each of the questions below:
    5—strongly agree
    4—somewhat agree
    3—not sure
    2—somewhat disagree
    1—strongly disagree

Part I: Job Satisfaction

A. *Individual Morale:*
    1. All things taken together, I am satisfied and fulfilled at working on this unit at this time. 5   4   3   2   1
    2. I am hopeful that working on this unit will be satisfying in years ahead. 5   4   3   2   1

B. *Esprit de Corps* (common spirit of warmth, pride, and high-performance standards):
    3. Most people are proud of belonging to this unit. 5   4   3   2   1
    4. A friendly atmosphere prevails among the people on this unit. 5   4   3   2   1
    5. Most people accept the goals of this unit. 5   4   3   2   1
    6. There is a continuing effort to improve personal and group performance on this unit. 5   4   3   2   1
    7. On this unit, there are very high standards of performance. 5   4   3   2   1
    8. When people need help, they can usually count on getting assistance from their coworkers. 5   4   3   2   1

9. There is warmth in the relationships between those in authority and those who work under them on this unit. 5 4 3 2 1

C. *Mental Support* (constructive help from supervisors, acceptance of responsibility by subordinates):

10. My supervisor, as a rule, is not excessively critical. 5 4 3 2 1
11. When people make a mistake on this unit, they will not be criticized harshly and unfairly. 5 4 3 2 1
12. The contribution I make to this unit is sufficiently appreciated. 5 4 3 2 1
13. On this unit, individuals generally accept responsibility. 5 4 3 2 1
14. One gets constructive help on this unit when one makes a mistake. 5 4 3 2 1

D. *Structure* (authority and jobs are clearly defined):

15. It is clear who has the authority to make a decision. 5 4 3 2 1
16. People are sure from whom they should take orders. 5 4 3 2 1
17. The policies and rules of this unit have been clearly explained. 5 4 3 2 1
18. "Red tape" is kept to a minimum on this unit. 5 4 3 2 1
19. In general, people have a clear idea of what is required of them in their job on this unit. 5 4 3 2 1
20. New and original ideas receive consideration. 5 4 3 2 1

E. *Lack of Conflict* (the feeling that those in authority want to hear different opinions; emphasis is placed on getting problems out in the open rather than ignoring them or smoothing them over):

21. On this unit, one may have open disagreements. 5 4 3 2 1
22. Talking over problems is more important on this unit than avoiding conflict. 5 4 3 2 1
23. My nursing care manager on this unit encourages us to speak our minds, even when it means disagreeing. 5 4 3 2 1
24. Conflict is accepted, faced, and worked out in this unit. 5 4 3 2 1

F. *Responsibility* (authority provides the opportunity for responsibility):

25. My nursing care manager delegates authority properly. 5 4 3 2 1
26. Supervision on this unit is mainly a matter of setting guidelines for subordinates. The nursing care manager lets them take responsibility for their work. 5 4 3 2 1
27. On this unit, the nursing care manager does not expect you to check everything with her (or him). If you think you've got the right approach, you just go ahead. 5 4 3 2 1

G. *Rewards* (recognition for excellence in performance):
  28. People are rewarded according to the excellence of their job performance on this unit. 5 4 3 2 1
  29. There is reward and recognition given for doing good work on this unit. 5 4 3 2 1
  30. The promotion system on this unit helps the best person rise to the top. 5 4 3 2 1
H. *Leadership* (is open, communicative, prudent, decisive):
  31. The unit nursing care manager holds meetings to make decisions and solve work-related problems. 5 4 3 2 1
  32. The unit nursing care manager seeks the opinion of department members and carefully evaluates their ideas. 5 4 3 2 1
  33. The unit nursing care manager does not merely inform department members of rules and goals she (or he) expects them to follow without discussion. 5 4 3 2 1
  34. The members of this unit have sufficient opportunities to express their views to the director of their department. 5 4 3 2 1
  35. The unit nursing care manager does not evade and delay decisions unnecessarily. 5 4 3 2 1
  36. The unit nursing care manager does not make decisions without proper data and evaluation. 5 4 3 2 1
  37. The nursing care manager of this unit keeps everyone properly informed. 5 4 3 2 1
I. *Effectiveness:*
  38. There is good coordination of effort on this unit. 5 4 3 2 1
  39. The quality of work or performance on this unit is good. 5 4 3 2 1
  40. Time is used efficiently on this unit. 5 4 3 2 1
  41. There is good communication between the members of our department. 5 4 3 2 1
  42. Work assignments are properly planned on this unit. 5 4 3 2 1
J. *Interdepartmental Coordination:*
  43. There is poor communication between our unit and other departments and nursing units. 5 4 3 2 1
  44. Other departments and/or nursing units, as a rule, cooperate well with our unit. 5 4 3 2 1
  45. Activities between our unit and other nursing units and/or departments are well-planned and timed. 5 4 3 2 1
  46. Our unit, as a rule, cooperates well with other departments. 5 4 3 2 1

K. *Opportunity for Self-Expression:*
   47. I have opportunities to try out my own ideas. 5 4 3 2 1
   48. I have many chances to feel I have accomplished something. 5 4 3 2 1
   49. I have opportunities to learn new skills. 5 4 3 2 1
   50. I have many chances to influence policies and decisions that affect my work. 5 4 3 2 1
   51. I have an opportunity to use my skills and abilities. 5 4 3 2 1
   52. I have a chance to share in actual decision making. 5 4 3 2 1
   53. I have a chance to do things my own way. 5 4 3 2 1
L. *Staffing:*
   54. There is adequate staffing in my department. 5 4 3 2 1
M. *Equipment:*
   55. My unit does not have up-to-date equipment. 5 4 3 2 1
N. *Physical Conditions:*
   56. The physical conditions—light, heat, space, cleanliness—on my unit are good. 5 4 3 2 1
O. *Reaction to the Survey:*
   57. This survey is a good means of communication. 5 4 3 2 1
   58. This survey will not really contribute to any worthwhile changes. 5 4 3 2 1
   59. I liked the survey. 5 4 3 2 1
Additional Comments:

Name (Optional) _____

Source: Courtesy of Linda Joos, RN, BSN, Nursing Care Manager, St. Francis Medical Center, Peoria, Illinois.

Nurse Administrator Evaluation

Rate your perceptions of agreeing or disagreeing with the statement on a 1–3 scale.

Scale: 1—Agree
2—Neither Agree nor Disagree
3—Disagree

STATEMENT	1	2	3
1. I enjoy my work 100% of the time.			
2. I enjoy my work 80% of the time.			
3. I enjoy my work 50% of the time.			
4. My staff respects me.			
5. My staff believes that I am fair.			
6. My director supports me with my goals for the unit.			
7. My director sets expectations of my role.			
8. I feel that I am a key person in administration.			
9. I am able to discuss my concerns with my peers.			
10. I am able to discuss my concerns with my director.			
11. I am able to discuss my concerns with my nurse administrator.			
12. The nurse administrator is concerned with providing a quality and cost-efficient nursing department.			
13. Some unit operational problems do not need to be shared with anyone.			
14. Decentralization has brought more authority to the nursing department.			
15. Decentralization has given me more authority and decision-making powers.			
16. I prefer decentralized nursing.			

STATEMENT	1	2	3
17. I can express my opinions in service meetings.			
18. I can express my opinions privately to my director.			
19. I can express my feelings to the nurse administrator.			
20. Many improvements have been made since decentralization.			
21. I am glad I selected the nursing profession as my work.			
22. I would like to change my profession if I could.			
23. Nursing administration is concerned with the education and professional development of managers.			
24. Many changes are needed in the nursing department.			
25. Nursing directors and the nurse administrators should develop more consistent policies to follow.			
26. Nursing directors and the nursing administrator should allow managers to develop their own policies specific to their unit.			
27. Managers should choose their own delivery systems.			
28. I feel confident in my position.			
29. I feel secure in my employment.			

The following is most frustrating to me in my work on a scale of 1–3.

Scale: 1—Least frustrating
2—Moderately frustrating
3—Frustrating!

ITEM	1	2	3
30. Time cards			
31. Schedules			
32. Rebellious staff			
33. Inconsiderate physicians			
34. Service meetings			
35. Staffing meetings			
36. Performance evaluations			
37. Budget monitoring			
38. Nursing care manager meetings			
39. Department manager meetings			
40. Staff problems			
41. Patient complaints			
42. Unit pot luck dinners			

ITEM	1	2	3
43. Unit parties			
44. Chart monitoring			
45. X-ray department			
46. Pharmacy			
47. Laundry			
48. Laboratory			
49. Admitting			
50. Surveys like this one			
51. Other: _____			
_____			
_____			
_____			
_____			
_____			

I feel that changes need to be made in the following areas. (Check if appropriate.)

52. _____ Patient advocacy program
53. _____ Charting system
54. _____ Nursing care manager role
55. _____ Assistant nursing care manager role
56. _____ Clinical nurse educator role
57. _____ Staff development
58. _____ Nursing administration
59. _____ Clerk program
60. _____ Budget system
61. _____ Staffing system
62. _____ Policy development process
63. _____ Forms development
64. _____ Career ladders
65. _____ Physician/nurse relationship
66. _____ Medication delivery
67. _____ Delivery systems

68. Other: _____

_____

_____

_____

69. My staffing (if positions are all filled) is:

_____ Not adequate

_____ Adequate

_____ Overstaffed

Chapter 4

The Marketing Process

The first phase of the marketing process is establishing the mission and organizational positioning. This chapter will discuss the second phase of the marketing process, the environmental assessment. Figure 4-1 shows the phases of the marketing process: phase 1, the mission and positioning; phase 2, the environmental assessment; and phase 3, the marketing plan. The marketing plan flows from a thorough examination of the internal and external forces affecting the organization's ability to carry out the mission. As a part of the assessment, the organizational strengths, weaknesses, opportunities, and threats (SWOTs) are analyzed.

ENVIRONMENTAL ASSESSMENT

The environmental assessment forms the baseline for the identification of organizational SWOTS. Figure 4-2 shows the dynamic process leading to profiling the nursing department, matching organizational strengths to market demand, and developing the marketing objectives. The assessment, also known as the marketing audit, is defined by Shuchman as

> a systematic, critical, and impartial review and appraisal of the total marketing operation: of the basic objective and policies of the organization and the assumptions which underlie them as well as of the methods, procedures, personnel, and organization employed to implement the policies and achieve the objectives.[1]

The purpose of the assessment is to diagnose problems, identify trends, and anticipate organizational performance. Performed annually, the assessment includes the internal and external environments.

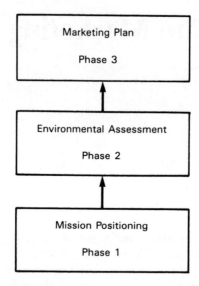

Figure 4-1 Phases in Marketing Process

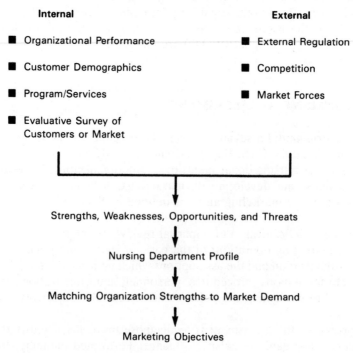

Figure 4-2 Environmental Assessment

Internal Environmental Assessment

Marketing principle 1 is to know the organization well. The internal environmental assessment involves a comprehensive analysis of the scope and function of the entire department and related activities. Initially, the collection of data reflecting the internal operation of nursing is a complicated task. However, once a system is developed, data can be accumulated throughout the year and reported in a meaningful format. The internal environmental assessment is subdivided into

1. organizational performance
2. demographics
3. organizational marketing mix
4. evaluative survey of customers

Organizational Performance

All of the indicators of productivity, costs, and quality are reviewed under organizational performance. Figure 4-3 shows some of the indicators. In order to identify important trends, data are collected retrospectively, preferably five years back. Budgeted data are compared to the actual by service or by unit. Some of the questions to be explored here are:

- How cost-efficient is the nursing department?
- How productive is the nursing department?

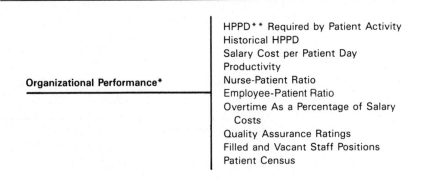

Organizational Performance*	HPPD** Required by Patient Activity
	Historical HPPD
	Salary Cost per Patient Day
	Productivity
	Nurse-Patient Ratio
	Employee-Patient Ratio
	Overtime As a Percentage of Salary Costs
	Quality Assurance Ratings
	Filled and Vacant Staff Positions
	Patient Census

*Five-year trends
**Hours per patient day

Figure 4-3 Organizational Performance

- What were the self-defined quality ratings by unit and service?
- Is there an inverse relation between quality and productivity?
- Are some services more efficient than others?
- Is overtime justifiable?
- Do salary cost increases exceed the consumer price indexes?
- Are there appropriate levels of professional care?
- Are negative trends sporadic or subtle indications of major problems?

In order to provide the highest quality for the best price (the best value), the nursing department monitors the cost, productivity, and quality indicators monthly and annually, plotting five-year trends. Financial, productivity, and quality problems are identified by service and unit. Other questions for analysis are:

- If productivity is increasing and hours per patient day (HPPD) decreasing, is quality affected? In other words, has short staffing affected quality?
- If overtime is increasing, are the actual staff positions less than budgeted (acuity data included in budgeted staff)? What justifies the overtime?
- If productivity is low and productive HPPD high, is low census the problem? If not, are vacations being given properly, or are there orientees on the unit?

Exhibit 4-1 shows an example of a tool that can be used on a monthly basis to monitor unit financial management, productivity, human resource management, quality of care, and organizational development.

Customer Demographics

Marketing principle 2 is to know the customer well. In order to know the customers well, demographic data are obtained and analyzed. Demographics include such data as age, sex, race, income, education, marital status, and religion, to name a few. Table 4-1 shows an example of the kinds of demographic data that are obtained on the three major customers of nursing: patients, nurses, and physicians.

Patients. Segmenting patients by demographic data allows managers to target specific patient populations for specific programs. For example, if a large number of obstetric patients are 15 to 18 years of age and originate from low-income zip code areas, the emphasis will be on education and community resources. Later, when programs are developed, the same demographic data are used to target specific population segments for new programs. For example, a health fitness program would be more successful in young, high-income, professional populations. Demographic data assist in

- planning programs for age ranges specific to the population of the organization
- narrowing the foci of programs to serve the major diagnostic groups
- planning appropriate use of after-care services such as home health and community services
- predicting future trends in order to plan accordingly
- assessing the appropriateness of current programs and services
- targeting the specific populations for promotion

Customer demographics are obtained about all aspects of patients, nurses, and physicians.

Nurses. Responsive nurse managers know the number of RNs employed both full-time and part-time; the part-time/full-time mix; and their race, average age, education preparation, turnover rate, and average length of stay. The implications here are:

1. Longevity will increase the salary cost per patient day.
2. The average length of stay will show the critical period where accelerated benefits should begin.
3. The educational preparation will determine orientation content and continuing education.
4. The age will determine the values. For example, younger nurses will be interested in tuition reimbursement and more senior nurses will be interested in the retirement plan.
5. Marital status helps determine mobility and possible turnover.
6. The unit turnover can be compared to the department as a whole in order to identify retention problems.

Physicians. Because nursing cannot serve all markets, physician data showing top admitting physicians, top surgeons, and top obstetricians carve out the targeted population for marketing and retention strategies. Physician age is a predictor of retirement. If two of the five top admitting psychiatrists on staff are approaching retirement age, the patient census on the psychiatry unit is in jeopardy.

Exhibit 4-1 Quality Assurance/Accountability Standards Monitoring Tool

Accountability Standards Monitoring Tool   **Unit:**

Code Accountability	Standard	Range	Oct	Nov	Dec	Jan	Feb	Mar	Apr	May	Jun	Jul	Aug	Sept	Total
1 Financial Management															
1.1 Salary Cost per Patient Day															
1.2 Salaries per Productive Hour															
1.3 Expense Ratio to Nursing Dept. Total															
2 Productivity															
2.1 Paid Hours per Patient Day															
2.2 Overtime Hours as a % to Total Hours															
2.3 Actual Productive/Budgeted Productive FTE Percent Variance															
3 Human Resource Management															
3.1 Absenteeism Rate															
3.2 Employee Opinion Survey Score in the Category "Supervision"															
3.3 Percent Performance Appraisals Completed by Due Date															
3.4 Turnover Percent															
3.5 Stability Percent															

4   **Quality of Care**
4.1 Percent RN Hours to Ancillary Hours
4.2 Patient Satisfaction Percent
4.3 Patient Incident/Accident Rate
4.4 % Medication Errors within Stnd Dev.
4.5 Nosocomial Infection Rate
4.6 Percent Documentation RN assessment
      every 24 Hours
4.7 Percent Compliance of Patient Care
      Plan Documentation

5   **Organizational Development**
5.1 Percent Staff Attendance at Mandatory
      Inservice Programs

Source: Reprinted with permission from "Accountability Standards Balance Quality and Efficiency" by V. Kunkle, *Nursing Management,*
© January 1987.

Table 4-1 Organizational Demographics*

Patients	Nurses	Physicians
Age ranges	Number	Top 10 by admissions
Sex	Part-time/full-time mix	Top 10 by patient days
Origin by Zip code	Sex	Top 10 by number of
Average income in zip	Ages	surgeries
code	Length of service by unit	Top 10 by number of
Marital status	Educational preparation	deliveries
Education level in zip	Marital status	Top 10 consulting
code	Clinical ladder level	Age ranges
Payer source		Number by specialty
Top 20 DRGs with		Number and types of
maximum reimbursement		specialties
Top 20 DRGs most		
frequent		
Top 20 DRGs lowest		
reimbursement		

*Five-year trends.

Generally speaking, marketing efforts are targeted to the top admitting primary care physician since specialists and consulting physicians will naturally follow with the referrals from primary care physicians. The exceptions to this are obstetricians, pediatricians, and psychiatrists, who are often selected by patients directly.

Programs, Services, and Marketing Mix

As part of the assessment, the department's programs and services are analyzed for

1. adequate volume or activity
2. appropriate content (programs)
3. revenue generated and profit margin
4. benefits other than revenue
5. profitability

Table 4-2 provides an example of possible programs and services, which are evaluated by the items in the marketing mix.

The marketing mix is the program/service mix of

1. position
2. product

Table 4-2 Programs, Services, and Marketing Mix

Programs	Services	Marketing Mix
Number of programs	Number of services	Positioning
Diabetes	Obstetrics	Price
Arthritis	Intensive care	Packaging
Pulmonary	Medical	Access and Delivery
Rehabilitation	Surgical	Promotion
Geriatrics	Pediatrics	
Oncology	Psychiatry	
Community outreach	Rehabilitation	
CPR instructor	Neurology and neurosurgery	
Refresher nurse course	Emergency	
Speaker's bureau		
Lamaze		

3. price
4. place (access and distribution)
5. promotion

The four *P*s of the marketing mix are expanded here to five to include *position*. *Position* is the name or theme of the program or service. Also, *access* and *distribution* are used here instead of *place* because services, not actual products, are involved. Each program/service is analyzed by the appropriate marketing mix. Questions to ask are:

1. Is the name easy to remember? (position)
2. Does the name fit the program? (position)
3. Is the price competitive? (position)
4. How is the program put together for purchase? Should the price include all of the program options or should the price be broken down for menu selection by customers? (product packaging)
5. Is the program/service site accessible to the customers? How can it be made more accessible? (access and delivery)
6. How is the program communicated to the public? Is the communication effective? (promotion)

The following is an example of assessing a program and its marketing mix. The volume of consults to pulmonary clinical specialists had decreased over the past few years with a concurrent decrease in revenue. In fact, the revenues generated by the nurse specialist no longer cover the salary costs. During the past year, one of the pulmonologists had been successful in concentrating the pulmonary patients in one medical unit. Because of this, the nurses on that unit became more specialized in pulmonary regimens. Consequently, neither the nurses nor the pulmonologists consulted the nurse specialists for patients on that unit. However, consults were increasing from a few internists on staff who consult the clinical specialist but not the pulmonologists. The nursing department is now faced with these facts:

- decreased utilization of the service
- decreased pulmonology interest in the service
- increased general medicine interest in the service
- decreased revenue generated by the service

Marketing mix issues are:

- Is the positioning right? Right now, the service is for patients and optional to pulmonologists. Internists have not been targeted for marketing.
- Is the price too high? Not high enough?
- How are the parts of the services organized, packaged, and priced? Are the subparts of the whole still appropriate and comprehensive?
- How easy or difficult is it for physicians to obtain a timely consult from the nurse specialist?
- How is the service being promoted to the medical staff?

Some of the options for the nursing department to consider are:

- Eliminate the position and reduce the cost.
- Let the program survive or fail on its own.
- Redesign the program with a new mission, target market, package, and price.

This example provides a brief sketch of how each program should be assessed in terms of its market demand and the marketing mix. In Chapter 5, this example will be included in the marketing objectives.

Evaluative Survey of Customers or Market

As a part of the internal assessment, marketing research is completed on how the customers perceive the nursing department in comparison to that of other competing hospitals. Survey questionnaires are used to obtain and organize the data. This survey differs from the monthly attitude questionnaire in two ways: (1) it is administered annually specifically for the assessment, and (2) its focus is comparison with other nursing departments (the competition). The two surveys are similar: both use simple, self-devised questionnaires. Probability studies are obtained later during marketing research for program development. As shown in Figure 1-3 in Chapter 1, research occurs in the market model at three points: (1) the environmental assessment, (2) the marketing plan for programs, and (3) the monitoring and evaluation of the program/service.

Figure 4-4 shows two basic types of surveys: the developmental and the evaluative.[2] Developmental surveys are concerned with obtaining customer opinions of new services or programs, and evaluative surveys are often used to obtain customer opinions of one product compared to another or compared to multiple products or services. Developmental surveys are either qualitative or quantitative. Qualitative surveys involve either focus group opinions or one-to-one interviewing. Quantitative surveys employ the scientific method to the extent possible and are, as a result, higher in validity and reliability. Each developmental survey has specific purposes, advantages, and disadvantages that are discussed in more detail in Chapter 5.

The evaluative survey is used at this point in the marketing process to determine the standing of the nursing department in the mind of its customers in comparison to competitors. The survey questions can be simple and devised by nurse managers. Administered annually, the results are trended from year to year to show increases or decreases in customer perceptions in the different categories of the survey tool. Patients, nurses,

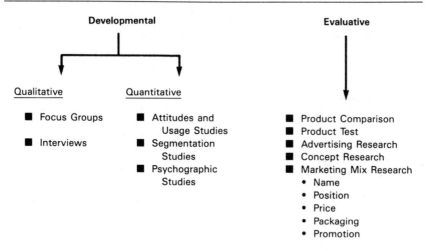

Figure 4-4 Types of Surveys

and physicians are the subjects, and some method is employed to ensure anonymity. Methods of administration vary, but one method that ensures an adequate return is the selection of a specific week day for administration and collection. The disadvantage of this method is that the respondents will represent only the opinions of the subjects present in the hospital on the day of the survey.

A simple survey that can be used for both physicians and nurses is shown in Appendix 4-A. In the place of Hospital X and Hospital Y, competitor hospital names are used. Appendix 4-B shows a similar survey tool for nurses. Again, the items on the tool are individualized by the qualities valued most by each of the customers as identified by the nursing administrator or manager. The data are analyzed by simple percentage difference and percentage change from the previous year.

External Environmental Assessment

Increasingly, hospital operations and performance are affected, influenced, and sometimes regulated by macroeconomic forces. Without analyzing these external forces and without forecasting, combined with strategic planning, hospitals cannot survive in the marketplace. The purpose of the external environmental assessment is to identify potential threats to and opportunities for the organization and to predict trends. Figure 4-5

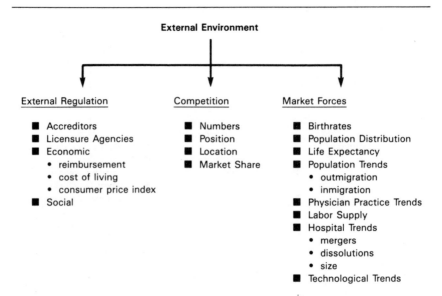

Figure 4-5 Components of External Environment

shows the three components of the external environment: external regulation, the competiton, and external market trends.

External Regulation

Examples of regulation affecting the operation of hospitals include

- accreditation
- hospital licensure
- economic regulation, specifically HSAs, reimbursement, cost of living, and the rising consumer price index
- political regulation
- social restraints

Licensure and accreditation impose many regulations on hospitals ranging from expensive physical facilities requirements to extensive and expensive auditing procedures. Important questions are:

- What are the trends in Joint Commission and licensure requirements?
- What preparations are needed now to meet the demands that are predicted to come?

Moreover, many economic regulations exist. Examples include government-established HSAs to determine where and when beds, services, and capital equipment are added. Additionally, the government has regulated reimbursement based on DRG, salary increases are regulated by the cost of living and area wage rates, and supply costs are regulated by the consumer price index. A global view of health care is essential. Appropriate questions are:

- What health care issues are arising in the pacesetter areas of the east and west coast?
- What health care bills are being discussed in the legislature?
- What is being discussed in the Blue Cross/Blue Shield arena?
- What is happening to the economy locally? Are women being forced into the work scene? Are they working part-time or are they heads of households? How will this affect birthrates? Are younger workers being laid off in the area and relocating elsewhere, resulting in a further reduction of the birthrate and hospital census?
- What does this have to do with nursing?

The last question requires reflection. If nursing could have anticipated the census drop in hospitals in the early 1980s, staff layoffs and downsizing throughout the country might have been avoided by conservative hiring and attrition.

Politically, hospitals are affected by the notions of a particular party and the person in power. Nobody can deny that "Reaganomics" had its impact, but the point is: Who is the contender and what is the target? Additionally, political forces fund or do not fund specific diseases, nursing education, medical education, and social programs. Hospitals leaping into home care were surprised to find the arena a crowded, political playground for government regulation accompanied by a new set of rules to follow.

Societal attitudes and values influence the way hospitals operate. For example, the health care consumer, more informed and less tolerant of errors, has regulated (to some extent) physician practice by the increase in malpractice suits. As a result, more laboratory and radiology tests are ordered, more consults are requested, and more time is spent by the physician documenting procedures. All of this translates into higher hospital bills, which are then passed off to the patient in the form of higher insurance premiums.

Because the risk is high for physicians in private practice, joint venturing with hospitals for all or part of the malpractice premium is becoming commonplace, specifically with the more high-risk specialties such as obstetrics, anesthesiology, and orthopedics.

Appropriate questions at this point are:

- What are the joint venture trends between hospitals and physicians?
- What are the trends in joint venturing with malpractice insurance?
- What does this mean to nursing?

Specifically, cooperative ventures between hospitals and physicians for malpractice insurance mean a smaller bottom line to be allocated among the various departments, nursing included, resulting in smaller expense budgets.

Competition

Marketing principle 3 is to know the competition well. A discussion of the competition is incomplete without including the thoughts of Ries and Trout. These authors maintain that instead of being customer oriented, firms must be competition oriented, looking for weak points, then launching attacks—tactics, not strategy.[3] It makes good sense that if success were dependent solely on expensive and extensive market research, one hospital would need only to copy the ideas of the competitor, saving marketing research dollars for something else. Obviously, something more is required.

In order to know the competition well, a thorough assessment of the competing hospitals is completed. Figure 4-5 outlines important subdivisions of this assessment as

- number of competitors
- rank position of competitors
- location of competitors
- market share
- comparison of services
- comparison of programs

The number of competitors may not equal the number of hospitals in the area since some hospitals are clearly not competitors because of a difference in philosophy or mission. The position is important since marketing strategies or tactics will differ depending on whether or not competing hospitals are leaders in the community or are in second and third place.

According to Ries and Trout,[4] leaders play defense and runners-up play offense. Thus, an appropriate tactic for leaders is to attack themselves by coming out with an improvement in their own product or service. On the other hand, runners-up look for weaknesses in the leader and launch an attack at that point. For example, large teaching facilities are often leaders but are also typically located in crowded inner cities, resulting in access problems. A runner-up located in a quiet suburb of the city attacks the leader's inaccessibility. The leader, then, admits the problem but improves access by announcing new valet and services for patients, families, and physicians. Some large inner-city hospitals also attack and improve service by providing vans for transporting patients and family members to and from the hospital for outpatient treatment, laboratory work, and admissions and discharges.

Market share is an excellent indicator of market performance. Organizations identify their percentage of the total market and follow it carefully to determine if they are gaining or losing customers to the competition. Nursing looks at market share by service. Once the real competition is identified, patient days of each hospital are determined by service and totaled. A percentage of the total is calculated for each hospital based on performance in the marketplace. Table 4-3 gives an example. Percentage of market share of Hospital W increased from 29.5 percent in April to 30.6 percent in June 1988, whereas the market share of Hospital X decreased from 39.3 to 38.3 percent in the same time period. This represents a gain of 16 patients for Hospital W and a loss of 17 patients for Hospital X. From April to June, there was a loss of only 2 patients in the total market.

Table 4-3 Market Share

Hospital	April 1988 Patient Days	Market Share (%)	June 1988 Patient Days	Market Share (%)
W	13,500	29.5	13,980	30.6
X	18,000	39.3	17,480	38.3
Y	9,000	19.3	8,940	19.6
Z	5,280	11.5	5,310	11.5
Total	45,780	100.0	45,720	100.0

It can be assumed that Hospital X lost 1 patient to the market and 16 patients to Hospital W. The question is, where did the loss occur? Table 4-4 shows a breakdown by service of the total market. Clearly, the loss occurred in pediatrics.

Unless dramatic, a one-month drop in market share is usually insignificant. A month-to-month analysis of market share data will show subtle

Table 4-4 Market Share by Service

Hospital	April	Market Share (%)	June	Market Share (%)	April	Market Share (%)	June	Market Share (%)
		Obstetrics				**Psychiatry**		
W	900	37.5	900	38.5	1,800	56.6	1,800	56.6
X	1,200	50.0	1,200	51.3	600	18.9	600	18.9
Y	300	12.5	240	10.2	0	0.0	0	0.0
Z	0	0.0	0	0.0	780	24.5	780	24.5
Total	2,400	100.0	0	100.0	3,180	100.0	2,580	100.0
		Medicine				**Surgery**		
W	6,000	26.7	6,000	26.7	3,000	25.0	3,000	25.5
X	9,000	40.0	9,000	20.0	4,500	37.5	4,500	37.0
Y	4,500	20.0	4,500	20.0	3,000	25.0	3,000	25.0
Z	3,000	13.3	3,000	13.3	1,500	12.5	1,530	13.0
Total	22,500	100.0	22,500	100.0	12,000	100.0	12,030	100.0
		Pediatrics				**Newborn**		
W	750	25.0	1,230	41.4	1,050	32.8	1,050	32.8
X	1,500	50.0	990	33.3	1,200	37.5	1,200	37.5
Y	750	25.0	750	25.3	950	29.7	950	29.7
Z	0		0		0		0	
Total	3,000	100.0	2,970	100.0	3,200	100.0	3,200	100.0

trends of growth or decline, which are analyzed in the assessment and addressed in the marketing objectives. Table 4-5 shows a method of documenting and analyzing the reasons for a market share loss to the competition.

External Market Forces

There are external market forces affecting the marketing plan that are neither regulatory nor the influence of the competition. Some of these forces are

- birthrate
- population distribution
- life expectancy
- mortality rates
- out-migration of the population
- in-migration of the population

National, state, and regional birthrate trends are assessed because of their impact on obstetrics and pediatrics. Regional birthrate trends are not absolute predictors in the presence of regional in-migration and out-migration of the population. National trends, however, can provide a base for predicting the rate of growth or decline in populations.

Population distribution data and life expectancy data are used to predict the predominate age groups from which hospitals will draw patients in the future. For example, life expectancy at birth increased from 47.3 in 1900 to 73.7 in 1980, going from a 9.8 percent distribution of the total population in 1970 to 11.3 in 1980.[5] Based on these data, hospital utilization by the elderly will increase, chronic diseases will be more prevalent, and health care expenditures will increase. Questions for analysis during this part of the assessment are:

- What will happen to obstetric and pediatric hospital utilization based on the birthrate trends?

Table 4-5 Market Share Analysis Example

Competitor	Market Share	Competitive Factor
Hospital W	41.1%	Pediatrics—Private Rooms
		With Sleep-in Facilities
		At Competing Hospital

- What role will the hospital play in keeping the older population healthier longer so that they will remain useful members of society?
- How will the hospital prepare for the increase in the prevalence rate of chronic diseases associated with older populations?
- What changes in practice and fees will be required for government reimbursement of care delivered to the elderly?
- What will be the health care demand of the "baby boomers," the major age category in the United States, as they pass through middle age and become elderly health care consumers?[6]

Additionally, mortality rates, in rank order by disease, establish leading causes of death. Trends are analyzed to identify major health problems and needed services and programs.

Likewise, trends in population in-migration and out-migration from surrounding zip code areas are analyzed to predict local shrinking or growing of the total market. With a dwindling of the total market, hospital-specific market share increases only with more competitive prices and services, or more specifically by a reduction of the market share of the competitor. In-migration represents an available market and is, therefore, carefully tracked and grouped by numbers, age groups, payment sources, and reasons for in-migration. In-migration populations bring with them different cultures, norms, social trends, and health care practices.

Other external market forces include

- physician practice trends
- labor supply
- hospital trends
- technological trends

Physician practice trends are assessed and analyzed for their impact on nursing. For example, the current trend is toward group rather than solo practices because group practices are more efficient. Other trends are hospital joint ventures with physician groups and HMOs. The questions for nursing to explore here are:

- How will physicians operate under the different management structures and how will patient care be different?
- How will group practice affect the census of the unit and the transfers in and out of the unit?
- Will emergency departments be used by physicians in off hours to evaluate and justify hospital admissions (rather than admitting for observation)?

- Will more patients be denied admission and be followed in the home?
- Will patients be discharged earlier and need more home care?
- What will weekend physician coverage mean to nursing when one physician is covering for a five-member group?
- How will the practice of hospital-hired physicians differ from those in private practice, and how will the difference affect nursing?
- How will nursing meet the demands of the increasing subspecialty physicians with all of the subspecialty protocols and procedures?
- How will nursing resolve nursing turnover problems and the resulting endless and expensive orientation of nurses to specialty nursing?
- How can nursing provide a climate that attracts and retains subspecialists yet prevents nursing burnout in specialty nursing?

In the external market forces assessment, labor supply is analyzed with data showing national and statewide trends, with emphasis on RNs. Important indicators are

- enrollment trends in schools
- number of RNs in the market
- percentage of RNs in the work force
- percentage of RNs employed in hospitals
- ratio of part-time to full-time RNs
- trends in number of RNs graduating from local schools of nursing
- utilization of RNs locally

This information is used to analyze and predict the future supply of nurses. The number graduating each year locally is compared with the local RN position vacancies. As stated previously, the total available market for nurses has been reduced because of other, more attractive and competitive options for women. The national and state labor supply of nurses can be used to predict what will happen locally. However, the problem of recruiting young women and men into the field of nursing is a much broader problem than can be addressed in individual hospital nursing department marketing objectives.

Hospital organization affects nursing. In this assessment, nursing analyzes data on trends such as

- mergers
- dissolutions
- takeovers

- downsizing
- bed reductions
- occupancy rates
- percentage trends of nonprofits versus profits
- diversification trends

For nursing, these indicators translate into budget cuts, organizational changes, mission changes, elimination of programs and services, and emphasis on revenue-producing departments. Predicting trends in hospital organization allows nursing to make adjustments and plan changes at a reasonable pace.

Technology affects the operation of hospitals both negatively and positively. For example, the lithotriptor, which is a technological innovation designed to crush renal calculi, has almost eliminated surgery for the removal of kidney stones and can be used to crush gall stones. This piece of equipment was initially placed in hospitals amid a frenzy of political entanglements commandeered by state health planning agencies. In order to obtain a lithotriptor, a hospital had to obtain a certificate of need (CON) approval and be associated with a medical school. Hospitals successful in obtaining the equipment replaced revenues lost from surgical patient days with revenues generated by the miraculous stone crusher. However, as soon as the public became aware of the existence of the lithotriptor, they placed themselves on a waiting list for the procedure. Consequently, not only did the total market for kidney stone surgeries decrease, some physicians found themselves unqualified or not credentialed to operate the crusher. Patients in surrounding communities were lost to the crusher and to the physicians who were trained to operate the equipment. Over time, however, the sought-after crusher will be more readily available, and technology, in the end, will replace patient days lost with a safer, more efficient improvement in the treatment of patients with renal calculi. In this assessment, new technology and the resulting changes in the delivery of care are identified and analyzed for the purpose of planning for the change.

As the total market of patients decreases, physicians, too, are experiencing a decline in chargeable visits and, ultimately, revenue. As the impact of technology is examined, the possibility of physicians purchasing such capital items as radiation equipment, lithotriptors, nuclear magnetic imaging equipment, and lasers cannot be excluded. Unlike hospitals, physicians do not need CON approval for these capital items. Already, physicians are installing laboratory facilities, small scale radiology equipment, lasers, neurophysiological equipment, and physical therapy equipment. This can represent a loss of revenue for the hospital.

Another consideration is that even if the hospital obtains CON approval and purchases new technological innovations, a physician must be both willing and educated to operate the equipment. The threats to hospitals are as follows:

- The technology is located at another institution.
- The technology is located in a physician's office.
- The technology is located in the hospital, but the physicians either cannot or will not use it.

In all of these scenarios, the result is loss of patient days and revenue.

On the brighter side, most technological improvements require nursing. In the assessment, the role of nursing with the new technology is anticipated then addressed in the marketing objectives.

SWOTS

Based on the internal and external assessment, the nurse manager or nurse administrator and the management team identify nursing department SWOTS. As shown in Figure 2-1, SWOTS serve as a building block to profiling the department. The definition of *SWOTS* and examples are provided here.

Strengths

Strengths are those assets belonging to a nursing department or service that translate into an advantage in the competitive marketplace. Specifically, strengths are both advantages that the competition does not possess and attributes that differentiate the nursing department from all others. These strengths tend to attract the major customers such as patients, physicians, and nurses. Some examples are as follows:

- experienced, senior nursing staff
- friendly, caring, professional staff
- clinical specialists in specialty areas
- exceptional nurse orientation and continuing education program
- primary nursing or primary nursing philosophy
- supportive administration
- small, efficient nursing units

- supportive medical staff
- special programs for patients such as a rehabilitation home evaluation program, Lamaze program, coronary patient education program, or formal discharge planning program
- spacious physical facilities and adequate parking
- lower nurse-patient ratios and more cost-efficiency

Weaknesses

Weaknesses are those qualities that create a disadvantage in the marketplace. Weaknesses are of two types: those that can be corrected and those that cannot. Major weaknesses that can be altered are identified here and addressed in the markeing objectives. Some examples are as follows:

- pulmonary program that is declining in activity and revenue (correctable)
- pediatric unit that is losing patient days to the competition because of better physical facilities elsewhere (correctable)
- obstetric unit that is losing patient days because of the declining birthrate and out-migration of young people from the area (uncorrectable by nursing)
- obstetric unit that is losing patient days to the competition because of progressive programs elsewhere (correctable)
- too-large hospital that is perceived to be inaccessible (correctable)
- high RN vacancy rate and ineffective recruitment efforts (somewhat correctable)
- "burned-out" nursing staff because of excessive overtime worked (correctable)

Opportunities

Opportunities are chances to accomplish something positive in the marketplace. These chances are fleeting in nature and require rapid planning in order to seize the opportunity that may never be available again. Recognizing the opportunity, timing, and follow-up is crucial. Some examples of opportunities are:

- Develop a new diabetes unit to capture the majority of the total available market.

- Develop an outreach telemetry program with other hospitals to capture the tertiary care market in coronary care.
- Develop exchange relationships with area nursing homes to capture more of the Medicare market.
- Establish flexible staffing programs to capture more of the new graduate nurse market.

The list of SWOTS is exhaustive. No issue is too small to consider.

Threats

Threats are potential or actual events in the environment that could have a negative impact on the nursing department or service. A negative impact

---

Exhibit 4-2 Sample Profile of a Nursing Department

Wilmington General Hospital has experienced a 5% decline in patient days over the last two years, primarily in the obstetrics area. Market share shows that Hospital X has gained 5% in patient days because of a short-stay maternal-infant program. Additionally, internal market data show that the former top admitting obstetrician is now in fourth place. The cost per patient day has decreased 1% overall but has increased 4% in the obstetrics area because of the decline in patient days and lack of staff attrition in that area.

Based on data from patient questionnaires, market share loss in pediatrics is due to the competitor's more attractive physical facilities. Also, the questionnaires showed that parental overnight accommodations at the competitor's pediatric unit has resulted in the defection of patients here.

Additionally, the Pulmonary Nursing Consult Program has experienced a 50% decline in activity and revenue. Data also indicated that the DRGs 240 and 241, Rheumatoid Arthritis (with complication and without) are the top DRGs with the least favorable reimbursement.

The average patient length of stay has decreased from 7.5 to 6.8. The patient acuity index shows an increase from an average of 5 hours per patient day to 5.5. These data indicate that patients are not only more acute but are discharging earlier.

The nursing survey shows less satisfaction with orientation and continuing education than last year's survey. Additionally, the turnover rate has increased by 2% from last year with the average length of stay for RNs, at 2 years, down from last year's 2.5. The RN vacancy rate has increased to 14 percent from 13 percent last year. The termination interviews show that the most frequent reason for leaving is better salaries elsewhere. Fifty percent of the nurses are diploma prepared: 25% associate degree, and 25% baccalaureate.

The physician survey shows satisfaction on all items in the survey. The patient focus groups show nursing to be higher in caring attitudes than the competition, but the patient questionnaires from inpatients show a decrease in caring attitudes from last year.

is any event that could result in a census decline, loss of market share, or decrease in the total available market. Some examples are

- physician defection to a competing hospital
- reputation of understaffing because of the nursing shortage
- duplication of a program by the competition or the competition being the first to offer a program

PROFILE OF A NURSING DEPARTMENT

The internal and external assessments as well as the SWOTS are summarized in the nursing department profile. This will become a part of the executive summary of the business plan, which is discussed in Chapter 7. The profile details major strengths and opportunities of the department, pinpointing specific indications of needed changes in programs and services. A sample profile is shown in Exhibit 4-2. The problems identified for Wilmington General Hospital are addressed in the marketing objectives and marketing plan.

NOTES

1. Abe Shuchman, "The Marketing Audit: Its Nature, Purpose, and Problems," in *Analyzing and Improving Marketing Performance,* AMA Management Report no. 32 (New York, N.Y.: American Management Association, Inc., 1959), 13.

2. Edward Epstein, "Market Surveys: Practices and Procedures" in *Marketing Handbook,* vol. 1, ed. Edwin Bobrow and Mark David Bobrow (Homewood, Ill.: Dow Jones-Irwin, 1985), 184–205.

3. Al P. Ries and Jack Trout, *Marketing Warfare* (New York, N.Y.: McGraw-Hill Book Co., 1986), 4–5.

4. Ibid., 55–56.

5. H. Stephen Leiber and Lauri Rustand, *Illinois Hospitals: A Decade's Perspective* (Naperville, Ill.: Illinois Hospital Association, 1984), 40–41.

6. Ibid., 40.

Appendix 4-A

Patient or Physician Survey Tool

On a scale from 1 to 5, with 5 being the highest and 1 the lowest, rate each hospital's nursing on the following items.

Item	Hospital X	Hospital Y	Hospital Z
Clinical competency[1]			
Knowledge base[2]			
Courtesy[3]			
Friendliness[4]			
Caring attitude[5]			
Nursing care[6]			

[1]Skill with procedures such as intravenous therapy, insertion of nasogastric tubes, etc.

[2]Able to explain disease process, action of medications, and treatment regimen.

[3]Receptive to questions, considerate of patients and family members.

[4]Establishes a warm, trusting relationship.

[5]Addresses concerns, remembers likes and dislikes, and considers patient individuality.

[6]Explains procedures before they are completed, involves the patient in the nursing care plan, and gives appropriate discharge instructions.

Appendix 4-B

Nurse Survey Tool

Please rate each hospital on the items below on a scale of 1 to 5, with 5 being the highest rating and 1 being the lowest.

Item	Hospital X	Hospital Y	Hospital Z
Adequate orientation			
Continuing education			
Challenging assignments			
Adequate pay			
Caring environment			
Good working conditions*			

*Fair shift assignment, available equipment and supplies, safe nurse-patient ratio, space to work.

Chapter 5

The Marketing Plan

This chapter discusses phase 3 of the marketing process (see Figure 4-1). Phase 3 includes the marketing objectives; marketing plan; marketing mix; and implementation, monitoring, and evaluation of the marketing plan. Chapter 6 discusses the participative process inherent in the three phases of the marketing process.

MARKETING OBJECTIVES

Marketing objectives differ from more traditionally inspired departmental objectives in many ways. Table 5-1 shows the contrasting points.

Traditionally, exhaustive lists of departmental goals are made by management for the projected year. These dream lists are often unrealistic expectations without controls to ensure achievement. Defined by management, focused on the organization, and driven by organizational needs, these goals rarely filter down to those in the organization who interface directly with the primary customer of the organization. Consequently, commitment to the objectives is weak at staff levels where implementation is carried out. Moreover, objectives that are not achieved in a fiscal year are often carried into the next fiscal year or dropped for lack of institutional readiness. Additionally, since controls are vague or absent, it is never clear who is responsible for achieving the goal.

In contrast, marketing objectives are few in number and are

- based on customer needs, wants, and demands
- based on major areas needing a focus
- limited to a specific time period
- delegated to specific individuals for implementation

- developed with input from the entire department
- changed as new information is available
- monitored and controlled by the degree of achievement of the objective

The marketing planning process provides the nursing department with five or six major objectives that are realistic, achievable, and measurable. The first step in developing the objectives is to list key result areas that need a focus in the nursing department.

Key Result Areas

An efficient way in which to begin the development of objectives is to list key result areas.[1] These are formulated by selecting areas needing improvement or a special focus taken from the nursing department profile. Used in this way, the profile is the final assessment from which customer needs, wants, and demands are drawn into focus. These key result areas are four or five major improvement or innovation areas that will form the basis of the objectives. Further defined, key result areas consist of only a few words that describe areas needing achievement or results, areas that without a focus would not be addressed. For example, in Chapter 4, Exhibit 4-2, key result areas from the profile are

- market share in obstetrics
- physical facility in pediatrics
- customer relations—patients and physicians
- RN turnover and vacancy rates
- pulmonary nursing consultation referrals
- rheumatoid arthritis home care program
- discharge planning

These, then, are just a few areas needing improvement or a focus for the projected fiscal year. These key result areas are merely small-scale examples. In actuality, key result areas can be exhaustive lists of areas for improvement, expansion, divestiture, and new growth.

Strategic Matching

The second step is to view the key result areas from the prospect of organizational capabilities and market attractiveness. Table 5-2 shows a

Table 5-1 Traditional Objectives and Marketing Objectives: A Contrast

Description of Objectives	MBO*	Marketing Objectives
Number	Exhaustive lists	5 or 6
Development process	Autocratic or democratic	Participative
Participant involvement	Management (top down)	All staff levels (bottom up)
Duration	Years	1 year
Stability	Static	Dynamic
Focus	Organization	Customer
Driving force	Organizational need	Customer need
Control	Vague/undefined	Achievement of objectives

*Management by objectives.

simple process to evaluate market attractiveness of programs and services and the capability of the organization to produce the programs and services.

Market attractiveness is defined here to mean programs and services that are profitable to the organization and can capture new, retain old, or maintain present markets. Organizational capabilities are the existing or potential abilities, skills, and knowledge of the staff to produce, manage, and control the programs and services efficiently, effectively, and competitively. Table 5-2 shows:

- Organizational capability for maintaining the pulmonary nursing consult program is high, but the market attractiveness is low because of duplication in-house and lots of competition in the community.
- Organizational capability for an innovative obstetrics program is high, but the market attractiveness is low because of competing programs at other hospitals.
- Organizational capability and market attractiveness are high for the rheumatoid arthritis home care program because the organization al-

Table 5-2 Strategic Match

Program	Organizational Capabilities	Market Attractiveness
Pulmonary	High	Low
Obstetrics	High	Low
Rheumatoid arthritis	High	High
Customer relations	High	High
Discharge	High	Average
Pediatric renovation	Low	High
Nurse retention	Low	High

ready has home care and there are no competing programs in the community.

- Organizational capability and market attractiveness are high for the customer relations program since staff is available to implement the program and the program has the capability of retaining physician and patient customers.
- Organizational capability is high and market attractiveness average for the discharge program.
- Market attractiveness is high for the pediatric renovation program, but organizational capability is low because the task involves outside consultation and board commitment.
- Market attractiveness is relatively high for the nurse retention program, but organizational capability is low because of budgetary constraints and salary structure limitations.

The strategic matching process is used in determining the content of the marketing objectives. Low market attractiveness and low organizational capabilities are not determinants of the program or service but are determinants of the focus of the objective. For example, the nursing department may decide to implement an innovative obstetrics program in spite of low market attractiveness in order to remain competitive and maintain the current market share. The objective then would be "to retain present patient days in obstetrics by offering a variable stay program." This is an informed objective developed in the realization that the competition offered the program first and that the program may not increase revenue and patient days or recapture the market lost to the competition. Additionally, the marketing mix (discussed later in this chapter) will be designed specifically to retain present customers rather than capture new markets.

In summary thus far, key result areas are listed from the nursing department profile and strategically matched within the grid. Then, five or six key result areas are selected by the process of prioritization for development into departmental objectives.

Objectives

The process by which five or six key result areas are selected by the nursing department to become major objectives is participative, involving both management and staff. This process is discussed in Chapter 6. The objectives are

- quantifiable

- time limited
- stated in behavioral outcomes
- assigned to individuals

Table 5-3 shows sample objectives derived from the key result areas listed in this chapter.

In the three examples given in Table 5-3, the obstetrics program objective is to maintain market share, the home care arthritis program objective is to reduce hospital inpatient costs and increase revenue and activity in another department, and the pulmonary program dissolution objective is to reduce nursing department costs. Achievement of the objectives will be measured by the market share retained, specific dollar amounts reduced in the department, and specific revenue and activity generated. These objectives will define the marketing mix of each program. As shown in Table 5-3, the first responsible party listed for each objective becomes the program manager and, along with others assigned, develops the program marketing plan, implementation subobjectives, target dates for completion, and responsibilities.

Table 5-3 Sample Marketing Objectives

Major Objective	Target Date for Completion	Responsible Party
Maintain present market share in obstetrics by implementing variable stay program	Between Fiscal Year 87/88 and 88/89	Director of Nursing, Obstetrics Director of Marketing, Obstetrics
Decrease inpatient cost for DRG 241 by $28,230 and increase activity by 300 visits and revenue by 1.4% in home care by implementing a home care program for rheumatoid arthritis patients	June 30, 1989	Director of Home Care Rehabilitation coordinator Assistant Director of Marketing
Decrease costs in the nursing department by phasing out the pulmonary nursing consult program	January 31, 1989	Director of Nursing, Medical Pulmonary nurse specialist

MARKETING PLAN

A marketing plan is formulated by the program manager of each objective. A simple, yet comprehensive, format for developing the marketing plan is to apply STRAP to each objective.[2] The letters represent each element of the marketing plan:

S Segment the market.

T Target the market.

R Research the market.

A Appraise the exchange relationships.

P Play with the five *P*s (the marketing mix):

- product/service/program
- position
- place (access and delivery)
- price
- promotion

Segmenting the Market

Market segmentation is the differentiation of buyers according to common characteristics. For example, a potential market for a service or program is segmented by age groups. Then, a specific age group is targeted for promotion of the service, or the entire market is targeted. Generally speaking, it is difficult to plan a promotional campaign to fit the needs of a total market. Market segmentation allows the organization to plan programs and services efficiently to meet the specific needs of one or more market segments rather than attempt to design one program to appeal to the entire market. There are several approaches to segmentation.[3]

Complete Market Segmentation

Market segmentation involves planning an appeal to each potential customer based on individual needs. In large markets, this is not realistic or cost-effective in the long run. However, this marketing strategy has been used successfully in the market for obstetric patients. One southwestern hospital in the United States offers individual contracts to obstetric patients. The contract spells out the length of stay, method of delivery, type of pain management, number of family support members either participating or observing, supplies and equipment used, hours and times of rooming in for the infant, and individualized fee.

In lieu of complete market segmentation and individual contracts for care, some hospitals provide service differentiation by offering two or three types of hospitalization plans for obstetric patients. Examples are

- routine delivery and care
- 36-hour stays with partial rooming in
- 24-hour stays with complete rooming in

The mix of service entities is limited only by the imagination.

Market Segmentation by One or More Attributes

Market planners segment a market by one or more attributes in order to select or target a segment(s) for a specific program appeal. These attributes are sex, gender, age, race, or geographic area to name just a few. Often the market is segmented by two or more attributes. For example, the market for a physical fitness program is segmented by sex, age groups, income, and geographic area of residence. Three markets are then segmented as follows:

1. Males, ages 40 to 55, within a 50-mile radius are segmented for the stress testing and cardiac fitness program.
2. Females, ages 18 to 40, within a 50-mile radius are segmented for the post child-birth fitness program.
3. Females and males, ages 25 to 45, in the middle to upper income level, within a 50-mile radius are segmented for the weight control, strength, and endurance program.

There are many ways to separate market commonalities or attributes. Some of these are

- geographic (region, county, city, state, zip code area)
- demographic (age, sex, income, education, occupation, religion, race, ethnic origin, payer source)
- psychographic (social class, life style, personality)
- behavioristic (buying behavior, heavy or light user status, repeat users, quality versus economy buyers, readiness to buy)

Demographic and geographic data are easily obtained, but psychographic data involve administration of questionnaires, which are usually administered during the research phase of the marketing plan. Market segment data are used at this point in two ways. First, identified market segments can be targeted for selective programs and services. Second, market segmentation within already established programs or services can be determined in order to discover which segments are attracted by the current program.

Targeting the Market

The organization or nursing department decides whether or not to target a specific market or markets. *Target marketing* means to select one or more market segments for the program and the appeal. The decision depends on the marketing objective. In the example of the obstetric variable stay, the objective may be "to restore former market share" not "to maintain market share." Therefore, differentiated marketing, offering several programs to more than one market segment of patients and physicians, is indicated. In this way, the present market preferring a more traditional delivery will not be lost, and the lost market preferring the more progressive services will be regained. If the objective were "to maintain market share," undifferentiated marketing or appealing to the entire market with one program might be selected.

On the other hand, if an organization were introducing a program that was new to the obstetric community and the objective was "to increase market share by two percent," concentrated marketing or targeting one market segment with one innovative program offer would be indicated. Likewise, the target marketing decisions would affect the marketing mix.

Using the obstetric variable stay program objective, the target markets would be the present population. The number of market segments within this population would be identified and targeted. Marketing research further defines the target markets.

Researching the Market

At this point in the marketing plan, some research has already been conducted to determine market demand for the program or service through the patient questionnaires. Research here is completed to determine which market segments will be attracted to the traditional and the proposed new program. In Chapter 4, Figure 4-4, segmentation studies were developmental, quantitative research aimed at obtaining information that could be generalized to the entire population segment. Because decisions concerning costly programs are based on marketing research, it is important that the marketing research is conducted in a scientific manner.

Nursing departments with access to hospital marketing research departments have a definite advantage since the survey design, implementation, and analysis tasks are completed by professionals in the field. Nursing departments without such services should use consultants for marketing surveys involving the development of costly programs. The problems inherent in developing a survey tool are obtaining a nonbiased tool with a high degree of validity and reliability and then converting the data into meaningful results for decision making.[4]

Quantitative research, which is conducted primarily by telephone survey, mail survey, or intercept survey, is used to identify the target market segments for new or current nursing programs. Additionally, information about appropriate packaging, pricing, and promotion strategies is obtained. Mail surveys are appropriate if a listing of all of the qualified members of a segment is obtainable. The disadvantage of the mail survey is that the return percentage is often low and the survey can be expensive. However, the mail survey is less costly than the intercept survey, which involves face-to-face interviews with a structured questionnaire and possible interviewer bias.

Exhibit 5-1 shows the steps in conducting segmentation studies by a mail survey. From the results of the returned mail survey questionnaire, important information about program feasibility, further target markets, pric-

---

Exhibit 5-1 Steps in Conducting Segmentation Studies

Step 1. Define the objective for the survey.
Step 2. List information that will be needed.
Step 3. Add appropriate demographic and geographic data.
Step 4. Add promotional questions such as commonly read newspapers and newspaper sections, commonly watched TV channels, etc.
Step 4. Add questions about pricing.
Step 5. Construct the survey tool.
  • Use multiple choice questions.
  • Use commonly understood language.
  • Use only 15 to 20 short questions.
  • Include demographic, price, and promotional information at the end of the tool.
Step 6. Administer the tool to 50 persons in order to evaluate the clarity of the tool.
Step 7. Submit the tool to someone with expertise in survey design.
Step 8. Revise the tool.
Step 9. Mail the tool to the targeted market along with a self-addressed, stamped, return envelope.
Step 10. Collect, organize, and analyze the data.

ing levels, and appropriate promotion is obtained. Depending on the program, the target market may be individuals other than persons who will be using the program. For example, the target markets for a home care program may be physicians and hospital discharge planners. In this case, a smaller sample size represents the larger potential consumer market.

The sample size for the survey tool is at least 150 respondents, which means that at least 300 survey tools are mailed initially. Some surveyors obtain only a 15 percent return rate; others obtain up to a 50 percent return rate. If the return rate is less than desired, multiple or repeat mailings are sent. The sample includes either everyone in the specified target population or a random sample of everyone in the target population. For example, if the survey is intended to measure the attitudes of physicians toward a home health care program for arthritis patients, the survey would be mailed to all of the physicians treating arthritis patients in the target area. However, if this were not feasible, a random sample of all of the physicians treating arthritis patients would suffice. The data are analyzed in a quasi-experimental design to test the differences in attitudes and responses between groups that are based on demographic data. The results determine feasibility and further segment the potential market.

Appraising the Exchange Relationships

Exchange theory is a complex theory founded in the social and psychosocial disciplines. The concept of *exchange behavior* is a part of most definitions of marketing. In a classic article, "Marketing As Exchange," written in 1975 by Bagozzi, exchange is described as "restricted, generalized, and complex."[5] In theory, the exchange between hospital and nursing program development and implementation fits into a complex exchange consisting of at least three parties, each of whom is involved in at least one direct exchange.[6]

In this scenario, the potential client sees an advertisement on television for a hospital program and persuades the physician to make the referral into the program. The physician benefits. The potential client becomes a patient or participant in the program. The hospital and patient benefit. The hospital allocates part of the program fee back to the television channel for more advertisements. The media benefits. The television station uses the funds for more television programing. The viewer benefits, and the complex cycle continues.

To appraise the exchange relationships is to describe the part of the market environment that is favorable to positive exchange relationships.

As an example, the exchange relationship environment for the rheumatoid arthritis home care program includes these facts:

- There is no home care arthritis program in the state.
- The program would be the first arthritis home care program in the city.
- There is an abundance of rheumatoid arthritis medical specialists on staff.
- There are rheumatology nursing specialists on staff.
- There is a well-established home care service in existence in the medical center.
- There is a well-established arthritis foundation in the city.
- There is a total market of 70,000 arthritic persons in the county.

From this perspective, the appraisal of the exchange relationships is favorable for the new home care program.

Marketing Mix

The last element of the format STRAP is "playing with the five *P*s," which is also called the marketing mix. The marketing mix is the appropriate emphasis on product, position, place, price, and promotion. The marketing mix is affected by the marketing objectives and whether or not undifferentiated or differentiated marketing has been selected, among other factors.

Product

McCarthy stated that "what we are really selling in a product is the capacity to provide the satisfaction, use, or perhaps the profit desired by the customer."[7] From this perspective, services and programs fit into the definition of *product* by satisfying a customer need.

The total product consists of the core product and all of the parts offered to the customer. It includes how the product is packaged. In product firms, packaging includes the product, its parts, and the wrapper. In services, the total service is the core benefit and its features, packaging, quality standard, and styling.

Using the variable obstetric stay as an example, the core benefit is maternal and infant care. It features a length of stay selection: 24-, 36-, and 48-hour stays. Another feature is the variable one-price option. This means that each length of stay selection has one price regardless of the number of procedures performed. It is packaged with one home health nurse maternal-infant visit. It is styled as progressive and family oriented. The quality standard is that it is abandoned if the delivery is not standard and routine.

Further, the product or service can be augmented to include other options. For example, the fifth variable stay delivery is offered free as an augmentation. Also, a part of the product is positioning and naming, which is discussed here as a separate *P* in the five *P*s.

Positioning

Positioning means identifying strengths of the program or services, matching the strengths with the specific customer need, naming the position, and achieving it in the mind of the customers. MacStravic effectively stated:

> The specific position that is your target should be the best possible fit between your capabilities, strengths (relative to your competition), and the kinds of products/place/prices your market is most interested in and likely to buy from you.[8]

Questions that will assist in developing a position are:

- Who is the market, and what does the market need?
- What market segments will be interested?
- What is it about the program that is unique to the strengths of the organization or department?
- What is the relation of the program to the programs of the competition? How is it different, more appealing to the market?
- What is the attractive mix of service, price, and access to the program?

Using the rheumatoid arthritis home care program as an example, the strengths of the program in terms of the customer and the nursing department are

- its appeal to patients with frequent arthritis "flare-ups"
- lower cost, effective care for the patient
- easy access for the patient (it's in the home)
- an alternative for the physician

- lower cost care for the hospital
- easily introduced by the organization
- first in the city to offer a packaged arthritis program in the home

The name and the theme set the positioning. For the arthritis program, the name is "Mercy Arthritis Home Care," and the theme is: "The First To Serve You Better." The hospital name is retained because its reputation in rheumatology and rehabilitation already speak of quality. "The First" positions the program as the leader, and "To Serve You Better" means easier access and lower cost than inpatient care.

Place

In product firms, the place is the total of the channels involved in getting the product to the customer. In short, it is the manufacturing, wholesaling, distributing, and retailing of the product. The place decisions, therefore, affect the price and promotion of the product. In product firms, the manufacturer often makes the place and promotions decisions.

In contrast, service firms have no official manufacturing, wholesaling, or distributing activities related to a tangible product. Service firms address the place issue by providing maximum access to programs and services. The degree to which customer convenience is provided is a place decision that has a major impact on the price of the service.

Frequently, for health care providers, the place is the site of the physical facility. However, hospitals are becoming increasingly more creative by providing the place closer to the customer. Examples are satellite clinics and outpatient facilities located at strategic suburban sites. Also, place is addressed in hospitals by creating easier access to the facility and services. For example, in recruiting nurses who must commute for long distances, part of the place issue could be free lodging on the hospital premises. Likewise, free lodging at a nearby hotel could be provided to patients who must travel long distances for outpatient services and programs. These place decisions are based on the strategic balance of place and price.

Price

Price strategy depends on the program objectives. Most program objectives will be stated in terms of increasing revenue or profit margins, increasing market share, or retaining market share. These program objectives, respectively, translate into

1. profit-oriented pricing
2. market share–oriented pricing
3. competition-oriented pricing

Profit-oriented strategies are aimed at maximizing profits either in the short run or over the life cycle of the service. This strategy is used where the objective is to increase revenue or profit margins. Such an objective is possible when little or no competition exists and there is price inelasticity of demand. In other words, the demand is not sensitive to price. Profit maximization strategies are successful with such programs as sports medicine, cardiac fitness, cosmetic surgery, and (most recently) lithotripsy. The effectiveness of profit-oriented pricing is dependent on the absence of pure competition, presence of inelastic demand, and lack of program substitutes in the marketplace.

The arthritis home care program provides a possible application of profit-oriented pricing. However, although there is no home care competition, the pricing must be competitive with inpatient care. Additionally, other similar programs can be expected to enter the same market soon. Therefore, a short-term target return price that is under the price of inpatient care is in order. The pricing strategy will change as other hospitals enter the arthritis home care market and as the cost of providing the service changes. Then, the price of the service may increase, stay the same, or decrease, depending on the market price. At any rate, profit margins will decrease over the life cycle of the program as the competition will create demand elasticity and an alternative to customers.

Occasionally, programs are priced to increase market share with the rationale that increased revenue will follow. Clearly, increased market share is not always synonymous with increased revenue since variable costs may also increase. However, since some programs and services are considered feeder services to other more profitable services, prices are set to increase market share rather than revenues. One example is a break-even price for an outpatient diabetes education program. The objective here is to increase market share in the inpatient and outpatient services. The strategy is that once the participants are aligned with the hospital through the low-cost education classes, they will use the hospital's inpatient and outpatient facilities later when such care is needed. Other programs designed by nursing can have the same effect. Examples include low-cost Lamaze, child development, cancer screening, and hypertension screening programs.

In competition-oriented pricing, the objective is to retain market share, and the strategy is to set prices at or below the market price. The variable obstetric stay objective discussed earlier in the chapter provides an example that is appropriate for competitive pricing. In order simply to retain the current market share in obstetrics, the department must

1. price at or below the market price
2. engage in nonprice competition

The nonprice competition is the development of the variable stay program. In order to break even in such an environment, costs may have to be decreased or the losses offset by another more profitable service.

In summary, price levels at, above, or below the market price are determined by a complex mix of the supply and demand, cost, projected activity, life cycle of the service, competition, substitution, marketing objectives, and hospital or nursing mission.

Promotion

The chief purpose of promotion strategy is to influence the purchase decisions of the targeted market favorably by providing information about the service or product. Promotion is essentially effective communications. MacStravic[9] defined four areas of health care communications:

1. personal communications (telephone, face-to-face, mail)
2. publicity (free public services)
3. sales promotions (fairs, exhibits, etc.)
4. advertising (purchased media)

Personal communications are used when the target market is small. For example, promotions for a tertiary care ventilator-dependent children's unit are successful with personal communications (mail, brochures, telephone calls) to the outlying hospitals' neonatal and pediatric directors. On the other hand, promotional decisions for a new diabetes unit require consideration of the larger target market of potential patients in the area, region, and state as well as physicians, other hospitals, and community agencies. Thus, the promotion decisions may include all four areas of communications.

Some considerations in the choice of promotion include

- size of the target market
- life style of the target market
- budget for promotion
- need for controlling the time and content of the promotion
- marketing objective
- amount of consumer education needed
- demand for the service
- program status as leader or follower in the market

Advertising by media is expensive but reaches a large audience and provides a high degree of control over the content and timing of the advertisement. Publicity is the least expensive, as it is free, but control over time of day and content is often inflexible. Sales promotions are expensive and are primarily used by large companies to augment other promotional channels. For example, a new car is raffled nationwide to promote a new car line.

One other type of promotion is word of mouth (WOM) advertising. WOM advertising experts maintain that information-seeking consumers rely on coworkers, family, and friends to make health care purchase decisions and that these decisions are sometimes based on name recognition and familiarity.[10] This means that ongoing WOM marketing programs that enhance the overall image of and create familiarity with the hospital significantly increase the chances that consumers will choose the hospital. Based on this, nursing is instrumental in WOM communications with programs that produce positive images of the hospital.

Promotion in hospitals is the responsibility of the communications department. Its staff are most qualified to make promotional decisions. Nursing assists by describing and narrowing the target markets for the various nursing programs and services.

IMPLEMENTATION

Once the marketing objectives are established and assigned, the responsible nurse manager selects key people in the organization (a project team) to set subobjectives, apply STRAP, design the marketing mix, develop the business plan, obtain approval, implement the program, and monitor the progress of the program. Nurse managers are assigned to objectives based on their qualifications and interest in the specific objective.

Ideally, there is an objective for each manager. Also, the project team members should be equally qualified for objective implementation. For example, the project team members assigned to the arthritis home care program include the home care director as project manager, a rheumatology nurse specialist, a home care occupational therapist and physical therapist, a home care nurse, a rheumatologist, a discharge planner, and staff members from the planning, marketing, and finance departments.

MONITORING PERFORMANCE

The marketing objectives state standards of acceptable performance. These standards are the measures of success. Stated simply, achievement of the objective occurs when the standard is met. For example, the obstetric variable stay program is successful if the market share in obstetrics is maintained. The arthritis home care program is successful when home health has increased revenue by 1.4 percent as a result of the program.

Monitoring the success or failure of a program or service is accomplished by developing a monthly performance analysis that is then compared to the standard established in each objective. These monthly comparisons are summarized in quarterly reports, which are discussed by the nursing administration staff. At this time, problems are assessed and corrected, and programs are changed based on new market information.

NOTES

1. Terrence J. Rynne, *Market-Based Strategic Planning* (Evanston, Ill.: Rynne Marketing Group, 1985), 52.

2. Ibid., 64.

3. Phillip Kotler, *Marketing for Non-Profit Organizations* (Englewood Cliffs, N.J.: Prentice-Hall, Inc., 1982), 217–18.

4. James Lazarus, "Finding the Right Research Resources," in *Marketing Handbook,* vol. 1, ed. Edwin Bobrow and Mark David Bobrow, (Homewood, Ill.: Dow Jones–Irwin, 1985), 180.

5. Richard P. Bagozzi, "Marketing As Exchange," *Journal of Marketing* 30 (1975): 32.

6. Ibid., 33.

7. E. Jerome McCarthy, *Basic Marketing: A Managerial Approach* (Homewood, Ill.: Richard D. Irwin, Inc. 1978), 237.

8. Robin E. Scott MacStravic, *Marketing by Objectives for Hospitals* (Rockville, Md.: Aspen Publishers, Inc., 1980), 117.

9. Robin E. Scott MacStravic, *Managing Health Care Marketing Communications* (Rockville, Md.: Aspen Publishers, Inc., 1986), 119.

10. Robin E. Scott MacStravic, "Word-of-Mouth Communications in Health Care Marketing," *Health Progress,* October 1985, 26.

Chapter 6

Integration of the Marketing Plan

Prior chapters discussed the economic environment as a factor precipitating the involvement of marketing in hospitals, positioning strategies for the nursing department, and development of a customer-oriented marketing plan. All of the strategies discussed are designed to identify and create growth opportunities as well as stimulate innovation and service improvements. This chapter discusses the role of the nurse manager in market-based planning, responsive philosophies, internal environments, and organizational structures facilitating the market-based planning model as well as the participative process of development and implementation. Also discussed is how the market-based planning model is integrated into the administrative planning cycle and the departmental strategic plan. The business plan is isolated as a mechanism for organizing the strategic plan, and product lines are discussed as a method of organizing based on services offered to customers.

ROLE OF THE NURSE MANAGER IN MARKET-BASED PLANNING

The role of the nurse manager or administrator is a difficult one. In addition to planning, organizing, leading, and evaluating, the nurse manager must possess (1) the nursing skills to be a credible leader, (2) the business skills to be a competent administrator, (3) the political skills to complement those of the administrative team, and (4) the human relations skills to inspire the growth and development of others from staff to management in the nursing department. The totality of administration is a synthesis of the disciplines of "psychology, sociology, social psychology, anthropology, political science, engineering, economics, mathematics and statistics, [and] physiology."[1]

Further, the administration of today has evolved from Taylor's scientific management beginning in 1911, to Weber's bureaucratic administration in the 1920s, to Mayo's human relations movement in the 1930s and early 1940s, to the decision-science movement in the 1940s and 1950s, to the behavioral movement in the 1950s and 1960s, to the organizational-humanist movement in the 1960s and 1970s, existing alongside the avant-garde systems movement and power dynamics movement.[2] The contingency movement,[3] which is an updated form of the systems movement, predominates in the 1980s and attempts to quantify variables in specific administrative situations that can be used to analyze, predict, explain, and control other similar situations. In other words, the contingency movement is an effort to form hypotheses leading to administrative theory.

Historical perspectives provide an understanding of the present and give insights into the future. Table 6-1 describes the major thrusts of each phase in the evolution of administrative thought.

The contingency movement maintains that the method of decision making and the structure of the organization are contingent on the needs of the organization, external environmental factors, and resources within the organization. In other words, the structure, strategy, and philosophy are consistent with the external and internal needs at the moment.[4] The nurse manager, then, is responsive to the changing environments and, by the

Table 6-1 Major Thrusts of Administrative Movements

Year	Movement	Originator(s)	Major Thrust
1911	Scientific	Frederick Taylor	Divisions of labor Time-in-motion studies
1920	Bureaucratic	Max Weber	Authority, rules and regulations
1930	Human relations	Elton Mayo	Informal, happy, social, work groups
1940	Decision-science	Simon and March	Scientific method
1950	Behavioral	Brown, Homans, Vroom, Porter, & Lawler	Goal oriented
1960–70	Organizational humanist	McGregor	Work participation, trust, work humanization
1970	Systems		Organization viewed as a subsystem in a larger system
1970	Power dynamics	Zaleznik and Salancik	Power and its influence on decision making
1980	Contingency	Fielder and Vroom	Relationship of parts to whole—different situations require different approaches

legitimate power of the position, establishes the climate for growth, innovation, quality, and excellence in the nursing department.

The market-based planning model requires a participative process for development and implementation. The primary functions of the nurse manager are

- communicating the facilitating philosophy
- acting as a change agent and facilitator
- developing facilitating organizational structures
- establishing the participative process

Facilitating Philosophy

The basic philosophical concept of the market-based planning model is that it is a top-down, bottom-up approach that involves the entire organization. Other concepts are that the model

- augments and supports the hospital marketing plan
- is research-based and consumer demand–driven
- requires teamwork and unification of goals
- focuses on growth and innovation
- is dynamic and changing
- drives the nursing department operational plan

Top-Down, Bottom-Up Approach

The concept of *top-down, bottom-up* means decision making is based on the input of the entire organization to the extent possible. The idea is that the customers and those closest to the customers are better able to define areas of need. It is crucial to acknowledge people as the single most valuable resource of a nursing department or organization. The business is nursing care, and the employees are both the producers and sellers. Employees exist for the patients, and the managers exist for the employees. Responsive nurse managers communicate a people-oriented philosophy by

- being visible on patient care units
- conversing with employees and patients
- establishing communication systems for employees
- acting on both positive and negative feedback from employees
- involving employees in goals and objectives

A few nurse administrators in the Midwest are involving themselves in the work of employees by actually caring for one patient each week. Although this does not solve staffing shortages and is not intended to do so, it does show the employees that patient care is the top priority and that management is interested in the business and the work of patient care. However, simply being visible on the units and conversing with employees and patients communicate a people-oriented philosophy.

Augmenting and Supporting the Hospital Marketing Plan

The nurse manager's role as departmental administrator is to move the nursing department toward the goals and objectives of the hospital. Each department manager participates in the hospital marketing and strategic plan in order to do the following:

- represent the needs of their respective department
- influence the direction of hospital goals based on departmental needs
- know and understand the direction of hospital goals
- interpret the hospital goals to the respective departments

As the largest department, nursing has a major role in the hospital strategic plan. The prevailing philosophy is that the nursing department acts in concert with other departments in meeting the objectives of the hospital and becoming a part of the unified whole. The point here is that nursing marketing plans augment and support hospital marketing objectives.

Research-Based, Consumer Demand–Driven Planning

One of the key concepts of the marketing model is that it is research-based and consumer demand–driven. The nurse manager's role here is education of the management team in market-based planning methods. Additionally, the nurse manager defines parameters of the research base and sets up systems for continuous data collection and analysis.

Teamwork and Unification of Goals

Just as the nursing department marketing plan is developed in concert with other departments and is consistent with hospital marketing objectives, the input from the various nursing units and services is synthesized and unified into the overall nursing department goals and objectives. The nurse manager guides and facilitates the marketing plan based on the input of each unit and service. The final objectives are the result of teamwork in the department and represent the efforts of as many team members as possible.

Growth and Innovation

Another key concept of the market-based planning model is the focus on growth and innovation. Quite simply, growth and innovation in services and programs contribute to market share and marketing objectives. These programs are developed and continued. Other programs without growth potential are discontinued unless associated with a market-share benefit.

Dynamic Orientation

Still another philosophy underlying the market-based planning model is that it is based on a dynamic and changing environment. Plans are changed even as programs are developed, based on new information obtained. The nurse manager creates an environment that facilitates rapid change in the department through simple organizational structure and delegated responsibilities and authority.

Marketing Plan As a Driving Force

Ideally, the marketing plan is the starting point in the administrative planning cycle (see Figure 2-2). The service improvements and innovations drive the nursing department goals and objectives, the financial operating projections, and the nursing strategic plan. The role of the nurse manager is to ensure the proper sequence of events in the administrative planning cycle.

The Nurse Manager As a Change Agent and Facilitator

The role of the nurse manager is to facilitate and effect change. This means that the nursing department staff and management will do more than participate in nursing department innovations; they will design and implement them. *Facilitation* means that the nurse manager will provide the structure and process for change. Special attributes of the manager as a change agent are the following:

- ability to establish an open, trusting relationship with the staff
- commitment to growth, innovation, and quality
- ability to delegate authority and responsibility
- self-confidence (required to take risks)
- tolerance for failure
- belief in the participative process
- knowledge of group processes and change theory
- legitimate power to make changes

- referent power for credibility in change
- personal power to use resources for change

The role of the nurse manager in the market-based planning model is to design and facilitate the process, problem solve, motivate, communicate, and evaluate. Although the process is participative, the nurse manager does not lose or delegate the accountability for the outcome of the process. The emphasis is always on the result, which is the product. The characteristics of the product are a direct reflection on the abilities of the nurse manager. Peters and Waterman[5] described this accountability best by the term "loose-tight properties" or the "co-existence of a firm central direction and maximum individual autonomy." This is accomplished by defining, then communicating, basic managerial expectations.

Facilitating Structures and the Participative Process

Five basic premises underlying facilitating organizational structures have emerged from marketing and organizational structure experts:

1. No one organizational structure is best.[6]
2. A relationship exists between internal and external environmental factors and the structure to achieve goals.[7]
3. The more complex the task and the larger the organization, the more appropriate is decentralization.[8]
4. Decentralization coexists with a trusting environment.[9]
5. Simpler structures and fewer management staffs facilitate innovation and goal achievement.[10]

The organizational structure, then, depends on the size of the institution, degree of change required, nature and complexity of the change, capabilities of the organization in terms of change, willingness of the organization to delegate responsibility and authority, and corporate philosophy. Organizational structures are merely communication channels. The ideal organizational structure is designed for rapid upward and downward communication. In the most basic and concrete form, the organizational structure provides

- responsibility and authority at the lowest possible level
- simple, flat chains of command
- top management accountability

The bureaucratic functional structure centralizes responsibility, authority, and accountability at the top, stifling creativity and innovation as well as impairing rapid communication. Divisionalization, which is a step toward decentralization, creates the same bureaucratic structure in the various segmented divisions. Here, responsibility, authority, and accountability rest with the division head. This is bureaucratic management one layer down in the structure. Other decentralized structures, such as matrix management and project management, delegate responsibility, authority, and accountability; promote rapid communication; and stimulate innovation. However, controls are either vague or absent. Because accountability has been delegated, fragmentation, loss of centralized control in significant issues, and frequent chaos occur. Many organizations "go back to the basics" after discovering that basic values and standards are lost in pure decentralization.

Recommended here is a structure whereby responsibility and authority are delegated to the lowest level possible, but accountability is retained by the nurse manager. This structure recognizes that accountability cannot be delegated. As a simple example, the nurse manager delegates the responsibility and authority to another for developing a marketing program. However, the success or failure of the program in terms of its financial, political, and social loss/benefit to the hospital is an accountability that rests with the nurse manager and cannot be delegated. Based on this concept, program performance analyses become the controls that are used as tools by the nurse manager in exercising accountability for the outcome of the program.

From this perspective, the nurse manager is not exercising supervision of others who have the responsibility for the program; rather, the nurse manager is building in a system of controls by which basic values and standards are met. Thus, the nurse manager is setting expectations, shaping behavior, and retaining accountability for the final product. It is during the participative process that these standards and values are established. Hence, participants define the accountabilities by which success or failure will be judged. Failure, then, rather than becoming a personal indictment, becomes the impetus for change, a learning experience in and of itself, and an opportunity for growth based on an increased knowledge base.

This concept is exemplified at the grass roots level in the shared governance model. Porter-O'Grady[11] described the set of accountabilities in nursing practice. These accountabilities are the credentialing and privileging process in which nursing sets the values, standards, parameters, and indications of successful practice. These parameters are the controls, mechanism, and tools by which the nurse manager retains the accountability for patient care. By the group process, the nurse manager assists with, facilitates, and guides the development of the accountabilities that determine success or failure.

An organizational structure that preserves accountability for standards and values yet stimulates change, creativity, and innovation is one in which the nurse manager becomes the product line manager or project manager. If responsibility and authority are delegated to the lowest possible level, operational management becomes a matter of facilitating, coordinating, guiding, developing, and monitoring. Without the responsibility of filling out forms, writing memorandums, and shuffling papers, the manager is free to use group process and human relations skills for developing programs and service innovations that have been identified as needs in the marketing planning process. In essence, the nurse manager is a part of both the operational and the matrix structures of the organization. Figure 6-1 shows the relationships.

Although a decentralized structure is preferred, the concept works with any type of structure. The major theme is that the manager is given the responsibility and authority for program development. Theoretically, and depending on how the organizational structure is designed, the nurse manager may or may not be cutting across lines of authority in his or her role as project manager. For example, the nurse manager of obstetrics is the project manager for the labor-delivery-recovery-postpartum (LDRP) program. The project team members are primarily from obstetrics, but the team also includes staff from planning, marketing, and home health. In other words, marketing objectives are assigned to nurse managers depending on their specific expertise and interest in the program area.

The work of the project team may cut across departmental lines depending on whether or not the marketing objective requires input from other departments. The pediatric rehabilitation unit will involve the project manager (rehabilitation nurse manager); a pediatrician; a physiatrist; a pediatric nurse specialist; a discharge planner; a rehabilitation coordinator; staff from planning, marketing, and public relations; the nurse recruiter; a staff development coordinator; and others as indicated. Core team members will be permanent members, and others will come in and out of the planning meetings as required by the stages of development. Departmental lines crossed may involve nursing and other hospital departments.

A critical factor in this concept is that the nurse manager is both the project or program manager and the manager of operations in the respective service or department. Obviously, this has implications for the selection of nurse managers. Because of their broad knowledge base, specialized clinical education, and nursing experience, clinical specialists are excellent program developers and marketing agents. Additionally, they possess the group skills required to lead a project or program team. These group skills

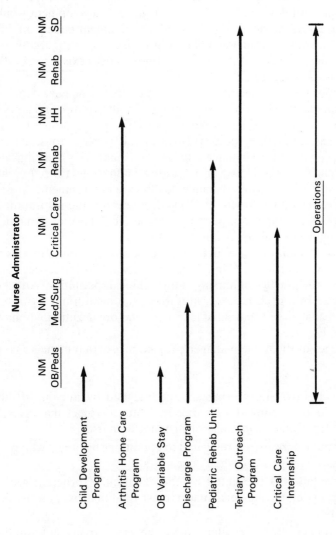

Figure 6-1 Programmatic Structure for Implementation of Marketing Objectives (Abbreviations: NM, Nurse Manager; HH, Home Health; SD, Staff Development)

are the same human relations skills required in the role of nurse manager. However, the missing elements in the education of clinical specialists are finance and budget. Proposed here is the consideration of clinical specialists for nurse managers. Their excellent leadership, group, and human relations skills combined with a specialized clinical focus can easily be supplemented with management development. This management development would include a formalized in-house management development education and selected administrative academic courses in budgeting and marketing. Additionally, many outside continuing education courses exist specifically for preparing nurse managers.

This proposition is in recognition of the fact that budgetary deficiencies can be supplemented but the clinical, programmatic, group, and marketing orientation of clinical specialists cannot. Also, this proposition is presented with the realization that some will consider it preposterous. After all, academia prepares nurse managers for management roles and clinical specialists for clinical roles. However, roles are blending, and the requirements are constantly changing in a dynamic health care environment. Academia cannot be expected to provide it all, and, therefore, the institution must share in the development of people to fill role demands of dynamic and evolving organizational structures.

Another consideration is: Will the clinical specialist want to fill this role? The answer is: of course. Clinical specialists want to influence, change, and enhance the practice of nursing in their clinical specialties. What better way is there? In a goal-directed, nurturing, and mentoring environment, the nurse manager will find satisfaction and the organization will have an invaluable resource.

Advantages of the nurse manager/project or program manager concept are:

- Programs involving nursing are spearheaded by nursing in the department of nursing. Other models feature project managers from other departments who may or may not be nurses.
- Nurse managers are not relegated to operations by others who develop innovative programs in their specialties.
- Fragmentation is prevented by consolidation of program accountabilities under the nurse manager most qualified by experience and education.
- Nurse managers are challenged by the role expansion, resulting in increased job satisfaction and productivity.
- The focus of departmental activity is directed to customer demand–based innovations designed to improve the delivery and quality of care as well as to stimulate and facilitate growth.

In order to manage this dual role, nurse managers utilize all the available resources and delegate responsibilities appropriately to others on the project team. The outcome, then, is the result of the coordinated efforts of the project team. Additionally, the nurse manager develops the unit staff to the fullest of their capabilities. The nurse manager who also manages a product line or program has a fully developed staff capable of functioning well during short absences of the nurse manager.

INTEGRATION

The participative process of development and implementation of the marketing objectives is paramount to the achievement of the objectives. The degree of participative involvement depends on the management philosophy and capability of the organization to involve the various levels of staff in the organization. The more involvement and participation, the stronger the commitment for goal achievement and the more likely that marketing goals will be met. If the nursing department is just beginning to use market-based planning, perhaps only the management staff will participate. In subsequent years, both staff and management will participate in all of the phases, from the mission development to the marketing plan.

As shown in Figure 2-1 in Chapter 2, the process begins with the hospital marketing plan. Once the overall focus is known, nursing, as a department, develops a marketing plan that supports and augments the hospital plan. The nursing units repeat the same process. Ideally, the marketing plans are incorporated into the nursing department management or business plans, which in their entirety represent the nursing strategic plan. The strategic plans of each department, then, become the strategic plan of the hospital. Obviously, the coordination of such an event requires careful timing and planning.

Administrative Planning Cycle

The hospital fiscal year is used to divide planning functions into months and quarters. Two planning cycles are ongoing in the same budget or fiscal year:

1. monthly activities focused on the strategic plan of the next fiscal year
2. quarterly progress sessions focused on the implementation and performance analysis of the current fiscal year marketing objectives

Figure 6-2 provides an example of a market-based nursing administrative planning cycle. The fiscal year differs from hospital to hospital, and the activities vary based on the preferences of the nursing department. At any rate, the planning cycle specific to the hospital is developed, written, communicated, and followed.

In Figure 6-2, the fiscal year is from July 1 to June 30. The outside solid lines represent the planning cycle for the next fiscal year, and the inside broken lines represent the program implementation and monitoring activities of the marketing objectives for the current year. Although, theoret-

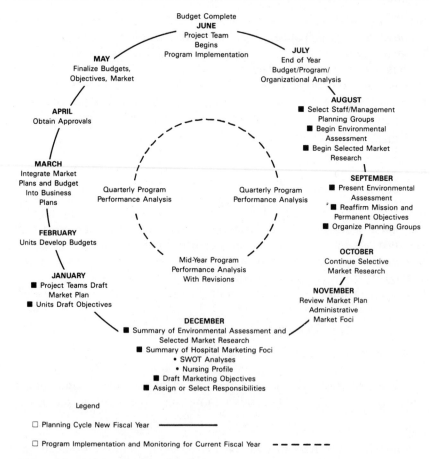

Figure 6-2 Administrative Planning Cycle

ically, marketing objectives are developed, submitted, and approved together in one organized package, reality often confirms that consumer needs and demands can define marketing opportunities mid-year. However, this is usually the result of inadequate environmental assessments and market research. At any rate, if not immediately seized upon, these unplanned marketing opportunities may be lost; therefore, the planning cycle is flexible with regard to changes, additions, or deletions based on new marketing information.

Strategic Planning for the Next Fiscal Year

The outside circle of Figure 6-2 outlines the months and associated activities of strategic planning for the next fiscal year.

July. July is reserved for collecting, organizing, and analyzing the end-of-year internal statistics, the results of which will be prepared in five-year trends for use in the environmental assessments. Some of the indicators are

- patient days, total and by unit and service
- market share month-to-month and five-year trends, total and by service
- performance analysis by program (use, profitability, achievement of objectives, effectiveness of the marketing mix, consumer evaluations)
- DRG census and reimbursement trends
- cost per patient day (total, direct, and indirect) and salary by unit and service
- productivity by unit and service
- staff hours per patient day (total, productive, and nonproductive)
- overtime utilization
- net revenue by unit, service, and program
- use trends (outpatient versus inpatient)
- procedure trends
- patient demographic data
- patient questionnaires (compiled results and trends)
- patient survey results
- physician demographic data
- physician utilization trends
- physician surveys (compiled results and trends)

- staff turnover rates and absentee rates by unit and service
- employee questionnaires (compiled results and trends)
- RN surveys
- RN demographic data (age, sex, race, education preparation, advanced degrees, etc.)
- patient care standards
- quality assurance results by unit and service
- professional accomplishments (number of publications, inservices and continuing education presented and attended, research conducted, tuition reimbursement trends, and professional awards)

When indicators are established and monitored monthly throughout the year, the end-of-the-year reports merely become an exercise in summarizing and trending for the years that data are available. Hospitals with marketing and planning departments will find that some information is already available and prepared.

August. During August, two activities occur in preparation for the marketing plan:

1. collection and analysis of market research data
2. selection of the staff for participation in the marketing planning process

Market research data include all of the data that will be used in the external environmental assessment. These data are obtained from hospital journals; state hospital associations; hospital-sponsored or nursing-sponsored consumer focus groups; government publications; and hospital planning, marketing, and public relations departments. As outlined in Chapter 4, the market research includes

1. competitive analysis
2. review of external regulations
3. review of market forces

The concept of market-based planning by consumer need and demand is formalized in the results of the data obtained from marketing research. These data combined with those obtained from the internal assessment are used to make predictions about health care needs in the future. Services are then planned accordingly.

Also, during August, planning for the planning occurs. One of the philosophies underlying the marketing process is that it involves the entire organization. Clearly, the involvement of each nurse manager is needed. The issues are how much and what kinds of staff involvement are needed as well as how to integrate the diverse inputs in the nursing department. Realistically, everyone cannot be involved in the numerous planning activities. However, everyone can be represented. A clear delineation of similar work groups is made and agreed on by the nursing management, and representatives are selected. Although the number of representatives depends on the size of the nursing department, the concern is that the total group could be too small rather than too large. Group tasks can always be broken down into smaller units for assignment to large groups. Figure 6-3 shows an example of how representatives from similar work groups are selected.

In smaller hospitals, one staff representative per unit may be the rule. Invited guests drop in and out as needed for the specific planning issue. Invited guests may be other departmental managers, administrators, physicians, or other specialists.

The method of selection is based on the selection processes that are comfortable for and common to the department. For example, in a shared

Figure 6-3 Marketing Planning Group Representation

governance model, the work groups are written into the bylaws, and elections define the appointment. In a more traditional setting, staff may be asked to represent the unit and category, or staff may apply and be selected by the management. The two most important criteria for selection of representatives are

1. willingness to serve
2. commitment to stay with the task

Because of their close contact with patients, physicians, and other employees, staff representatives are able to articulate accurately customer needs and strengths and weaknesses of the department. Additionally, involvement of staff at the planning level facilitates staff acceptance and implementation of the marketing objectives. Therefore, staff involvement is important to the process. However, representatives selected must be willing not only to serve but to commit themselves to the process until completion.

September. The September meeting is the first group meeting of the first quarter of the new fiscal year. The purposes of the meeting are the following:

1. organize into smaller planning groups
2. present the environmental assessment
3. reaffirm the mission and permanent objectives

The organization of the large planning group into smaller work units facilitates the input of the entire group through a designated or elected leader for each small group. The designated leader of each group not only represents the inputs of the small group but accepts work-study projects to be completed and presented at the next quarterly meeting in December.

At the September meeting, the internal and external environmental assessments are presented to the marketing planning group. Actually, the group members present the material. The data analysis is divided into categories that are selected by the nurse managers for presentation prior to the meeting. These categories are parallel with the categories in the internal and external environmental assessment and are

- organizational performance
- patient data analysis
- employee data analysis
- physician data analysis
- marketing research

Each nurse manager presents a major category of the prepared analyses to the marketing planning group. Also at this time, the mission statement and permanent nursing objectives are reviewed, and changes are made where appropriate.

During the presentations, specific issues are isolated for additional marketing research. For example, if the data analyses show that a significant market share in pediatrics has been lost to the competition and that admissions are down for a specific pediatrician, these issues are identified as needing further research. Each small group leader accepts an issue for study by the work-study groups. This additional research will be presented at the next quarterly meeting in December by the small work-study group leaders.

Specifically for the pediatric market share issue, the assigned group may want to interview the defecting pediatrician. The defecting pediatrician may state that she has not truly lost patients but is admitting at the competitor hospital because of a juvenile diabetes program and nurse specialist at the competitor hospital. She may also mention that parents are more welcome at the competitor hospital, there are closer parking facilities, and the laboratory and pharmacy are more efficient. It may still be difficult to gain insight into the major problem. Does the pediatrician reflect the current thinking of all of the pediatricians or has she raised these issues as an excuse for leaving for other reasons (e.g., a joint venture with the competitor). The work-study group may decide to interview other pediatricians, hold focus groups with the parents of former patients from both hospitals, and survey parents of small children in the community. The results, which will be presented at the December meeting, may show an excellent marketing opportunity in pediatrics, either to make up for the lost market share from the pediatrician or to lure the defector back into the fold.

October. In October, the marketing research on selected issues continues, and plans are made for the second quarter meeting. Also, environmental data and the competitive analysis from the hospital marketing activities are shared with the planning group.

November. The marketing objectives and major marketing foci from hospital administration are presented to the planning group in November. Nursing marketing objectives include a support system for the hospital marketing objectives. In some cases, nursing may be designated by the administration to develop and implement some of the objectives. It is critical to the achievement of hospital marketing objectives that the top nursing executive be directly involved in the marketing plan of the hospital. As an example of nursing support for a hospital focus, perhaps the hospital marketing objective is to increase the patient days of patients 65 years of age and older (the Medicare population) by recruiting and hiring a gerontologist. Nursing, then, would develop an objective to develop and implement a geriatrics program or unit to complement and support the hospital objective.

December. The December meeting is the second quarterly meeting and also the mid-year point in the planning cycle. The activities of this meeting are

1. summarizing the environmental assessment
2. presenting the selected marketing research issues completed by the small work-study groups
3. reviewing hospital marketing objectives
4. identifying strengths, weaknesses, opportunities, and threats
5. profiling the nursing department
6. matching organizational capabilities with market demand
7. defining areas needing improvement or a special focus
8. drafting marketing objectives
9. selecting of objectives by project managers
10. organizing the project teams

The process of these activities are discussed further in this chapter, and the concepts underlying these activities were discussed in Chapters 4 and 5. The major concept, however, is that the nursing department objectives are the result of a group effort involving the input of the entire department.

The result is the drafting of at least five or six major objectives. These objectives represent areas needing improvement, growth, or a special focus, areas that if not addressed in the marketing plan would most likely be left to chance. This is not to say that the nursing department cannot be working on other objectives; rather, these objectives are the major foci of the department. They number five or six because, in reality, this is the limit of what can be expected from the planning group within one year.

The selection of objectives by the nurse managers increases the likelihood that strength and expertise will be matched with the objective. Some nurse managers may feel more comfortable pairing with another as an associate for the objective.

The organization of project teams occurs similarly. The planning team members select the objective that fits their specific interest and expertise. The result is five or six project teams that will continue to meet outside the main group to develop the objectives and marketing plan.

January. In January, the nurse project managers work with their project teams, further quantifying the marketing objective and developing the marketing plan (market segmentation and targeting, marketing research, and marketing mix). Simultaneously, nurse managers present the hospital and nursing marketing objectives to the unit staffs. The units then draft unit objectives, which when approved will become a part of the nursing department strategic plan. The same marketing planning format is used at the unit level, with organization of on-unit groups based on the preferences of the nurse manager.

February. In February, the units draft the unit budgets based on the objectives. The budgets reflect expenses and revenue associated with the operation of the unit as well as the expense and revenue associated with the marketing objectives.

March. In March, the unit budgets for objectives and nursing department objectives and associated budgets are organized into business plans and integrated into one strategic plan for the nursing department. The business plan is discussed further in this chapter.

April. In April, all of the hospital department business plans are submitted for approval and, once approved, become a part of the hospital strategic plan. Far in advance of approval time, the nurse executive keeps the administrator informed of the nursing marketing planning activities. Strategic plans, then, come as no surprise and are continued with tentative approval until budget approval time.

May. After submission of the strategic plan in April, May is set aside for budget and objective revisions outlined in the approval process. This time period provides nursing the opportunity to review the completeness of the marketing plan as well as ensure that associated expenses are included in the budget.

June. The revised budget, objectives, and business plans are submitted as the final strategic plan. Rather than being a time to relax and reflect, June is the beginning of the implementation of the objectives. Therefore, the events described on the inside circle of Figure 6-2 are initiated.

Project Implementation and Monitoring

Program or project implementation begins in June (Figure 6-2). Then, quarterly meetings of the initial marketing planning group are held where project managers and their respective teams report progress with the objectives as defined by program performance analyses. The measurable objectives established are used to measure the achievement of the objectives. In the example given in Figure 6-2, the quarterly meetings and performance analysis reporting occur in June, September, December, and

March. At the December, or mid-year, meeting, program revisions are made if necessary since the collection of data for six months is sufficient to determine whether the programs are on or off target.

Although program objectives are established for one year, the financial and long-range strategic plan may define program implementation phasing in for up to three years. In this case, the program is divided into three phases over the three years, with each phase and associated objectives set for completion in a one-year period. With this approach, a high degree of control over outcomes is achieved.

Forum for Action

Whether the hospital is large or small, planning sessions with the nursing management team are crucial in today's competitive environment. The nurse executive's primary responsibilities are to ensure that strategic planning occurs by setting aside time and organizing a forum for the planning activities. To elaborate on the specific point here, day-to-day, face-to-face conversations among management staff are not enough. Strategic planning sessions are more than communication, more than meetings, and more than committee work. *Strategic planning* is plotting out a course of action for the nursing department after considering the mission, market, financial and programmatic issues, and feasibility of such action. It is a continuous, dynamic process. This requires the input, combined knowledge and expertise, and creative ideas of the entire management team. As previously stated, staff representation is ideal.

Since the administrative planning cycle is separated into quarters with two simultaneous activities occurring, planning sessions are structured to include both the activities of planning for the next fiscal year and project implementation and monitoring for the present year. During the months between, the sessions are brief presentations or analysis reporting sessions held in-house. The mid-year meeting, which is in December in Figure 6-2, is a management retreat, lasting one or two days, preferably away from the hospital environment. The major activities of the group (drafting the marketing objectives) are conducted at this mid-year retreat.

Mid-Year Retreat: First Day

Although the mid-year retreat is specifically designed as a one-day working session, it can be combined with professional or management development into two days, depending on the nursing department budget. If conducted as a two-day retreat, the first day consists of the discussion of timely topics that fit into the scheme of strategic planning. Again, depending on the budget, speakers may be in-house specialists; free university, college, or civic leaders; or professional fee-for-service workshop leaders. Also, the first day of the retreat may be open to other hospital nursing departments for a small fee to cover the cost of the retreat. With a little creativity, an inexpensive two-day retreat can be planned. A few topics for the retreat include

- national health care forecasting
- reimbursement trends
- care delivery trends
- political climates
- new directions in nursing
- creation of an environment for professionalism in nursing
- trends in health care education
- the role of hospitals in the future
- creative health care programing
- demand-based programing
- leadership within financial restraints

The purposes of this first-day agenda are the following:

1. Enhance or develop management skills and philosophies.
2. Create enthusiasm and anticipation for the all-important second day.
3. Stimulate team spirit and group cohesiveness.
4. Provide topic information needed for participating fully on the second day.

The cost of the two-day retreat must be viewed in terms of the outcomes. It is expensive to take management and selected staff from patient care for two days even if the speakers are free. To meet and develop objectives are not enough. The outcomes that will justify the cost are

1. improved care to patients
2. programs designed to increase patient days and revenue
3. programs designed to retain nurses, saving costly recruitment and orientation dollars
4. programs designed to retain physicians

The objectives must concretely specify program outcomes, program implementation plans, persons responsible for the objectives, and financial and service projections.

Mid-Year Retreat: Second Day

The size of the nursing department will not alter the content of the strategic planning session on the second day of the retreat. However, size will affect how it is organized. Large nursing departments plan months in advance to ensure that all data are ready for presentation and that the participants are selected and placed into planning groups. The planning groups are organized at the first quarterly meeting, and some will have completed selected marketing research for this mid-year session. Since there will be six objectives, six smaller groups of participants are organized with any number in the groups. Although the number in each group is not an issue, the composition of the groups needs discussion. Since this session consists of a summary of the environmental assessments, SWOT analysis, and development of marketing objectives (not the actual marketing plan development), groups can be assigned heterogeneously. For example, management and staff from different areas can be grouped together. In fact, it is better to ensure that participants from the same area are not together for the purposes of this session. Some of the advantages of heterogeneous small groups are

- free flowing ideas in the absence of line relationships
- contrasting views and opinions because of diverse backgrounds, facilitating idea generation and the use of persuasive and negotiating skills
- sharing of diverse ideas, enhancing problem-solving skills

Table 6-2 shows a typical agenda for the day. Group leaders are prepared since they were designated or elected by each small group at the first quarterly meeting of the new fiscal year. During the SWOT analysis, each group member develops a list of strengths, weaknesses, opportunities, and threats. Each group leader then solicits the top five or six SWOTs from each member, and the group prioritizes them. The result is five or six SWOTs from each small group. The retreat leader then does the same for the entire group. The outcome is five or six SWOTs prioritized by the entire group representing the input of each member.

With the environmental assessments and the SWOTs in mind, the small groups repeat the process of development and prioritization of key result areas. At this point, the key result areas consist of one or two words representing areas needing a focus or improvement. The entire group assisted by the retreat leader develops the key result areas into measurable objectives.

The last hour of the retreat consists of assigning marketing objectives to appropriate nurse managers, who will become the project managers for the marketing objective and leaders of the project teams. Each group member present, by selection or assignment, becomes a member of a

Table 6-2 Sample Agenda for Strategic Planning Retreat

Hour	Activity
1	Review and reaffirmation of the mission, philosophy, objectives, and hospital marketing focus
2	Summary of the environmental assessments Summary of the hospital marketing plan Presentation of selected marketing research
3	Small group development Prioritization of SWOTs
4	Entire group prioritization of SWOTs Profiling the nursing department
5	Small group development Prioritization of key result areas Strategic matching
6	Entire group prioritization of key result areas
7	Development of marketing objectives by entire group
8	Assignment of marketing objectives Selection of project teams Initial meeting of project teams

project team. This team will meet independently to develop the marketing plan. Resources from planning, marketing, and finance are utilized by the nurse managers in preparing the business plans, which will be integrated into unit and departmental budgets and submitted for approval.

MARKET-BASED PLANNING AT THE UNIT LEVEL

All of the concepts and techniques for market-based planning can be applied at the unit level. In fact, market-based planning at the unit level is the fine tuning and detailing of service issues that set the nursing department apart from all others. The customers are the same customers of the nursing department. The internal environment is the unit, and the external environment is the nursing department, hospital, and community. The competition is other units in-house as well as similar units at other hospitals. The same market-based model is applied at the unit level, with staff serving as planning group leaders and project leaders.

A planning cycle is established to coincide with that of the nursing department, and marketing objectives augment and support those developed by the nursing department and hospital. Key result areas are defined from unit SWOTs and are focused on improvements in

- care and service to patients
- relationships with physicians
- working environments for nurses

Improved Care and Service to Patients

Nurses may identify in the unit SWOT analyses that patients in a major disease category are receiving different standards of care based on physician differences, nursing differences, or shift differences. Additionally, the SWOT analyses may show that the competition has developed promotional programs to attract patients that are becoming a threat to the unit census. General unit standards of care, patient care standards, and promotional programs are then identified as areas needing improvement or a focus. Objectives are written and assigned to or selected by staff nurses who become team project leaders to develop the marketing plan for unit standards, disease standards, and unit promotions. The team develops and implements the marketing plan, reporting progress in meetings established to monitor the achievement of objectives.

Unit Standards

Basic unit standards outline expectations and ensure that care delivery is consistent between caregivers and across shifts. Unit standards of care may address

- unit objectives
- structure and function of the unit
- admission of patients to the unit
- transfer of patients to another unit
- discharge of patients to home
- routine vital signs
- staffing requirements
- documentation requirements
- staff-patient ratios
- care delivery system
- charge nurse responsibilities and expectations
- staff nurse responsibilities and expectations
- auxiliary staff responsibilities
- float nurse responsibilities
- procedures not performed by nurses on the units
- unit certification requirements
- unit orientation plan for staff and patients
- method of ensuring quality of care

- standard unit meetings and committees
- shift routines and expectations

Once developed, unit standards provide the framework for developing tools to monitor and measure the compliance with and effectiveness of the standards.

Patient Care Standards

Patient care standards ensure that all patients receive consistent and agreed-on nursing management that reflects both current practice and the latest in scientific thought. Two levels of care can develop on the same unit for the same type of patients in the absence of standards. For example, diabetes patients are admitted on the same unit by both internists and endocrinologists. Patients of the endocrinologists receive teaching on insulin administration based on self-administered capillary blood glucose testing, and patients of the internists administer their own insulin based on self-administered urine glucose levels and a sliding scale. Additionally, patients of the endocrinologists are referred by consult to the diabetes nurse specialist for teaching and the teaching protocol varies from that given by unit nurses. Nursing in this case bridges the gap with patient care standards for diabetes patients. The development of such standards will require the input of all the physicians, nurses, and allied health professionals involved in the care of diabetes patients. The finished standards will address

- assessment methods
- diagnosis patterns (nursing)
- intervention methods
- teaching
- discharge teaching
- consult and referrals

Using this example as an issue arising from the units' SWOT analyses, a staff nurse with a special interest in the care of the diabetes patient would select the objective "to standardize the nursing management of the diabetes patient," using the market based planning format for achievement of the objective. A diabetes program, then, would be planned, incorporating indicators from the patient classification tool into the interventions of the various nursing diagnosis categories, which would then be integrated into the DRG that includes diabetes. The result would be an improved and consistent level of care given to all diabetes patients. Written and formalized, such programs are highly marketable to patients and physicians.

Promotional Programs

Promotional programs designed to attract or retain patients are based on programs or services that are already developed but that need special promotions in order to compete. These strategies are primarily based on augmented services rather than on price, although, occasionally, price competition is one of the strategies. Highly competitive areas or services design special promotional services to link current patients and potential patients to the institution. This is especially common in obstetrics and pediatrics but can also occur when there is more than one of any specialized program in the community such as oncology, rehabilitation, home, emergency, and ambulatory care. Although these promotions are often designed by the marketing and promotions departments, staff at the unit level are indeed creative in generating ideas for the promotion of their specific services. Examples include

- birthday cards for newborn nursery infants
- free pictures for newborns at birth and ages 1 and 2
- videotapes of infants receiving the first bath by their mother
- exercise classes for obstetric patients (designed with physician input)
- child development classes for parents of young children
- quarterly health update newsletters for cardiac patients
- reunions for rehabilitation patients
- support groups for relatives who have lost loved ones
- hotlines for obstetric, emergency, and psychiatric patients with qualified response staff
- follow-up telephone calls to the patient from the primary nurse
- unit tours for elective patients
- unit tours and receptions for the public
- CPR certifications for the public

Promotions such as these are topics of controversy in health care and are often labeled *gimmicks* by critics. Actually, they are augmentations of already developed services and programs. Although they are designed to attract patients, these augmentations also improve services to the customer. Additionally, such promotions provide increased top-of-mind name awareness of the hospital in the mind of the customers.

Improved Relationships with Physicians

One of the stark realities a nurse manager must face when planning strategies designed to maintain census is that physicians are still the major determinants of hospital selection by patients.[12] As such, physician satisfaction with patient care is paramount. Although nursing as a department plans programs and services to attract and retain major physician admitters, services planned at the unit level are often more effective because staff working directly with physicians are in a better position to know the needs and wants of these major customers. As mentioned in Chapter 3, marketing programs for physicians are not intended to perpetuate the "handmaiden" role of nurses but rather to view the physician from a purely business perspective. The "bottom line" is that if physicians continue to admit patients, the hospital will prosper and so will the staff. Problems with individual physicians are managed in the same manner that a business firm would manage customer problems, and this is through an established customer relations service. The equivalent of the customer service department in hospitals is the patient care committee discussed in Chapter 3.

The needs and wants of physicians are similar to those of nurses. In elementary terminology, both nurses and physicians want patients to improve with care, be satisfied with the care, and return when services are needed again. Additionally, both physicians and nurses want to go about the work of caring for patients safely and efficiently with adequate support (supplies, equipment, and ancilliary and support services). Further, each desires adequate compensation for this important work.

In one unit SWOT analyses, it was identified that physicians are complaining that nobody seems to know what is going on with the patients and that it takes them hours to complete their rounds. In response to last year's competitive analysis, one nursing unit implemented a decentralized approach to nursing care by eliminating the charge position and having each nurse function as the charge for their specific patients. Although it was one year in the planning, and physicians were informed of the change, they seemed to lack patience with the new system at the onset. An interested nurse volunteered to lead a marketing research team that will study the problem. No objective was formulated until the research was completed and presented. After one month of interviewing physicians and nurses as well as observing physician rounds, the study team reported:

1. As many as five nurses are caring for the patients of one physician.
2. The patients of one physician may be located in rooms at opposite ends of the hallway.
3. Nurses are signing off to other nurses at break time or lunch time, but this is not communicated to the physicians.
4. The physicians do not know how to find the primary nurses because the nurses are in the rooms giving patient care when physicians arrive on the unit for rounds.

5. Several physicians stated that nursing at the competitor hospital did this and after a year, "it [was] still disorganized and it will never work."

The nurse manager immediately recognized this as a marketing opportunity instead of a threat. If the unit makes the new system an improvement over the old one and that of the competition in the eyes of the physicians, the unit will have a competitive advantage with both physicians and nurses. The project team developed the objective "to increase physician satisfaction with the new system by 85 percent within the next three months." The subobjectives were:

1. Divide the unit into modules.
2. Classify the modules by physicians or physician groups.
3. Assign patients to rooms according to their physician module.
4. Assign nurses to modules for two-month rotations, retaining the primary nurse concept.
5. Install a larger assignment board listing the patients, their physicians, the primary nurse, the nurse caring for the patient for the day, the associate, and the name of the alternative (to whom the patient is signed off at the time).
6. Place the name of the nurse caregiver on each patient's door.
7. Establish nurse/physician rounds, with the nurse being notified by the unit secretary when the patient's physician arrives for rounds.
8. Include other professionals in the rounds as appropriate to patient needs such as dietary, physical therapy, social service, nurse specialist, or discharge planning personnel.
9. Name the nurse/physician rounds and position them as patient/physician/nursing patient care conferences.
10. Have the unit secretary place the medical records of each patient on the outside door of each patient's room in preparation for the rounds.
11. Evaluate the effectiveness of the program in three months by a physician and nurse survey questionnaire.

The 11-point strategy was given target dates for completion and assigned to nurses who would be responsible for implementing each subobjective.

This is just one simple example of how market-based planning conducted on the unit level is used to improve the relationship with physicians. Programs to improve physician relationships with the unit or service are focused on

1. improved unit efficiency
2. improved or augmented services
3. increased physician input into services

Although the example presented here is simple, comprehensive physician/nurse–planned programs that are highly competitive and marketable can arise from the unit market-based planning process. Examples are pediatric rehabilitation programs, outpatient rehabilitation evaluation programs, cancer screening programs, and same-day admission programs.

Similar to the nursing process, market-based planning begins with an assessment that identifies problems, and out of the problems, programs are formulated as solutions. Whether or not these programs are planned at the unit level or departmentwide depends on the amount of support required for the program. Usually, unit-based programs are augmentations of present services involving only specific unit staff and physicians. On the other hand, departmentwide planned programs involve new services, new units, and new programs requiring a broader spectrum of support. In either case, these programs, new or augmented, ultimately benefit the patient.

Improvements in Working Environments of Nurses

Clearly, filling nurse vacancies is no longer a matter of attracting the market share. With the total available market for nurses dwindling, filling nurse vacancies is accomplished at the expense of the market share of other hospitals and health care institutions. The very best market share strategy is retention of nurses already employed with the hospital. Therefore, unit-level marketing strategies are focused on internal marketing, i.e., improving the working environments of nurses. This ultimately will improve the marketability of the nursing department and recruitment. Issues of nurse marketing on the supply side are discussed in Chapter 8.

The American Hospital Association, Division of Nursing, completed a research study in 1987 on the nursing shortage. Some of the possible solutions to the current shortage of nursing cited in this study were:

- Upgrade the educational system.
- Establish two levels of nursing—professional and technical.
- Differentiate staff nurses in the hospital.
- Initiate clinical ladders.
- Increase pay.
- Give recognition.
- Allow nurses to participate in key decisions.
- Permit nurses to work flexible hours and/or design their own work.
- Institute group nurse practices contracting with the hospital.
- Align schools and hospitals.
- Communicate to the public a realistic view of nursing.[13]

Some of these issues can be addressed at the unit level.

The unit SWOT analyses will most likely identify weaknesses and threats associated with the nursing shortage. These are

- burnout because of excessive overtime
- excessive responsibility because of an increased nurse-patient ratio
- unreasonable shift rotations
- lack of recognition
- lack of promotional avenues
- inadequate salary
- lack of respect from physicians, administration, and the community
- lack of professional challenges

Salary is an issue. The perception of inadequate salary is accurate in most instances when the relative worth and job demands of RNs are compared (as they often are) to those of executive secretaries, grocery checkout clerks, and skilled trade positions such as plumbers, carpenters, etc. However, the real aggravating factor is that nursing is a profession comparable to pharmacy, physical therapy, speech therapy, psychology, and dietary. Yet, compensation disparities exist. The issue of salary becomes magnified in times of shortages because money is perceived as a due reward for tolerating impossible working conditions.

Another issue is overtime, which is intimately associated with salary and the perception of being underpaid. Nurses begin the cycle of continuous overtime because of the belief that they are assisting the unit through a temporary situation. Although payment for overtime is important, the expectation is that the contribution is temporary and that it will be appreciated and remembered (recognition). Unfortunately, nurses are caught in a permanent situation, and their contributions are rewarded with requests for more overtime. An entrapment cycle begins when nurses have worked enough overtime to increase their standard of living. Then, new cars, new furniture, and perhaps better housing require overtime to meet expenses. Overtime is no longer an assist to the unit in a temporary crisis, but rather it is required to meet living expenses. With the new standards of living achievable only under impossible working conditions, the frustrated nurses perceive inadequate salary, poor working conditions, and no way out.

Compounding the issue is the fact that not all nurses are working the overtime, hence the perception of unfairness in schedules and assignments. Further, the nurses who are working the overtime, with all of the bonuses, shift differentials, and overtime pay, are making more than the nurse managers, hence the perception of inequity at the management level. When management makes less, what is the message to the nurse at the bedside?

Further compounding the issue is the use of agency staff. These nurses, who are paid a high hourly rate, sometimes double that of the unit staff, choose their days and hours, and have less responsibility than the unit staff, and their high hourly rates are paid from the nursing unit budget. Working alongside one unit nurse may be a nurse on overtime making more with less responsibility and an agency nurse making much more with much less responsibility. What is the message here? The message is that if "they" have the money to pay overtime, why don't "they" just increase the salaries of staff nurses and fill the positions? Eventually, this simple logic will prevail. Until then, nursing is left to creative and ingenious methods to staff for patient needs.

Some of the solution strategies are developed by the nurse administrator for the entire department and include

- realistic budgeting of needed staff positions
- reviewing nursing tasks to determine which tasks could be done by another department (medical records, pharmacy, dietary, housekeeping, laundry, and volunteer services) or by other unit staff such as the unit secretary or unit aide
- negotiating adequate and competitive salaries
- abolishing wage compression and inequity
- providing a career ladder to include promotional pathways for nurses in staff nursing, management, and education
- exempting and paying salaries to RNs
- aligning with schools of nursing providing clinical practice sites and joint staff/faculty positions
- piloting entrepreneurial practice models
- providing in-house registries for supplemental staffing
- discouraging the use of outside agencies for staffing
- discouraging the use of overtime as an accepted method of staffing
- defining *absenteeism* and following up on excessive and unexcused absences
- budgeting and establishing an effective recruitment strategy
- establishing and preserving an adequate orientation and continuing education program
- establishing criteria for excellent units and a recognition program

At the unit level, many strategies are employed to retain and ultimately recruit nurses. Some of these include

- implementing a thorough unit orientation program
- creating flexible positions
  —straight shift
  —rotation shift
  —12-hour seven on/seven off
  —12-hour, three-day week plus 8
  —part-time, every other weekend
  —10-hour, four-day week in outpatient areas where procedures can be shifted to overlap hours
- creating flexible employment programs
  —faculty/staff summer work
  —nurse internships
  —student nurse summer program
  —on call program
  —job sharing (three nurses filling one full-time equivalent [FTE] and the replacement)
  —job pairing for same days off and on
  —unit rotation programs
  —float pool
  —observe a nurse program
  —minishifts for peak times in outpatient areas, delivery, surgery, emergency, ambulatory care
  —burnout rotation in and out programs
  —cross training of several units
  —cross training of unit secretaries and unit aides
- creating promotional avenues
  —preceptor
  —mentor
  —charge nurse
  —module leader
  —clinical ladders
  —assistant nurse manager
- creating educational opportunities
  —leadership course for nurses
  —preceptor course
  —critical care course
  —certification programs in specialties
  —advanced skills certification

- establishing criteria for excellence in nursing and a recognition program
- establishing staff led committees
  —quality assurance
  —documentation
  —policy and procedure
  —standards of care
  —care planning
  —patient teaching
  —social planning
  —orientation and inservice
  —primary nursing
- promoting the concept of primary nursing from admission to discharge of patients
- establishing regular feedback sessions with nurses to develop and monitor progress with professional goals
- developing entrepreneurial programs

The last item, developing entrepreneurial programs, deserves special discussion. The concept of shared governance is only a step away from group practice and direct billing for nursing service. It provides the framework for an organized professional nursing staff similar to the medical model. Mitnick and Crummette[14] described an entrepreneurial contracted group practice model in which nurses formed partnerships and contracted their services to hospitals to provide 24-hour care to patients. The partnership in this model would provide supplemental staffing out of the contracted fee when needed for patient care. This model is similar to the practice model of physicians except that the hospital is still responsible for paying the contracted fee. Although this takes nurses off the payroll, they are still under the control of the contracting hospital.

A possible evolution of this model is the nursing partnership or group practice that is credentialed under the nursing staff organization and receives consultations for nursing care of hospitalized patients by physicians and receives reimbursement by direct billing. This role creates a different relationship with physicians, one that is not unlike the relationship of physicians to psychologists, speech therapists, and other consulting physicians.

At the unit level, a precursor of this model is the shared governance model and the unit franchise model described by Donna Davidson, Vice President of Nursing at Santa Monica Hospital.[15] In this model, owners of the franchises are the clinical nurses who run the unit as a business. The point here is that with the current problems in nursing, such as image, the shortage, lack of respect, lack of autonomy and inadequate salaries, entrepreneurial experimentation at the unit level provides insights into possible solutions not only for the unit but for the profession. The market-based model applied at the unit level facilitates identification of problems and generation of unique and ingenious solutions.

NOTES

1. Stephen P. Robbins, *The Administrative Process* (Englewood Cliffs, N.J.: Prentice-Hall, Inc., 1980), 56.

2. Ibid., 34–45.

3. Ibid., 46.

4. Thomas C. Kinnear and Kenneth L. Bernhardt, *Principles of Marketing,* 2d ed. (Glenview, Ill.: Scott, Foresman & Co., 1983), 644.

5. Thomas J. Peters and Robert H. Waterman, Jr., *Search of Excellence* (New York, N.Y.: Harper & Row, 1982), 318.

6. Kinnear and Bernhardt, 632.

7. Ibid., 644.

8. Robbins, 234.

9. Ibid.

10. Peters and Waterman, 311.

11. Timothy Porter-O'Grady, *Creative Nursing Management* (Rockville, Md.: Aspen Publishers, Inc., 1986).

12. Kathy Luciano and Lu Ann W. Darling, "The Physician As a Nursing Service Customer," *Journal of Nursing Administration* 15, no. 6 (June 1985): 17.

13. Neale Miller, ed., *The Nursing Shortage: Facts, Figures, and Feelings* (Chicago: Ill.: American Hospital Association, 1987), 22–23.

14. Steven David Mitnick and Beauty D. Crummette, "Hospital Nurses As Entrepreneurs," *Nursing Management* 18, no. 11 (1987): 58.

15. Pricilla Scherer, "Hospitals That Attract (and Keep) Nurses," *American Journal of Nursing* 88, no. 1 (1988): 40.

Chapter 7

Structures and Methods

Chapter 6 discussed organizational structures facilitating the participative process of market-based planning. This chapter presents product line management as a conclusion to the discussion of facilitating concepts and structures. Additionally, this chapter discusses business plans as a method of organizing and presenting programs and services developed in the process of market-based planning. Finally, Chapter 8 presents an example of a business plan for an arthritis home care program.

PRODUCT LINE MANAGEMENT AND PRODUCT LINE STRUCTURE

Product line management and product line structure were first introduced by Proctor and Gamble in 1927 as a result of success with a product line experiment with Camay soap.[1] Since then, product-oriented organizational structures have been common in businesses. Traditionally, each product line has its own product manager, and the product line is treated as a business within the business. Product lines and product structures have most recently appeared in market-oriented hospitals along with the evolution of the marketing function. The ways in which product lines are differentiated are as many and varied as the accompanying organizational structures.

Product Lines Defined

A *product line* "is a group of products within a product mix that are closely related, either because they function in a similar manner, are made available to the same consumers, or are marketed through the same types of outlets.''[2] A product mix (width of consumer offerings) is defined, then each product line in the product mix is lengthened by the product items. Table 7-1 shows a simple example applied to nursing education.

As shown, product lines are developed by product items that are similar in function. The product mix is composed of all of the product lines (science, psychiatry, humanities, business, practicum, and curriculum development). In these product lines are the various courses offered. This is a more traditional definition in which *product lines* are divisions of similar courses, sometimes labeled *the science department* or *the department of psychiatry*.

Table 7-2 shows a variation that defines product lines more progressively. As shown, six product lines comprise the product mix and and are organized by the similarities of consumers using the programs. For example, the generic nursing program is marketed to high school graduates; the degree completion to diploma and associate degree graduate nurses; the master's to baccalaureate degree nurses; health education to students in other majors such as physical education, business, education, physical therapy, or social sciences; and continuing education to RNs. Marketing, then, is a separate product line featuring

- recruitment
- planning (marketing research, program planning, and development)
- curriculum design and development
- advertising
- promotion

Whereas the product lines in Table 7-1 are organized by similarities of the products, the product lines in Table 7-2 are organized by similarities of the consumers who use the product lines. The product lines in Table 7-1 are oriented toward the organization, and the product lines in Table 7-2 are oriented toward the consumer.

Table 7-1 Product Mix and Product Lines, University School of Nursing

Science	Psychiatry	Humanities	Business	Practicum	Curriculum Development
SC 101	PSY 101	SOC 110	BUS 110	MS 110	Revision
SC 300	PSY 102	ENG 110	BUS 210	PED 110	New courses
SC 310	PSY 200	SPN 110	COM 110	OB 110	Textbooks
SC 312	PSY 310	REL 110		RHB 110	Sequencing

Table 7-2 Product Mix and Product Lines: University School of Nursing

Generic	Degree Completion	Master's	Health Ed	Continuing Ed	Marketing
Course A	Course A	Courses	Mental Hlth	Course A	Recruitment
Course B	Course B	Clinical	Child Dev	Course B	Planning
Course C	Course C	Thesis	Nutrition	Course C	Curriculum
Course D	Course D		Family	Course D	Advertisement
			Planning		Promotions

A change in the way products or services are differentiated has major implications for the organization, one of which is a change in structure to facilitate the success of the product line. The other major implication is that product lines require product managers. For example, in Table 7-2, the product *health education* requires a product manager, and this product manager will cross departmental lines in developing and implementing the product items in the product line. That is, the product items in the product line will be developed from the offerings of other departments such as psychiatry, pediatrics, sociology, nutrition, etc.

Product line management is different from program or project management. Project or program management is identifying and marketing major strength areas. Pure product line management involves

- identifying major areas of strengths
- organizing areas of strengths into product lines
- changing the organizational structure to accommodate each product line

Product Line Structure

Technology, environments, and consumer needs determine the organizational structure that will best achieve the goals of the institution at any specific point in time. "[A] more realistic view of organizational design should recognize that in many cases, it is emergent rather than purposely planned."[3] In other words, the organizational structure is dynamic, evolving, and driven by the goals of the institution. As product lines and goals are defined, organizational structure changes to achieve the correct fit.

Matrix Organization

The matrix structure is one example of a structure that has emerged in some hospitals in response to the competitive environment and the need to specialize according to organizational strengths and consumer demands.

For example, the hospital identifies major areas of organizational strengths and then builds a dual organizational structure around traditional functions and the functions of product lines. This facilitates specialization and increases the attractiveness of these product lines in the competitive marketplace yet maintains traditional lines of authority. The product line manager is a specialist who manages a team comprised of staff from various departments and services. Therefore, staff in the team may have two bosses: the product line manager and the traditional department manager. Such structure requires teamwork, cooperation, and flexibility. Figure 7-1 shows an example of a matrix organizational structure.

In this example, the hospital identifies several areas of strength, either because of specialized staff in the identified areas or space and equipment advantages. Strong areas include the diabetes center, women's health, wellness center, ophthalmology, and cardiology. Additionally, market research shows that these strengths have a high degree of consumer demand and market attractiveness. Following the concept of the matrix structure, these strengths are then organized as product lines and placed under the direction of a vice president of marketing. Each product line will have a product line manager who is a specialist employed or hired by the hospital. Further, the product line managers will develop product line teams who are also specialists employed by the hospital. The teams cut across traditional departmental lines of authority. Team members will report to the product line manager for programmatic issues and to traditional department managers for departmental issues.

The product line managers develop product items in the product line. Table 7-3 shows the product items in the product lines of the wellness center and the diabetes center. Depending on the hospital's capabilities and the market demand, more product items are added to the product lines, increasing the length of the line. More product lines are added as the hospital adds specialties, increasing the product line width.

Product items in the product line determine the team composition. For example, in Table 7-3, the occupational health program will require a physical and an occupational therapist on the wellness center team. These therapists will then report to both the project manager and the director of the hospital's department of physical and occupational therapy.

The matrix organizational structure facilitates the development of product lines as like services are grouped under lines of specialization that appeal to more narrowed markets. Such a structure creates more efficiency in

- coordinating highly marketable specialties
- developing marketable expertise in an area
- narrowing and defining the target markets

	Vice President of Marketing				
	Wellness Center	Women's Health	Ophthalmology	Diabetes Center	Cardiology
Nursing					
Physical Therapy					
Occupational Therapy					
Human Resources					
Finance					
Dietary					
Sports Medicine					
Psychology					
Pharmacy					
Surgery					
Radiology					
Medical Services					

Figure 7-1 Matrix Structure in a Hospital

Table 7-3 Product Line Offerings

Wellness Center	Diabetes Center
Executive fitness program	Diabetes outpatient program
Occupational health program	New onset classes
Community physical fitness	Juvenile program
Stress reduction	Ophthalmology assessment
Nutrition assessment and classes	Podiatry assessment
Obesity program	Dietary consult
Exercise program	Diabetes inpatient program
Smoking cessation	Update course
Athletic clinic	Medication management
Divorce adjustment program	Dietary management
	Diabetes support group

- reaching the target market
- competing with similar services in the community

Since there is "shared authority," one of the disadvantages of the matrix structure is confusion because of the dual reporting system.[4]

With the matrix structure, nursing is one of the departments crossed by the dual authority concept. Because of the specialization in nursing, the nurse manager provides specialty staff to the product line team. As presented in Chapter 6, the nurse manager can be the product line manager (project manager) for a product line, which simplifies the reporting system for nursing but does not address the issue in other departments. Because nurses are both generalists and specialists, they are excellent product line managers and product line team members. "[N]urse executives [nurse managers] possess the clinical knowledge and the communication and management skills and the understanding of today's health care issues crucial to the successful management of a SL [service line or product line]."[5]

Pure Product Line Structure

"[T]rue product lines have their focus on the marketplace, not on operations or productions."[6] A pure product line structure is developed by organizing under customer services, not hospital departments. Traditional lines of authority are used, but the scope of responsibility includes cost centers for services identified by the hospital as major strength areas. The major areas of strength are the hospital's product mix. For example, one hospital vice president is responsible for rehabilitation services, a product line including the following:

- rheumatology center
- spinal cord injury center

- stroke rehabilitation center
- head trauma center
- vocational rehabilitation center
- pain control center
- developmental pediatric rehabilitation center
- rehabilitation inpatient care
- rehabilitation outpatient care

Each product item has a business plan identifying budgetary income and expense included in a cost center under rehabilitation services. Each product item is a separate business within the hospital. Additionally, each product item has a product manager who develops a product team and reports to the vice president of rehabilitation services. Under this organizational structure, the vice president of nursing also manages a product line.

The emphasis in this organizational structure is service to customers, not operations or traditional departmental issues. The entire organization, staff to management, is brought into the product lines through participation in product teams. Administration and marketing are represented on the product teams, with the marketing representative being a facilitator and educator. The cost and revenue of nursing services, professional services, ancillary services, and support services are allocated appropriately to each product item cost center. This structure provides

- increased unity in implementing hospital objectives
- increased focus on customer service
- increased creativity in developing programs
- increased specialization and enhancement of expertise
- increased efficiency in defining the target market
- increased market attractiveness and competitiveness because of specialization

The disadvantages include the lack of attention to operations, policies, procedures, and detail as well as loss of some time-honored values of the organization. The matrix organizational structure addresses the disadvantages with the retention of traditional lines of authority but in the process creates the confusing dual authority relationships.

Regardless of the hospital organization, nursing can organize under major product lines as discussed in Chapter 6. However, in the absence of a hospital model, integrating nursing product lines into cost centers is difficult. Matrix and project organizational structures are innovative approaches designed to change the organizational focus from departmental operations to services. This customer-oriented approach recognizes that services and programs are both more important and marketable than operations. In fact, nursing, with its image problems and oppression, needs to experiment with and conduct research into entrepreneurial organizational designs.

Selecting Product Lines

Various methods are used by hospitals to define appropriate product lines. Certainly, the driving force is the market-based planning process itself. The environmental assessment identifies customer needs and wants, the SWOTs identify organizational strengths and weaknesses, and the process of matching organizational strengths and capabilities to customer demands defines an organizational fit for selected programs that can become product lines. Criteria, then, are

- recognized strength in the marketplace (includes clinical, educational, and research expertise)
- marketability in the area of strength (includes high profitability, high demand, and positive exchange relationships)
- capability for expanding the area of strength
- compatibility with the mission
- consistency with the interest of the program experts

Examples for some hospitals include cancer care, ophthalmology services, cardiology services, women's health services, etc. Again, the market-based planning process identifies the five or six major areas that need development, and these can be used in defining the product lines. During the annual market-based planning process, the product mix is widened, the product lines are lengthened, and existing product lines are continued, dropped, or expanded.

Attempts have been made to fit product lines into DRGs.[7] Typically, the top 10 to 15 DRGs are selected for product lines. The rationale here is that these diagnoses are the most frequent and therefore represent the hospital's strength in providing care as well as the consumers' preference in selecting care. Since DRGs are disease oriented and the desired connotation is health or wellness, DRGs are categorically combined and labeled for market appeal. For example, malignant neoplasm becomes the cancer care center.

Nursing uses the market-based planning model to identify product items and product lines. If product lines determine the organizational structure, only the most significant product lines are developed, product line managers are named, and separate cost centers are allocated. If traditional lines of authority are retained, product lines and product items can be integrated under the already established structure. Exhibit 7-1 shows an

Exhibit 7-1 Organizing Product Items or Product Lines Under Traditional Lines of Authority

Title	Service	Product Line	Product Items
Nurse manager	Pediatrics	Children's center	**Inpatient Pediatrics**
			Routine Care
			Intensive care
			Orthopedics
			Juvenile diabetes
			Rehabilitation
			Leukemia
			Same-Day Surgery
			Unit tours
			Preadmission screening
			Parental Education
			Child development
			Pediatric toxicology
			Pediatric nutrition
			Support groups
			Death and dying
			Diabetes support
			Pediatric emergencies
			Pediatric newsletter
			Outreach Education
			Intensive care course
			Annual seminar
			Physician Relations
			Office nurse seminar
			Physician/nurse
			mini–grand rounds
			Primary nurse program
			Nurse retention/recruitment program

example of product lines and product items organized under traditional organizational structures. The nurse manager of pediatrics manages the inpatient and same-day surgery units as well as the various other programs. In this example, the unit staff nurses become the project managers for the various product items. Cost centers include only the inpatient units of routine care and intensive care. The same-day surgery income and expense are included in the routine care unit cost center. The costs of the various programs are written in a business plan format but are a part of the units' budget. Since there are no official product line managers and there are no separate cost centers, Exhibit 7-1 cannot be said to illustrate product line management even though the process of development is the same.

In contrast, Exhibit 7-2 shows how pediatric cardiology is organized under product lines. In this example, pediatric cardiology is a product line that emerged from the market-based planning process. Because it meets all of the criteria for becoming a product line, pediatric cardiology is given its own cost center and product line manager, who reports to the vice president of marketing or pediatrics. How pediatric cardiology is placed under administration depends on the needs of the program. If the product line is well developed and needs a marketing focus, it is placed under marketing. On the other hand, if the product line is yet to be developed, it is more appropriately placed under nursing or professional services. Another method of placement is the allocation of certain product lines under certain administrators up front in a planned mass reorganization under product line management.

At any rate, a more important issue is the pediatric cardiology product line manager. Ideally, a pediatric nurse specialist is hired for the position, or a qualified nurse from within is promoted. If the administrator responsible for the program is not a nursing professional, the nurse specialist reports to the product line administrator for programmatic aspects and to

Exhibit 7-2 Pediatric Cardiology Product Line

Title	Product Line	Product Items
Product line manager	Pediatric cardiology	Surgery Inpatient care Diagnostic services Physician referral service Parental education Follow-up care Marketing

the nurse administrator for standards of care issues. Qualifications for product line management are developed, and a job description is written.

Responsibilities of the Product Line Manager

Once a product line is established and a product line manager is placed in the position, the product manager becomes responsible for further development, implementation, and monitoring of the product lines against the objectives. A more detailed list of responsibilities includes

- fine tuning the product line objectives and subobjectives
- organizing and leading an effective product line team
- implementing the product line objectives
- researching all aspects of the product line
- analyzing and preparing forecast reports based on research
- establishing a format for monitoring the objectives of the product line
- changing objectives based on new market information
- ensuring profitability of the product line
- coordinating team efforts with other departments
- developing periodic reports to go to the responsible administrator
- developing annual business plans

This list is not exhaustive, and responsibilities vary according to product lines and the requirements of individual hospitals. Since project management is similar, the responsibilities of project managers are the same. In project management, the variations are that cost centers are not developed around the product and the project is a smaller segment of a larger undeveloped product line. However, projects or single programs ensuring positive exchange relationships are often just as important. This is because some projects or programs cannot be directly measured in terms of profitability yet they contribute to the market attractiveness of the hospital. For example, the variable obstetric stay program is designed to retain market share. Although market share is monitored, a decline or an increase cannot be directly attributable to the variable stay program because other variables may also be concurrently intervening.

The qualifications of product line managers are not addressed here because of the lack of research available on the subject for hospitals. However, product line managers filling the positions in hospitals range from industry marketing experts to progressive individuals promoted from within.

Indeed, the lack of standard qualifications for this position is an opportunity for nurses to develop the role and establish the qualifications.

In summary, product line management and structures are efforts to become more competitive and marketable by focusing on the specialization of specific strengths that appeal to a specific market segment. These specific strengths are best defined by the market-based planning process, and full implementation of product lines means a change in the organization of the hospital or nursing department. In the absence of a hospital model for product lines, nursing can implement the philosophy of product lines through project management. Nurses are excellent candidates for the position of product line and project managers because of their broad-based generalist undergraduate education and their specialization at the master's level.

BUSINESS PLANS

In 1973, Ganong and Ganong[8] wrote about annual business plans for nursing administration. Since the health care world was not ready for such a progressive industry term, they called business plans budget plans. After 15 years, budget plans are now called business plans, perhaps in response to the more businesslike environment. However, today's business plan is more sophisticated and comprehensive. As shown in Chapter 2, Figure 2-1, the business plan is composed of the marketing plan, goals and objectives, and financial projections. The business plans of each nursing unit and program comprise the nursing strategic plan. The nursing strategic plan is formalized in the business plan for the entire department. Discussed here is the business plan developed for presentation and approval of a specific program or service. The purpose of the programmatic business plan is to "provide the framework for assessing the viability of a program before a major financial commitment is made."[9]

Business Plan Formats

Various formats for writing business plans exist. The format, style, and presentation are highly individualized by the type of program or service being established. For example, labor-intensive programs or services will focus more on staffing allocations and human resource budgeting, but equipment-intensive services will stress equipment cost, depreciation, assets, revenue from equipment, and space allocations. However, it is possible to present general guidelines that apply to all business plans.

Exhibit 7-3 shows a sample format for developing a business plan. The executive summary is just that. It summarizes key points in the business plan and includes alternatives and recommendations. The profile developed during the market-based planning process is the foundation for the executive summary. With the addition of a financial summary, start-up costs, and internal organization, the business plan is complete.

The strategic assessment, marketing plan, and implementation plan were discussed in previous chapters. In the financial plan, start-up costs are separated from the first year income/expense statement. The cost allocated for start-up is generous enough to include additional expenses that are due to delays in equipment purchases or renovation. On the other hand, the predicted activity for years 2 and 3 is conservative and somewhere between the least favorable and the most favorable activity projections. In some business plans, it is appropriate to include three-year pro forma statements based on the least favorable, the most favorable, and realistic market conditions. The purpose of this exercise is to analyze the risk of activity being less than predicted as well as the impact of activity being more than predicted. Obviously, the less costly the program, the less risk.

Pro forma statements are profit and loss statements that estimate financial needs as a percentage of annual revenue generated by the predicted activity. With accurate activity projections, ratios are applied to obtain pro forma statements for years 2 and 3. Exhibit 7-4 shows an example of a pro forma statement for a for-profit hospital inpatient unit. Profits in pro forma statements for years 2 and 3 are estimated as a percentage of gross revenue by the percentages established in the base year. In actuality, the taxes and dividends cannot be estimated as a percentage of the gross revenue. Pro forma statements are also projected for five years if break-even points extend beyond two or three years.

Style and Presentation of Business Plan

The business plan is usually presented to the board of directors of the institution. Therefore, the packaging of the business plan is conservative, yet professional. Some general guidelines are:

- The maximum length is 50 pages. In order to keep the agendas moving, the board members review business plans before the meeting. Lengthy business plans are skimmed, but brief business plans leave the impression that the plan was developed in haste or that it is deficient in content.

- Numbered pages and a table of contents facilitate easy reference in the presentation.

Exhibit 7-3 Format for a Business Plan

I. Executive Summary
  A. Product/service/technology
  B. Market potential
  C. Financial projections
  D. Internal management team
  E. Start-up costs
  F. Alternatives
  G. Recommendations
II. Strategic Assessment
  A. Mission
  B. Brief history of product/service
  C. Description of product/service
  D. Existing product/service
  E. Environmental assessment
    1. External
    2. Internal
    3. Competitive analysis (service similarities and differences)
    4. Potential customers
    5. Market share
  F. Implications of environmental assessment
    1. Strengths
    2. Weaknesses
    3. Opportunities
    4. Threats
  G. Marketing objectives
III. Marketing Plan
  A. Product strategy
    1. Product characteristics
    2. Exchange relationships
    3. Market segmentation
    4. Description of the target market
  B. Positioning
  C. Price
  D. Place (access and distribution)
  E. Promotion strategy
IV. Implementation Plan
  A. Pert chart
  B. Management team/organizational chart
V. Financial Projections
  A. Income/expense sheet
  B. Balance sheets
  C. Start-up costs
    1. Capital equipment
    2. Supplies
    3. Staff
    4. Marketing costs
    5. Promotion costs
  D. Pro forma financials for years 2 and 3
VI. Alternatives
VII. Conclusions/Recommendations

Exhibit 7-4 Base Year Pro Forma Statement (Without Start-Up Costs)

Activity: 4,500 patient days		
Revenue		
Revenue	$2,250,000	100%
Allowances	250,000	10
Gross Profit	$2,000,000	90
Expenses		
Fixed		
Indirect physical plant	$450,000	20
Administrative	135,000	6
Total	$585,000	26
Variable		
Salaries	$1,125,000	50
Other direct	157,500	7
Total	$1,282,500	57
Total Expense	$1,867,500	83
Profit Before Tax	$132,500	6
Taxes	$53,000	
Net Profit	$79,500	3.5
Dividends	$20,250	
Transfer to Surplus	$59,250	

- The type style and spacing are designed for rapid reading, and the business plan is tastefully bound by an inexpensive spiral binder holding the pages together and covered with an attractive yet inexpensive single color cover.
- The executive summary is concise (a maximum of three pages), is placed at the beginning of the business plan, and summarizes the major points of the plan.

Even the best business plan is ineffective if not presented well. A strong presentation is brief and concise and emphasizes major points. General guidelines are:

- Believe in the proposal, and the enthusiasm will flow during the presentation.
- Organize the presentation in writing, and practice·so that both the presentation and time for questions do not exceed the scheduled agenda time allocated to the presentation.
- Anticipate the questions, and prepare the answers.
- Know the material well, and know the members of the board well. For example, will the board be primarily interested in the profit margins or will they also be interested in the community impact, com-

munity service, and missions? Emphasize the positive points, and soften the disadvantages.

- Use audiovisuals to hasten the understanding of major points and to complement the presentation.
- Make the presentation strong by assuming approval in the concluding remarks. For example, the closing statement, "This proposal has received unsurpassed support and widespread approval by key staff and interest groups in the Medical Center and will be promptly implemented upon the receipt of your signatures," leads them right to the signature line.

Excellent material exists in the literature on developing and presenting business plans.[10] The focus here is on the marketing process, with business plans being the mechanism for documenting the process and obtaining approval for the nursing strategic plan. Appendix A shows an example of a business plan proposing the renovation of a coronary intermediate care unit. Appendix B shows a sample business plan for a home care program.

INFLUENCE OF PRODUCT LINE MANAGEMENT ON UNIT STRUCTURE

Top management philosophies, trends, and environmental responses filter down to the structure and organization of the nursing units. For example, past centralized nursing organizational structures were associated with the more centralized team nursing structures at the unit level. Likewise, with the advent of more decentralized nursing organizational structures, primary nursing came into being. Undoubtedly, these filtering down phenomena are indications of the organization's adaptive response to the needs of its customers as well as the resources available in the time frame. These lend additional credence to the notion that organizational structure is dynamic and is not a function of management theory but is simply an adaptation to the external and internal environments.

Thus, with the advent of prospective payment, resulting in decreased patient lengths of stay and increasing patient acuity, combined with the shortage of professional nurses, a new or at least different organizational structure and focus emerged in hospitals. This organizational focus, centering on product lines and business plans for targeted populations, resulted in the need for nursing to adapt to the changing environment, integrating nursing organizational structures and care delivery systems with the philosophical focus of the hospital.[11] Hence, the concept of *case management* at the unit level prevails in some hospitals as an emerging evolution of primary nursing.

As early as 1985, Zander, a noted primary nursing specialist and author, introduced the concept of "second generation primary nursing."[12] This concept was that primary nursing could be maintained in spite of the prevailing socioeconomic environments. The second generation primary nurse would carry a caseload of primary patients from admission to discharge, planning and evaluating the care of the patient, giving the direct care in some instances but relinquishing direct care to others when appropriate. In other words, the basic principles of primary care, planning and evaluating the care of a selected group of patients, would be retained.

Nursing case management evolved from the concept of second generation primary nursing. In this system, a group of nurses from various related nursing units form a group practice, collaborating to determine which nurse could best function as "case manager."[13] The case manager is initially the primary nurse for the patient, and collaboration with the medical case manager or physician is a requirement for developing patient management plans. In some models, as the patient improves or is transferred to another unit, the primary nurse continues to function as case manager even though direct care is given by another health care provider. In other models, case managers are selected according to defined qualifications and function only as case managers, with others providing the direct care.[14]

Case management, then, is the coordination of a management plan for the patient—a management plan that outlines predicted interventions and outcomes within a specific time frame, designed in collaboration with the physician. Depending on the specific model adopted by the nursing department, the case manager may or may not be the primary nurse and may or may not be involved in direct care.

The point here is that care delivery at the bedside is often redesigned in response to the changing organizational structure of the hospital and the nursing department. Second, case management evolved from primary nursing because of the environmental influences of product line management. To those who question whether or not nursing will ever stop changing modes of delivery, the answer is probably *no,* unless nursing operates in isolation or in a stagnant environment.

NOTES

1. Thomas C. Kinnear and Kenneth L. Bernhardt, *Principles of Marketing* (Glenview Ill.: Scott, Foresman & Co. (1983), 635.

2. Phillip Kotler, *Marketing for Nonprofit Organizations* (Englewood Cliffs, N.J.: Prentice-Hall, Inc., 1982), 289.

3. Stephen P. Robbins, *The Administrative Process* (Englewood Cliffs, N.J.: Prentice-Hall, Inc., 1980), 218.

4. Kinnear and Bernhardt, 644.

5. Pamela S. Bruhn and Donna Hill Howes, "Service Line Management: New Opportunities for Nursing Executives," *Journal of Nursing Administration* 16, no. 6 (June 1986): 18.

6. James C. Folger and E. Preston Gee, *Product Management for Hospitals: Organizing for Profitability* (Chicago, Ill.: American Hospital Publishing, Inc., 1987), 44.

7. Ibid., 45.

8. Joan Watson Ganong and Warren L. Ganong, *Help With Annual Budget Planning* (Chapel Hill, N.C.: Joan and Warren Ganong, 1976), 13.

9. Joyce E. Johnson, ed., *The Nurse Executive's Business Plan Manual* (Rockville, Md.: Aspen Publishers, Inc., 1988), xv.

10. Ibid.

11. Catherine E. Loveridge, Susan H. Cummings, and Jim O'Malley, "Developing Case Management in a Primary Nursing System," *Journal of Nursing Administration* 18, no. 8 (October 1988): 37.

12. Karen Zander, "Second Generation Primary Nursing: A New Agenda," *Journal of Nursing Administration* 15, no. 3 (1985): 18–24.

13. Karen Zander, "Nursing Case Management: A Classic Definition," *The Center for Nursing Case Management* (New England Medical Center, Boston, Mass. Spring 1987): 6.

14. Loveridge, Cummings, and O'Malley, 38.

Chapter 8

The Supply of Nurses: A Marketing Problem for Service and Education

Problems exist for educators in the marketing of nursing to potential nursing students. Equally problematic is the marketing of hospitals to RNs. As discussed in Chapter 1, the economic forces of supply and demand are not operating in nursing because of the substitution of nurses and because of monopolistic forces suppressing the economic worth of the nursing position. Further, as discussed in Chapter 2, exchange theory is a key phenomenon in the process of marketing; that is, during the exchange, something of value is given in exchange for something of equal or exceeding value. Still further, as discussed in Chapter 3, in order to market programs and services, the services must have market attractiveness. Finally, as discussed in Chapter 7, one of the criteria for defining a marketable product is that the product is recognized and valued by the community. From a marketing perspective, the problems in nursing on the service end, such as economic oppression, faulty exchange relationships, and image and identity shortcomings, have created a marketing dilemma for the supply end, which is nursing education. In brief, and somewhat understated, nursing is not easily marketed. This chapter explores the facts surrounding the shortage and the service-end origin of the nursing education dilemma, discusses how academia is responding, and applies the marketing model to nursing education. This topic is appropriate here because without an adequate supply of nurses, marketing in hospital nursing departments is difficult if not impossible.

NURSE SUPPLY

Hospitals employ approximately 68 percent of all practicing RNs.[1] In a December 1986 survey of 1,000 plus hospitals in the United States, the

American Organization of Nurse Executives found that 13 percent of RN full-time equivalent (FTE) positions were vacant, with an average of 10.9 full-time and 5.3 part-time FTE vacancies.[2] In 1984, 6,872 hospitals were in existence in the United States.[3] With these data, it is easy to estimate that the number of nurses needed to fill the vacancies are 74,905 full-time and 36,422 part-time FTEs, for a total of 111,327. However, this represents only 68 percent of the needs. More recent data estimate that there are 1,090,077 nurses employed in hospitals and that 138,872 more are required to fill a vacancy rate of 11.3 percent and that 26,073 more nurses are required to fill a vacancy rate of 20.3 percent in nursing homes.[4] This total of 164,945 nurse vacancies does not include vacancies in clinics, free standing home health agencies, HMOs, or other alternative settings.

Clearly, a shortage exists. However, vacancy data are meaningless without some indication of what is happening in nursing education. Table 8-1 shows the five-year trend from 1983–84 through 1987–88 in generic baccalaureate nursing enrollment. Although these data show trends only in students enrolled in baccalaureate programs in American Association of Colleges of Nursing (AACN) member schools, baccalaureate programs comprise a significant 30 percent of the nursing programs reported in existence in 1985 by the National League for Nursing.[5] Therefore, the trends shown here represent a considerable proportion of the nursing education community.

At this time, when the emphasis is on baccalaureate education as the minimum requirement for entry into professional nursing practice, an increase, not a decrease, in enrollment and graduations from these schools is expected. However, as shown, there are significant decreases in total full-time enrollment, part-time enrollment, combined full-time and part-time enrollment, and the total number graduating (29, 4, 27, and 1.5 percent, respectively).

From 1983 to 1987, 89,828 nurses graduated (not shown in Table 8-1). If all of these nurses had been employed and retained by hospitals, 55 percent of the total vacancies (163,945) would be filled. This indicates that even with the enrollment and graduation declines, schools may be supplying adequate numbers, but service is not attracting or retaining the graduates. However, what is not reflected here is the number of graduates actually passing state board examinations permitting them to work as RNs.

Table 8-1 shows the greatest declines to be in the Northeast, which has the only negative decline from 1983 to 1987 in graduating nurses. This may indicate that a geographic maldistribution exists or that the trend in fewer graduates in the remaining regions is yet to come. The latter may be the case since the Midwest and the South did not experience a decline in

Table 8-1 Five-Year Trend in Generic Baccalaureate Nursing Enrollment and Percentage Change from 1983–84 to 1987–88 by Student Status and Region of Schools*

Region and Student Status	1983–84	1984–85	1985–86	1986–87	1987–88	% Change 1983–84/1987–88
Northeast						
Full-time	18,145	17,995	16,395	14,240	12,399	(32.0)
Part-time	2,320	2,002	2,281	2,034	1,876	(19.0)
Graduates	4,643	4,578	4,706	4,618	4,291	(7.6)
Midwest						
Full-time	19,856	20,742	18,972	16,714	14,052	(29.0)
Part-time	2,339	2,484	2,924	2,478	2,401	.02
Graduates	5,577	5,888	5,924	5,904	5,582	.08
South						
Full-time	17,862	18,041	16,559	14,468	12,989	(29.0)
Part-time	2,079	2,428	2,186	2,158	2,025	(02.5)
Graduates	5,428	5,849	5,861	5,789	5,500	1.3
West						
Full-time	6,323	6,150	5,755	5,059	4,426	(30.0)
Part-time	607	746	714	720	755	24.0
Graduates	1,882	1,961	1,959	1,993	1,895	.6
Totals						
Full-time	62,186	62,928	57,681	50,481	43,866	(29.0)
Part-time	7,345	7,660	8,105	7,390	7,057	(4.0)
Full- and part-time	69,531	70,588	65,786	57,871	50,923	(27.0)
Graduates	17,530	18,276	18,450	18,304	17,268	(1.5)

*These data represent full-time and part-time students enrolled in baccalaureate programs in AACN member schools and the percentage returning questionnaires (360 of 391 in 1987).

Source: Adapted with permission from *Report on Enrollment and Graduations in Baccalaureate and Graduate Programs in Nursing: Public, Private, Religious, and Secular, 1983–1988,* American Association of Colleges of Nursing, © 1988.

graduating nurses until the 1986–87 year and the West, until the 1987–88 year. However, the decline in regions other than the Northeast did not drop below the base year of 1983–84. The West is the only region showing a trend of increased part-time enrollment.

The South, which is experiencing large decreases in enrollments, is the only region to recover the 1983–84 graduating status significantly. Again, since the first drop in graduating nurses occurred in the 1986–87 academic year, the downward trend may just be starting in the South. Actually, the first hint of general declines in enrollment and graduating nurses occurred in the Northeast and the West (the location of the pacesetter states of New York and California) in 1984. The Midwest and the South followed the trend in the 1985 academic year.

In summary and totally, there are downward trends in full-time and part-time enrollment and in graduating nurses from these baccalaureate schools and in other schools throughout the nation. The question is: Can these declines be shown as increases in other fields, and how does the general enrollment in higher education correlate with the decline in nursing enrollment?

Trends in Higher Education

There is speculation that there is a drop in the number of younger people applying to college.[6] This may be true of the younger age category, but the actual enrollment of women in institutions of higher education steadily increased in the decade 1976 to 1986. In fact, the percentage distribution of women enrolled in higher education has surpassed that of men. Table 8-2 shows enrollment in institutions of higher education by gender, number, and percentage distribution by gender between 1976 and 1986.

As shown, enrollment has not declined in either gender category. What has changed dramatically is that the percentage distribution of women

Table 8-2 Enrollment in Institutions of Higher Education by Gender, Number, and Percentage Distribution by Gender: 1976–1986 (in Thousands)

Year	Men	Women	Total	% Distribution Men	% Distribution Women
1976	5,794	5,191	10,985	52.7	47.3
1978	5,621	5,609	11,230	50.1	49.9
1980	5,868	6,219	12,087	48.5	51.5
1982	5,999	6,389	12,388	48.4	52.6
1984	5,859	6,376	12,235	47.9	52.1
1986	5,885	6,615	12,500	47.1	52.9

Total Variance and % Change: 1976–1986

	Men	Women	Total
No. Students	+91,000	+1,424,000	1,515,000
% Change	1.5	27.4	14

Source: Data are summarized from U.S. Department of Education, Office of Educational Research and Improvement CS 88-201. Available from Information Services, Office of the Assistant Secretary for Education Research and Improvement, Washington D.C. 20208.

enrolled in 1986 exceeded that of men. In fact, the distribution has actually reversed from 1976. The increase in number for women from 1976 to 1986 is 1,424,000. Several variables may explain this increase:

- increase in the participation rate of young women in higher education
- increase in the older, more nontraditional women learners returning to school after years of homemaking or working in nonskilled jobs
- increase in the population of women

At any rate, the increases are not reflected in nursing enrollment, as shown by the data presented in Table 8-1. Therefore, the speculation that women are not selecting nursing as a career in the 1980s because of the increased options available to them may be accurate. These increased options include such fields as law, medicine, business, and engineering.[7] Data available on degrees conferred between 1974–75 and 1985–86 reveal trends by gender and discipline as shown in Appendix 8-A. Table 8-3 presents these data,

Table 8-3 Bachelor's Degrees Conferred upon Women As a Percentage of the Total and Variance: 1974–75 and 1985–86

Field	1974–75 (%)	1985–86 (%)	Variance
Architecture	17.5	36.0	18.5
Business/management	16.2	45.7	29.7
Communications	40.5	59.0	18.5
Computer science	19.0	35.7	16.7
Education	73.3	76.0	2.7
Engineering	2.2	13.0	10.8
English and literature	63.5	66.6	3.1
Foreign language	77.0	72.6	⟨4.4⟩
French, German, and Spanish	3.5	3.0	⟨0.5⟩
Health professions*	77.8	85.0	7.2
Life sciences	33.0	48.1	15.1
Mathematics	41.8	46.5	4.7
Physical science	19.2	27.4	8.2
Psychology	52.6	69.0	16.4
Public affairs and services	63.0	66.0	3.0
Social sciences	37.3	44.0	6.7
Arts	61.5	61.0	⟨1.0⟩

*Excludes professional degrees requiring 6 plus years for completion.
Source: Adapted from "Degrees and Other Formal Awards Conferred," U.S. Department of Education, Center for Educational Statistics, 1987. Available from Information Services, Office of the Assistant Secretary for Education Research and Improvement, Washington, DC 20208.

calculating women as a percentage of the total and the variance percentage increase or decrease.

As speculated, major shifts have occurred within a decade. The major positive shifts in degrees conferred upon women are in the fields of architecture, business/management, communications, computer science, engineering, and life sciences. A mass exodus has occurred from foreign languages. Unfortunately, nothing can be inferred from the data on health professions because all health professions except dentistry, medicine, chiropractics, and pharmacy have been placed in this one category. The variance of the percentage increase in degrees conferred upon women in health professions is +7.2. Since a decline in nursing has been established, it is logical to assume that this increase reflects increased participation of women in other medical fields such as physical and occupational therapy, public health, biomedical communications, speech and audiology, and medical and radiology technology. Also, because the data in Table 8-3 are arranged by degrees conferred upon women as a percentage of the total, Appendix 8-A more accurately shows the mass exodus of both men and women out of the field of education. The total number of degrees conferred upon women in 1974–75 was 122,458, and for men, 44,567. Then, in 1985–86, the number decreased to 66,235 and 20,986 for women and men, respectively.

In summary, the enrollment of women in higher education

- increased generally
- increased in the disciplines of business, engineering, computer science, management, and health professions (excluding nursing)
- decreased in nursing

Nursing education is faced with fewer qualified applicants, fewer enrollees, and fewer graduating nurses. Marketing efforts have increased in nursing education, but as discussed later in this chapter, the focus of marketing in education has changed to meet the new challenge.

Underlying Problem

The 1980s must go down in nursing history as the decade of reports, studies, and recommendations. Yet, the closing of schools, serious hospital nurse vacancy rates, and unsafe nurse-patient ratios continue. Despite the fact that salary and working conditions appear to be the causes of the current nursing shortage, the helplessness of the profession, resulting from the way in which nurses are socialized into submissive roles, is the root of the underlying problem. The assumption here is that nurses are socialized to be submissive and dependent by the community, academic institutions, and practice settings.

The general environment of hospitals in the past has been one in which nurses had to conform to authoritarian rules, with the reward systems based on efficiency in carrying out physicians' orders, efficiency in caring for increased numbers of patients, loyalty to the hospital, and cooperativeness (not verbalizing complaints). The point is that most faculty members are first socialized in the hospital setting and that nursing students form their definition of nursing by interaction with the faculty. Sixty-eight percent of all nurses are employed in hospitals, and as they enter this practice setting, they receive further socialization by authoritarian managers and domineering physicians who reinforce submissiveness, dependence, and subordination.

Further, nurses are viewed by the community as physician extenders. In fact, physicians believe that nurses are physician extenders. A case in point is the recent AMA proposal to resolve the shortage of nurses by training registered care technicians. This is a serious issue. Regardless of whether or not this is a viable proposal, the very act of proposing a solution to the problems of another discipline implies that the physicians feel ownership of and responsibility for the discipline. The question is: Would these physicians feel compelled to impose technicians on the disciplines of social services, pharmacy, psychology, or physical therapy for similar shortages?

In 1983, the Institute of Medicine of the National Academy of Sciences published the report entitled *Nursing and Nursing Education: Public Policies and Private Actions,*[8] which included 21 recommendations to improve the distribution and supply of nurses to underserved areas. The report was the result of a two-year study mandated by Public Law 96-76, the Nurse Training Act Amendments of 1979. Some of the recommendations addressed

- job turnover and attrition (24 percent of the total RN population is not employed in nursing)
- improved career opportunities and working conditions
- improved opportunities for career progression
- improved salary
- improved working conditions

- flexible scheduling
- increased benefit options
- re-entry opportunities

Following on the heels of the report was the report of the National Commission on Nursing, a commission sponsored by the American Hospital Association, the Hospital Research and Educational Trust, and the American Hospital Supply Corporation, which, after three years of study, published 18 recommendations designed to resolve nursing problems in the provision of high-quality care. Some of the recommendations addressed

- authority of nursing over its management processes
- qualifications of nursing management
- working conditions of nursing
- salaries and benefits of nursing
- support systems for nursing
- integration of nursing constituencies in formulating nursing policy
- promotion of nursing research
- pursuit of baccalaureate entry and advanced degrees
- provision of educational mobility and re-entry opportunities for those desiring baccalaureate and higher degrees[9]

Four years later, in 1987, the American Hospital Association's report on the nursing shortage was published and included the identification of solutions made by a focus group of ten administrators and nurse administrators. Some of these solutions were:

- Upgrade the educational system (to be comparable with other professions by demanding a master's degree with appropriate salary).
- Establish two major levels of nursing: professional and technical.
- Differentiate staff nurses in the hospital by education, licensing examinations, duties and responsibilities, title, and pay.
- Institute a clinical ladder.
- Increase pay.
- Give recognition.
- Allow nurses to participate in key decisions.
- Permit nurses to work flexible hours and/or design their own work schedules.
- Institute group nurse practices, contracting with hospitals.

- Align schools and hospitals.
- Communicate to the public a realistic view of nursing.[10]

The problems of supply and poor working conditions are not new in nursing. The numerous reports and documentaries on the nursing shortage merely echo reports, statistics, and recommendations that have followed nursing throughout its history. In 1946, the short supply of nurses was attributed to long working hours, night work, physical working conditions, salary ($170 per month), lack of opportunity for advancement, the politics of physicians, and authoritarian nursing administrations.[11] Then, in 1979, the nursing shortage in the United States was between 45,000 and 65,000 nurses, with more than 395,000 working only part time and another 420,000 not even employed in nursing.[12] Although part-time nurses are needed to complement the full-time positions as relief, the staggering number of part-time nurses combined with the number of nurses not employed in their profession is a strong indication of problems in the work setting.

The point in presenting these reports is that the reports are just that: reports. Government reports, special interest group reports, and physician reports are all just repetitions of similar themes that come back again and again only to become a part of the troubled history of nursing.

Nursing, however, *is* in deep trouble. The nursing shortages of the earlier years differ dramatically from the shortage of today. Previously, the solution was to increase enrollment by accelerating recruitment efforts and increasing government funding for nursing programs until there were more qualified applicants than available student positions. Meanwhile, nursing education continued pumping the supply into a bottomless pit. Unfortunately, today, problems on the service end and increasing career options for women are resulting in shrinking applicant pools, decreasing enrollment, fewer graduates, and crises in the work place. Nursing has not changed, but the women of America have.

Kalisch and Kalisch described the women's movement in the 1970s and 1980s and its effect on nursing: "[T]he movement represented an effort to alter the nature of the family, to change the way in which children were raised, and to overthrow conventional attitudes concerning who should hold which jobs."[13] This new freedom and equality and the diminished differences between the sexes opened up new career options for women never before explored. Along with the new career options came new directions in education in fields of study previously predominately male. Nursing as it is today is not marketable. The underlying problems are not wages and working conditions but the history of wages and working conditions and the inability of nursing to resolve its own problems effectively.

Impact on Nursing Education

The impact of a smaller total market depends on the philosophical base of the educational institution and the market from which the school draws students. Some of the variables include

- whether or not the philosophy of the school permits reaching out into the community with nontraditional education
- extent of the geographic area served
- status of the college or department of nursing in the college or university
- existing competing options available to potential students
- flexibility of admission standards
- economic status of the market from which the school draws students
- funding and philanthropic support of nursing education program
- qualifications, ingenuity, and flexibility of faculty to diversify

Students today are concerned with the product of nursing education. As the cost of education continues to escalate, students will begin to examine the exchange relationships. In other words, how will they benefit postgraduation? What are the job opportunities, relative responsibilities, job demands, advancement potential, and salary potential? Certainly in nursing education, the investment is precious time, enormous costs, and rigorous study. Today's student examines the return on the investment. Indeed, the issue is the marketability of the outcome of nursing education, which is a nursing community dissatisfied with the profession but ineffective in producing change.

The factors that affect education as summarized by one Midwestern education director are

- fewer applicants, as major enrollment shifts are from nursing to other more highly esteemed professions and fields
- more applicants with lower American College Testing (ACT) scores
- fewer qualified applicants because of the lower ACT scores
- fewer students accepted and enrolled
- more minority applicants
- more social and emotional problems with students because of economic factors
- surplus faculty hours
- more emphasis on retention of students

The ultimate impact may be fewer schools. A sudden, shocking example in the Midwest was the closing of the undergraduate and graduate nursing programs at Northwestern University in Chicago because of declining enrollments and budget deficits. The provider cost of nursing education at the baccalaureate level can exceed that of other disciplines because of the additional faculty needed to supervise students out of the classroom in their clinical experiences.

Impact on Nursing Service

From the perspective of staff nurses, the nurse-patient ratio is the critical indicator of a safe and therapeutic or an unsafe workload. One of the major thrusts in nursing administration in the last decade has been to describe and quantify this workload in order to develop standards for safe, therapeutic care to patients. These efforts are documented in a voluminous amount of nursing literature on budgeting and staffing by patient acuity. Because acuity factors vary with individual patients and nurse competency varies with individual experience and maturity in the profession, such quantification efforts add to the research base on the subject but, thus far, are not absolutely reliable in predicting workload.

Additionally, other intervening factors exist. For example, the perception of short or adequate staffing is influenced by intermittent low and high productivity rates. To clarify further, because of the extreme variations in census and acuity, periods of high productivity may follow periods of low productivity. During periods of low productivity, staff nurses adjust, developing new standards of care that cannot be accomplished during times of high productivity. To caution, the label *short staffed* is used to describe perceptions (real or unreal), but the exact point where adequate staffing becomes inadequate is not defined. At any rate, with or without patient acuity, extremes in the nurse-patient ratio are deduced by common sense. For example, on an acute medical unit in a hospital, a ratio of one nurse to eight patients on the day shift in a primary, modified primary, or total patient care delivery system constitutes understaffing.

A recent survey in the *American Journal of Nursing*[14] reported that of the 392 medical-surgical nurses responding:

- 51 percent were caring for 6 to 10 patients (1 nurse to 6 to 10 patients)
- 36 percent were caring for 3 to 5 patients (1 nurse to 3 to 5 patients)
- 9 percent were caring for 11 to 15 patients (1 nurse to 11 to 15 patients)
- 3 percent were caring for 16 to 25 patients (1 nurse to 16 to 25 patients)
- 1 percent were caring for 1 or 2 patients (1 nurse to 1 or 2 patients)

Significant variables not reported in this survey were shift and whether or not the RNs were working alone with 6 to 10 patients or had the assist of an LPN or graduate nurse. If the worst conditions are assumed, possibly 63 percent of the RNs are working in understaffed units. The impact of the shortage is overutilization of RNs and, certainly, less than desirable care given to patients.

With the shortage of RNs, the expectation might be that the cost of nursing is under budget. However, the amount of money available from vacant RN positions is rapidly consumed by increased recruitment, overtime, and agency costs. The impact on nursing administration is increased nonpredictable costs and overbudget reports. The patients are ultimately paying more for less care.

Response of Academia

Because the downward trend was not clearly established in most areas until the 1986–87 academic year, schools have not had much time to change direction. However, some interesting patterns have emerged. According to one proactive and visionary nursing education chief in an upper-middle-class, secular university in the Midwest, the first step is to increase the clout (and thus the power) of the college of nursing in the university milieu. This begins with the hiring of qualified faculty. As discussed previously in this chapter, the underlying problems of nursing, which are dependency and submissiveness, adversely affect the image, status, and power of both nursing practice and education. For example, in education, there are few faculty who become full professors. Faculty cannot attract students to nursing education opportunities by isolating themselves within the confines of nursing. They must reach out into the mainstream of education and into the community, making nursing visible, viable, and equal in status with and in its contribution to that of other disciplines in the university.

Some innovative strategies developed and implemented by this nursing education director include involving faculty in planning and teaching health courses that have market attractiveness to the community. Examples are

- crises intervention
- alcohol and society
- loving relationships
- single parenting
- children and television
- family planning
- child nutrition and health

Unlike other disciplines, nurses, who are both generalists and specialists, bring to the university, as faculty, their broad knowledge base and diverse experiences, qualifying them to teach a variety of courses to multiple interest groups. The potential value of nursing faculty to the university is limited only by the imagination. The visibility of the faculty in the community

- markets nursing to the community
- markets the university
- markets nursing opportunities to other disciplines in the university
- affects the health status of the community
- increases the value of nursing to the university
- increases the status of nursing in the university
- increases the productivity of the faculty
- increases the job satisfaction of the faculty

This same nursing education director has planned another nursing education marketing strategy. The school of nursing offers a minor in health to other disciplines. Not only is this vertical integration strategy in line with the mission of the university, it enhances the image and identity of professional nursing. Additionally, it increases the value of the college of nursing to the university and contributes to university objectives. Some of the courses include

- introduction to health policy
- personal health management
- international health
- health and life style management
- medical terminology
- environmental health
- stress management
- teaching in health
- literature in health care
- sexually transmitted diseases, history and policy
- poverty and the homeless
- interdisciplinary teaching
- first aid
- nutrition

These courses are marketable as electives to the general student population or as a minor in health for English, business, and physical education majors, to name a few.

The idea of marketing to other disciplines is catching on. The nursing education directors of 100 baccalaureate schools (randomly selected) in the United States were surveyed about the response of their institution to the enrollment declines. Of 100 surveys sent, 55 were returned, 10 of which were not included because the programs were RN degree completion schools. Table 8-4 shows the results. The response numbers are unequal because some questions were unanswered. The schools that are not experiencing a decline in enrollment are located in large cities and are the same schools that are not increasing marketing efforts. The purpose of this small survey was not to show decline in enrollment, as that has been established, but simply to show how some schools are responding. The comments included with the survey were most interesting and revealed that some schools are compensating for enrollment declines by increasing various recruitment efforts. Table 8-5 shows some of the comments. The answer for some schools is downsizing to accommodate fewer students. If vertical or horizontal integration strategies are not employed, downsizing is an appropriate strategy.

The major compensation activity is increasing recruitment efforts for the RN degree completion program. Until baccalaureate nursing becomes the minimum requirement for entry into the profession of nursing, RN degree completion will continue to be big business for schools, and emphasis on degree completion will perhaps buy the time required for changes to take place in nursing, making it a marketable profession. The data shown in Table 8-6 reinforce the fact that there is a market demand for degree completion and graduate education in nursing. Schools of nursing can offset declining enrollments in generic nursing programs by expanding present services to include RN degree completion programs and graduate programs. However, the life cycle of the degree completion programs is ques-

---

Table 8-4 Survey Responses of 35 Generic Education Directors of Nursing Programs on Enrollment Declines: June to August 1988

Questions	Yes	No
Experiencing a decline in enrollment?	22	12
Expanding recruitment to include a broader geographic area?	17	14
Offering classes off campus?	17	14
Marketing courses to other disciplines?	25	12

Table 8-5 Survey Response Comments: Declining Enrollment Compensation Mechanisms

Comments	Number Commenting
More flexible scheduling of classes	1
Increasing recruitment in high schools	6
Increasing recruitment for RN completion program	10
Involving faculty in community service and nursing practice	1
Increasing MSN program activities, shifting faculty to MSN program	2
Teaching personal health as a general health requirement	1
Recruiting the nontraditional learner	1
Marketing to other disciplines	1
Revamping curriculum for fewer students without changing admission requirements	5

tionable. Thus, expansion of services in other areas as well is advised in order to ensure viability. However, these strategies will not directly increase the supply of RNs.

The Rush University model is one in which the general philosophy and mission are broad enough to encompass expansion of services as well as vertical and horizontal integration strategies. The characteristics of the Rush nursing concept aptly describe the strategic positioning discussed here. These concepts are

1. a quality of nursing care that surpasses existing norms
2. educational programs that range from the baccalaureate to the doctoral level (a complete school)

Table 8-6 Enrollment and Percentage Change in RN, Master's, and Doctoral Nursing Education: 1983–88

	1983–84	1984–85	1985–86	1986–87	1987–88	% Change 1983–88
RN enrollment	21,700	22,298	21,946	22,676	22,128	1.9
Master's enrollment	15,882	17,034	17,356	17,910	18,385	15.8
Doctoral enrollment	1,341	1,489	1,648	1,850	2,056	5.3

Source: Adapted with permission from *Report on Enrollment and Graduations in Baccalaureate and Graduate Programs in Nursing: Public, Private, Religious, and Secular, 1983–1988,* American Association of Colleges of Nursing, © 1988.

3. clinical research in nursing in sufficient scope to provide a substantive base for improving the quality of nursing practice
4. demonstration projects designed to show how multidisciplinary efforts can be more effective
5. continuing education constructed to enable nurses to be prepared for future developments in practice
6. demonstration projects that reach into the community so that nurses can better contribute to the general raising of levels of care
7. programs of international value[15]

In brief, good marketing strategies are to establish a broad mission and philosophy, expand services, employ vertical and horizontal integration strategies, and if necessary, diversify to improve the quality of nursing; thus, the status, identity, image, and power will follow for a marketable profession.

RECRUITMENT OF NURSES TO THE PROFESSION

Although the nursing profession has problems with marketability, nursing schools are still competing for enrollees in the shrinking market of available applicants. Chapter 1 established that marketing services are appropriate when competition and oversupply exist. In education, the oversupply is vacant qualified student positions and faculty hours.

Competition with other educational institutions exists for qualified faculty and students. Therefore, the marketing model is applicable to nursing education. As marketable programs and services emerge during the process of market-based planning, nursing education realizes at least two positive outcomes:

1. improvement in the status and image of nursing with the increased visibility of the faculty in the community
2. improvement in the market attractiveness of nursing education programs

The basic format of the market-based model shown in Chapter 2, Exhibit 2-1, serves as a guide to developing marketing objectives for nursing education departments. Although each nursing school must develop a marketing plan specific to the organization, basic marketing principles are applicable to all schools. Because of the extensive market research required, large university schools that attract students nationally may prefer employing marketing consultants to direct the activities of the first marketing plan. Although professional consultations are expensive, the return on the investment pays off with timely increases in utilization and revenue. Significant elements of the marketing process are discussed here.

Positioning

The central issues of positioning are mission, community image, desired image, theme, name, and appeal. The mission is examined to determine whether or not it fits the current beliefs about the services offered at present or in the future. The mission is closely aligned with the philosophy; therefore, modifications of the mission statement require the consensus of all appropriate constituents.

Specific questions guiding the analysis of the mission statement are:

- Are services restricted? For example, does the statement permit growth in a variety of services such as undergraduate, graduate, continuing education, education/practice cooperative ventures, demonstration projects, research, and community service? Use of the term *health care education* in lieu of *nursing education* permits expansion of services into other related areas.
- Is the population served restricted? For example, does the statement define narrow or broad segments of the market served? Does it permit expansion of services to other market segments such as nontraditional students, students from other disciplines, and members of the community?
- Who are the customers of the school? Potential students and participants come from a variety of population segments in addition to high schools. Some examples are all employees of hospitals from dietary aides to central supply aides, other health-related occupations such as dental assisting, and other non–health-related professions such as teaching, to name a few. The point is that customers are elementary and high schools; parents; hospital workers; benefactors; employers of the graduated students; nursing departments of hospitals; and young, middle, and older age groups. The mission narrows or expands the customer base according to the philosophy and capabilities of the school.
- Is the stated geographic area served broad enough for growth? Local, state, and national areas are considered.
- Does it state the goals of the services and the markets served? In other words, what is the positioning of the institution? Positioning includes

such attributes as flexibility, individual and personal programing, low cost, "high tech," "high touch," job oriented, science oriented, arts oriented, or graduate preparation.

Positioning is defining a desired image and identity, differentiating the program from all others, or carving out where the school wants to be in the marketplace. What is it that makes the program different? What will participants miss by attending another program?

One private high school in the Midwest prepared students well for the ACT test. As a result, the high school rapidly attracted the "college bound" student. In order to attract the graduate student at the baccalaureate level, a nursing school may benefit by positioning the program as the "graduate prep program" with a track record of excellent student Graduate Record Examination (GRE) scores. If this is too narrow a differentiation, a three-track program position could be adopted: track 1, focusing on job skills and rapid entry and placement into employment; track 2, a well-rounded liberal arts education with electives in other fields, preparing students for various graduate opportunities; and track 3, the nursing graduate prep program including GRE test preparation.

One graduate business school in the Midwest attracts students because it offers a work-study program with guaranteed placement upon graduation. After nursing graduate school, placement is an important issue. A graduate school could differentiate and therefore position the program by becoming the "placement program." Placement is guaranteed, but acceptance of placement by the student is optional. If this position is adopted, the school must have the capabilities of following through with a nursing placement department.

Positioning can be based on the marketable strengths of the nursing program or on the strengths the nursing program desires and is capable of attaining. Once the position is determined, the school must then convey this image and identity to the public by name, theme, and promotions, e.g., "St. Mary's Nursing Graduate Education and Employment Placement Program" as a theme with "guaranteed placement in your field." *Positioning* is determining what has market appeal, matching this appeal with organizational capabilities, and communicating this position to the targeted market.

The positioning, image, and identity of the school must match those of the community's perceptions. If the community holds negative perceptions, these must be changed. In order to determine the image held by the community, the school conducts surveys and focus group interviews. The participants must come from the area within which the school draws students (potential students and their parents), and must include those other than students and faculty who have biased opinions. Their opinions are important but are more appropriately solicited during the environmental assessment. Questions are structured so that a comparison with other institutions is obtained. Examples include:

- What have you heard or what do you know about the advantages of attending X school of nursing and Y school of nursing? The disadvantages?
- If you were entering nursing school, which school would you select? Why?
- If your child were entering nursing school, which school would you promote? Why?
- What should be changed in X school and in Y school?
- What should be added in the same schools?
- What are the most important criteria in selecting a school of nursing?
- Discuss the importance of school size and proximity, program length, and cost in the selection of a school.

Responses in the interviews are then used to obtain generalized, global community perceptions of the school.

Environmental Assessment

A thorough assessment of the environment includes the external and internal environments. The internal environmental assessment provides data to analyze organizational performance and capabilities. Indicators include

- faculty credentials
- length of service of faculty members
- faculty turnover
- faculty age, sex, and race
- enrollment and graduate data for the last five years
- student age, sex, race, religion, and geographic origin
- employment locations of students in the last five years
- average ACT scores of entering students in the last five years (GRE scores for graduate programs)
- National League for Nursing (NLN) scores of students in the last five years

- state board testing scores in the last five years
- student retention percentage for each of the last five years
- number and disposition of students dropping or dropped from the program in the last five years
- percentage of students employed in the last five years
- results of student surveys designed to determine the reasons for selection of the school (i.e., cost, proximity, length of program by the age of respondents)
- results of student evaluations per program in the last five years
- results of an annual faculty questionnaire trended over the last five years
- cost of the nursing education program over the last five years
- ratio of the nursing costs to total university cost in the last five years
- cost per student in the last five years
- tuition trends over the last five years
- tuition dollars funded by scholarships, the Nurse Training Act, grants, and other funding sources
- percentage of tuition costs covered by student loans
- revenues generated by the nursing program per year trended over the last five years (tuition, fees, books)
- revenues generated by the nursing program and credited to other departments
- percentage of the revenues generated to the total
- faculty-student ratios over the last five years
- faculty-clinical ratios and classroom hours per week
- faculty preparation time in hours per week
- number of publications by nursing faculty in the last five years
- research conducted by faculty in the last five years
- NLN accreditation results in the last five years
- number of community service hours given
- number of classroom hours taught in other departments
- number of classroom hours in the nursing program taught by faculty in other departments
- number of recruitment events
- cost of recruitment over the last five years
- curriculum changes in the last five years
- number and dollar amount of grants in the last five years

The internal assessment factors will depend on the offerings of each school and definitions of *quality* and *productivity*. For example, if continuing education is offered, an entirely different set of indicators may be used, depending on expected outcomes defined for the faculty, participants, and contribution to the community, school of nursing, and university.

Data from the external environmental assessment are used to forecast market demand and analyze competitiveness. Indicators include

- government trends in funding nursing education
- legislation passed or pending affecting nursing education
- number and type of nursing scholarships, grants, and loans used statewide and nationally
- nursing and higher education enrollment and graduation trends nationally, statewide, and locally (number; participation rates by race, sex, and age)
- national and local practice and specialty trends
- national and local nursing utilization trends (number employed, where, and doing what)
- national, state, and local utilization trends in high schools and grade schools
- national and state population birthrate trends
- national and state population migration trends
- national and state population mix of minorities
- national and local trends in the delivery of health care (traditional versus alternative delivery systems)
- national and local trends in hospital and health care utilization
- activities and major thrusts of nursing and medical associations
- major trends from review of the literature
- trends in education (number of schools, type, and preparation foci)
- national and local costs of education trends
- national and local trends in tuition expenses
- national and local work force trends specifically in the employment of women
- national, state, and local data on state board testing results
- market share trends in the community and state
- local tuition expense comparisons
- local curriculum comparisons
- survey or interview results of major employers of graduating nurses
- survey or interview results of graduating nurses

The data obtained from indicators in the external environmental assessment show external forces that will affect schools. Specifically, population trends predict the global number of students available in the total market in the future. The mix of minorities and the number of women in the work force predict a potential change in the type of student. Increased minority enrollment means that the curriculum will have to be changed to accommodate the needs of students with cultural and language differences. An increased number of women in the work force indicates a depressed economy and that students may be women with full-time or part-time jobs, creating the need for more flexible curricula. Additionally, the more depressed the economy, the greater the need for increased tuition funding sources in the form of grants, scholarships, and loans. Still further, the more depressed the economy, the greater the need for student social and emotional support systems.

Schools must remain competitive with other schools in the marketplace. The competition is identified, and market share as well as other indicators is monitored. Certainly, market share is a well-recognized indicator of competitiveness, but the results of a thorough examination of competing programs may explain market share increases or decreases. For example, is competition in the area based on economic or noneconomic factors (tuition or services)? When the competition is local, competitive factors are more easily identified. However, when the competition is state or national, a market share determination and competitive analysis are more complex.

Practice patterns and utilization of nurses in the work place are indicators of educational need and demand. For example, if nurses are being employed as product line and project managers, what are the additional qualifications that make nurses marketable for the positions and how can education enhance that marketability? On the other hand, education directors cannot keep changing the curriculum to accommodate the rapidly changing utilization patterns. The practice setting must bear some of the responsibility for the education of nurses in these roles. Collaboration between practice and education can accommodate the needs of students studying for such entrepreneurial roles. Specifically, this is accomplished through innovative collaborative projects in which students meet the academic objectives in field studies in the practice setting. The concept of extending and projecting learning experiences of students into practice settings under the joint supervision of qualified faculty and nurses in practice expands the educational resources of schools, provides competitive positioning in the marketplace, and upgrades skills in the practice setting. Additionally, the concept places some of the accountability for the outcome of education on the users of the product. With increasing accountability, those in the practice setting will become more interested and involved in the process.

The internal and external environment data are analyzed and used to describe current trends and to predict trends for the future. From these data and data obtained from the SWOT analysis, capabilities of the institution and market demand for educational programs are determined.

SWOTs

The market-based planning process is a participative process in which SWOTs are best defined by those who interface directly with customers. The faculty members are in direct contact with students, employers, high school counselors, and the community. The SWOT analysis is completed by the faculty after a thorough review and examination of the results of the environmental assessment. Because educators are indoctrinated to the concept that it is education that produces a change in behavior, they are most vulnerable to the product mentality described in Figure 2-1. This means that there is the potential to assume responsibility for determining the needs of the student based on expert knowledge. Further, the assumption is that the product will be sold once the student is educated to the benefits of the program. Therefore, weaknesses in the program are attributed to lack of education or knowledge about the benefits of the program. In order to avoid this, an exhaustive list of SWOTs (perceived and real) are developed in an objective, brainstorming fashion without regard to justifications. The perceived weaknesses and threats are treated as real because perceptions, not realities, affect the success or failure of programs and services. Further, consumers are capable of articulating their own needs, wants, and demands for education, and faculty members are able to translate these market demands into strengths and weaknesses that affect the marketability of the nursing program.

Identified strengths and opportunities are treated as areas of expertise that can be developed into specialized niches in the marketplace, differentiating the program from all others. Market demand for educational programing is then matched with the resources of the school and capabilities of the faculty. The capabilities of faculty members are not underestimated. These professionals, who are the role models of nursing, have the capability of developing new programs of high quality in a short time. The rapid conversion of diploma schools to baccalaureate schools, the development of RN completion programs, the expansion to master's programs, the extension of satellite programs, and the development of flexible scheduling affirm the capabilities of the faculty once these goals are established.

Marketing Objectives

Depending on the results of the environmental assessments and the SWOT analysis, market objectives and therefore strategic plans range from simple community programs to major reorganizations to accommodate graduate education. Marketing objectives are stated in behavioral terms and are assigned or selected by faculty members according to expertise in the area. Subobjectives break the whole into smaller parts, with target dates for completion. Although some objectives will span two to three years, as in the case of developing a master's or doctoral curriculum, detailed objectives are made for a one-year period so that progress can be monitored and objectives revised accordingly. Major objectives meeting the criteria discussed in Chapter 7 are expanded into product lines.

Project teams are coordinated by faculty members assigned to the objective. Team members are selected in and out of the nursing school, depending on the objective. For example, a stress management program might include

- a faculty member with a psychiatric background
- an exercise physiologist
- a doctoral student interested in teaching and research
- a faculty member from the psychology department
- a practicing clinical specialist in psychiatric nursing

The project team develops the subobjectives, and the faculty member coordinates and implements the plan. Team members can be brought in to teach parts of courses.

Some innovative programs emerging out of market-based planning in education are

- health education courses for students in other disciplines
- health-related courses for the community
- a fast-track, one-year graduate nursing master's program
- an upper division nursing baccalaureate capstone program
- a weekend completion program
- joint faculty positions in the practice setting
- co-op programs with major employers who provide paid specialty work experiences, theory, and clinical supervision by qualified staff within parameters set by the school (the clinical practicum becomes a part of the students' position orientation and the school's academic curriculum)

• field studies in which graduate students are paid by major employers to plan, coordinate, and implement projects in a nursing practice setting

With field studies, the project becomes a field study with credit hours going toward the master's degree. This concept is not new. Hospitals hire business administration students to do time and motion and productivity studies. These studies are a part of the academic credit for certain courses. In nursing, some of the projects include implementation of primary nursing, development of standards of care and patient teaching materials, evaluation of the patient acuity tool and career ladder for nursing, development of a patient satisfaction with care survey tool, or a nursing geriatrics program.

Another nontraditional market is providing fee-for-service contracts to hospitals and other health care institutions for faculty-taught courses. Such courses include physical assessment, critical care, emergency care, and other courses for certification. Depending on the sophistication of the hospital staff development staff, faculty members could also teach principles of adult learning to staff development nurses and preceptorship to staff nurses. Additionally, hospitals need nurses who could be supplied through college refresher nurse courses and aides who could be supplied through college aide training courses. These ideas are only a few of the possibilities.

The marketing plan for nursing education identifies new markets. These new markets supplement or replace the shrinking market for generic nursing students. It is possible that the applicant pool for nursing will never return to its previous state as nursing is defining new roles in the work place for RNs. With smaller numbers, nurses may manage the health care of clients in outpatient clinics and in the home with the actual care being given by others. Nurses in hospitals may contract with the hospital to deliver care to a group of patients. With less dependency on hospitals, who will provide the required certifications and specialty education?

NOTES

1. Neale Miller, ed., *The Nursing Shortage: Facts, Figures, and Feelings* (Chicago, Ill.: American Hospital Association, Division of Nursing, 1987), vii.

2. "AONE Takes the Lead on Nursing Shortage Issues," *The Nurse Executive* 12, no. 2 (March-April 1986): 10.

3. "Hospitals: 1960 to 1984," in *The World Almanac and Book of Facts* (New York, N.Y.: Pharos Books, 1988), 816

4. *Interim Report: Secretary's Commission on Nursing* (Washington, D.C.: Department of Health and Human Services, July 1987), III–12.

5. Miller, 40.

6. Ibid., 51.

7. Marilyn Peddicord Whitley and Anita Lee Malen, "Market Research and Nursing's Dwindling Applicant Pool," *Nursing Economics* 5, no. 3 (May-June 1987): 130

8. *Nursing and Nursing Education: Public Policies and Private Actions* (Washington, D.C.: National Academy Press, 1983), 190–210.

9. *Summary Report and Recommendations* (Chicago, Ill.: The Hospital Research and Educational Trust, 1983) 1–34.

10. Miller, 21–22.

11. Esther Brown, *Nursing For the Future* (New York, N.Y.: Russell Sage Foundation, 1948), 46–47.

12. Jerome Lysaught, *Action in Affirmation: Toward an Unambiguous Profession of Nursing* (New York, N.Y.: McGraw-Hill Book Co., 1981), 33.

13. Phillip A. Kalisch and Beatrice J. Kalisch, *The Advance of American Nursing*, 2d ed. (Boston, Mass.: Little, Brown & Co., 1986), 725.

14. Florence L. Huey and Susan Hartley, "What Keeps Nurses in Nursing: 2500 Nurses Tell Their Stories," *American Journal of Nursing* 88, no. 2 (February 1988): 185.

15. Luther Christman, "How Do We Market: A Private Perspective," in *Marketing Programs and Products* (Washington, D.C.: American Association of Colleges of Nursing), 5

Appendix 8-A

Bachelor's Degrees Conferred: Women as a Percentage of the Total and Variance, 1974–75 and 1985–86*

Discipline	1974–75			1985–86		
	Men	Women	Total	Men	Women	Total
Architecture	6,791	1,435	8,226	5,824	3,295	9,119
Business/Mngmnt	111,411	21,599	13,010	129,271	108,889	238,160
Communication	11,456	7,793	19,248	17,647	25,444	43,091
Computer Science	4,080	953	5,033	26,923	14,966	41,889
Education	44,567	122,458	167,015	20,986	66,235	87,221
Engineering	45,838	1,014	46,852	83,372	12,581	95,953
English and Literature	14,727	25,570	40,297	9,150	18,210	27,360
Foreign Language	3,914	13,204	17,118	2,686	7,124	9,810
French, German, and Spanish	1,077	200	5,745	409	86	3,015
Health Professions	10,856	38,003	48,858	9,683	54,852	64,535
Life Science	34,612	17,129	51,741	19,993	18,531	38,524
Mathematics	10,586	7,595	18,181	8,725	7,581	16,306
Physical Science	17,353	4,112	21,465	15,769	5,962	21,731
Psychology	24,190	26,798	50,988	12,578	27,943	40,521
Public Affairs and Services	5,465	9,265	14,730	4,670	9,208	13,818
Social Science	84,813	50,362	135,165	52,654	41,049	93,703
Arts	15,532	25,250	40,782	14,284	22,665	36,949

*Disciplines not segmented by gender were excluded; therefore, a grand total will not yield total degrees conferred.

Source: Adapted from "Degrees and Other Formal Awards Conferred," U.S. Department of Education, Center for Education Statistics, 1987. Available from Information Services, Office of the Assistant Secretary for Education Research and Improvement, Washington, DC 20208.

Chapter 9

Marketing To Affect Social Change

The concept of utilizing marketing principles to influence social change is the final aspect of marketing in nursing to be explored. The marketing process produces rapid changes in the types of programs implemented and the manner in which the programs are developed and implemented. In fact, the process sometimes results in the reorganization of management structure and methods of planning. Consequently, a reorientation or change in basic attitudes and beliefs of nursing staff must occur. In short, the change is from an organization-driven philosophy to a consumer demand–driven philosophy. All plans, goals, actions, and programs are patient oriented, with customer satisfaction with the product being the outcome of the efforts of management and staff. Obviously, some method of change strategy is in order. Proposed here is the utilization of marketing principles to affect social change.

Social marketing is defined as "the design, implementation, and control of programs seeking to increase the acceptability of a social idea or use in a targeted group(s)."[1] The approaches are legal, technological, economic, and informational.[2] The elements are the same as described in the marketing plan:

- segmenting the market
- targeting the market
- researching the market
- developing the product
- pricing (incentives, rewards)
- placing
- promoting

Described here, as an example, is the use of marketing strategies to change the behavior, attitudes, beliefs, and values of staff to view the delivery of care to patients as a business and to see patients as customers of the business. A reorientation campaign is planned in the form of a customer relations program. Three of the four approaches are used.

The informational approach consists of

- promotional campaigns to raise the level of awareness of the importance of good customer relations
- meetings with staff to define good customer relations, identify obstacles, and demonstrate techniques of good customer relations

The legal approach uses the legitimate powers of management by praising appropriate behavior and controlling inappropriate behavior. The visibility of management staff in the clinical area reinforces the claim that "patient care is our business." The visibility and management interest in patient care activities reinforce the legitimate power of management to ensure that the manner in which care is given is in line with the defined customer relations principles.

The economic approach is used by including the use of the principles of good customer relations in the job descriptions and evaluations of staff. This increases the cost of nonconformity. Also, such a strategy clearly communicates role expectations.

Segmenting, Targeting, and Researching the Market

The defined market is employees who come in contact with the customers of the hospital. The market is segmented because different informational sessions are planned according to levels of staff responsibility for the management of patient care. For example, RNs will both implement and reinforce customer relations strategies. Nurse managers will role model and reinforce the desired behaviors, and administrators will reinforce and reward desired behaviors. Informational and behavior modification sessions are then individualized to each group.

Researching the market consists of determining existing responses to consumers. For example, what actions and behaviors are the current norms for a patient complaining about the food, nursing care, housekeeping services, and physician? What major trends are identified in the patient questionnaires? What are some of the obstacles that prevent staff from applying the defined customer relations principles? How can management remove the obstacles so that the patients' perceptions of care will be improved? What are the current beliefs of staff about the rights of patients? What are the long-standing institutional cultures that reinforce or permit negative behaviors? What are the current staff beliefs about their role in operating the hospital as a business? In other words, do they believe that they, individually, influence return business? Do they relate organizational prosperity to their own? What do they believe about the present reward system in the institution? Results of this research provide information on the type and extent of change required.

Developing the Product

What products or services will make it easier for the staff to change attitudes, values, and behavior? Certainly, some of the answers are found in the research on the obstacles to the application of the principles of good customer relations. Inadequate supplies and equipment are often sources of staff frustration that are passed off to patients. Of course, staff must learn how to cope with inadequacies without reacting negatively to other personnel and patients, but the concept here is to determine which products or services will best help them implement the program?

Pricing

Price here means rewards and incentives. Rewards are built into the concept by integrating customer relations principles into the merit systems. However, other awards are recognition and praise for demonstrating the desired behaviors. These include special columns in the newsletter mentioning employees and their courteous deeds, special buttons and pins for exceptional acts, and small bonuses for meritorious service.

Placing

Place here is staff access to needed support systems in implementing the program. Certainly, nurse managers must be sensitive to and respond to staff who report barriers to customer relations and situations creating poor public relations. If attitudes and behavior are to be changed, old attitudes and behaviors must be extinguished by rapid confrontation. Additionally, staff must feel that they have the support of the entire administration. Interdepartmental problems affecting the quality of patient care are addressed swiftly without cumbersome reporting through a long chain-of-command process.

Promoting

Promotion consists of using in-house media and publications to reinforce the importance of customer relations. This includes the use of posters, newsletters containing complimentary letters from patients, special bulletins containing names and pictures of staff and acts of courtesy, and the positive responses from patient questionnaires, to name a few. The idea is to magnify even the smallest act of courtesy through the in-house media in order to convey the value message that the business is patients and care and service to patients and other clients.

In order to maintain enthusiasm and compliance with the program, the emphasis on patient care and patient services is continuous, with desired behaviors repeatedly reinforced with recognition and rewards.

NOTES

1. Phillip Kotler, *Marketing for Nonprofit Organizations* (Englewood Cliffs: N.J.:, Prentice-Hall, Inc., 1982), 490.

2. Ibid., 491.

A Sample Business Plan for the Establishment of a Coronary Intermediate Care Unit

MISSION

St. Theresa's Medical Center is a level 3, full-service trauma center servicing the acute health care needs of the surrounding communities and five counties contiguous to the Medical Center in the southern half of the state. As the only trauma center in the area, the Medical Center staff is committed to providing this care in a changing technological and socio-economic environment. Therefore, the establishment of a Coronary Intermediate Care Unit (CICU) would provide the technology and the medical and nursing resources required by an increasing coronary patient population. The mission of this unit is to meet the health care needs of the coronary patient in the defined area, to enhance and augment the reputation of the Medical Center's Heart Center, to provide the same standard of care to the coronary patient, and to offset the expense of the high intensity of care presently being given to these patients on the general medical unit.

HISTORY OF EXISTING SERVICE

Over the past five years, use of the six-bed Coronary Care Unit (CCU) in the Medical Center has surpassed the number of available beds. Patients are being transferred out of the unit to the general medical unit earlier in their hospitalization. Additionally, some patients are placed in the general Medical Intensive Care Unit (MICU) when the CCU is full. This has resulted in

- appropriation of a lower nurse-patient ratio on the medical unit of 4 West without a corresponding increase in charges

- delivery of two standards of care to patients with myocardial infarction (MI) in the MICU and CCU
- early patient transfers from the MICU to other units, affecting the level of care required on general care units
- diversion of 20 patients in the last year to other centers for medical intensive and coronary care, resulting in the loss of patient days and credibility in the community

As a part of the Heart Center, the Medical Center provides open heart surgery, cardiac catheterization, coronary patient and family education, inpatient and outpatient diagnostic testing, inpatient coronary care, and cardiac rehabilitation. The inpatient unit, which has been in existence for ten years, has shown a steady increase in admissions in the last four years. Because of the anticipated growth in the Heart Center, the Medical Center's strategic, long-range plans include the design and development of a modernized 10-bed CCU and 24-bed CICU. Until then, the proposed plan will

- alleviate the shortage of MICU and CCU beds
- provide the same standard of care to MI patients
- provide reimbursement to cover the expense of the lower nurse-patient ratio on 4 West
- prevent the loss of patients to other centers
- enhance the reputation of the Heart Center

DESCRIPTION OF PLAN

This business plan proposes to establish a 12-bed CICU. The projected census of ten would allow some flexibility during census peaks. The plan is to convert the six semiprivate rooms on 4 West Medical adjacent to the CCU on either side of the hallway to an intermediate care unit for post-MI patients transferring out of the CCU and for other patients meeting the criteria for admission as developed by the medical and nursing staffs. This plan will not change the number of licensed medical and intensive care beds. The spacious, presently unused, supply room bordering the north wing will be converted to a nursing station featuring central station monitoring capabilities for the 12 soft-wired telemetry units and conference space for the medical and nursing staffs. Monitoring capabilities will include central station, bedside, and telemetry. These will provide flexibility for the type of patient admitted to the CICU. Although the unit will be designed for intermediate care, it may be necessary to expand the CCU into the area to accommodate increased growth prior to the implementation of the long-range plan. Existing and proposed monitoring equipment will be upgraded upon moving to the permanent unit as outlined in the long-range plan. Support areas, such as linen and supply rooms, will be shared with the CCU.

Presently, the length of stay of MI patients in the CCU is seven days. This average was obtained from the unit log book rather than by diagnostic group from medical records to obtain an accurate patient census. Consequently, the length of stay also reflects those patients who were ruled out and discharged as well as patients (other than MIs) staying longer than seven days. The proposed plan is centered on a four-day CCU stay and a three-day CICU stay. Obviously, this will vary by patient and represents a projected average based on current utilization. The patients will be discharged from the CICU.

ENVIRONMENTAL ASSESSMENT

Environmental assessments include only significant internal and external factors affecting the development and implementation of the renovation plan. The internal environmental assessment includes the impact of the unit on the rest of the facility, nurse staffing, medical staff utilization, patient days projected, and patient demographics *including* payer mix. The external environmental assessment includes a discussion of the life cycle of the unit, the competition, and the impact of technology and innovation.

Internal Environmental Assessment

The internal assessment determines both the capabilities of the organization to implement the proposed plan and the market demand for such a plan. Because this is not a new service, but an extension and expansion of present services, systems and processes are already in place for the establishment of the unit.

Impact on Facilities

The Medical Center presently has the space to accommodate this expansion service. The 46-bed unit called 4 West has been running at 75 percent occupancy for the last three years. Six of the census of 10 projected for the CICU unit consist of patients presently in the census of 4 West.

The four additional patients per day are projected as a result of the displacement of four patients from the MICU and CCU to the CICU. With an average daily census of 33, 4 West can easily accommodate the additional four.

Nursing Staff

Fortunately, because of increased patient acuity on the unit, 4 West has the nursing staff to care for patients in the proposed unit. The lower nurse-patient ratio has been provided without additional charges to patients. These nurses are supportive of the proposed plan, which includes the education of nursing staff to electrocardiogram interpretation and arrhythmia detection.

Medical Staff

Two physician groups comprise the medical specialists of the MI patient population. Table A-1 shows the physician utilization of the MICU and CCU as well as patient days during the last fiscal year. Although both groups of physicians are on staff at the Medical Center, physician group 1 admits primarily to the competing hospital. Group 2 physicians admit some patients to the competing hospital. All cardiologists are supportive of the proposed plan. It is anticipated that with the establishment of the CICU, group 1 physicians will admit more patients to the Medical Center.

Patient Days

Table A-1 also shows that the total MI patient days are 3,854. With an average length of stay of 7, this translates into a total of 551 patient admissions annually. The objective is to provide the CICU as an extension

Table A-1 CCU and MICU Physician Utilization and Patient Days during the Last Fiscal Year

Physician	CCU Patient Days	CCU Census	MICU Patient Days	NICU Census	Total Days	Total Census
Group 1						
A	372	1			372	1
B			425	1	425	1
Group 2						
C	760	2	742	2	1,502	4
D	725	2			725	2
E	380	1	450	1	830	2
Totals	2,237	6	1,617	4	3,854	10

of the CCU, thereby creating space for the four MI patients in the CCU. As shown in Exhibit A-1, this is exactly what happens.

Exhibit A-1 describes the rationale of the projected census of six patients in the CCU and ten patients in the CICU. As shown, the six CCU patients will create a daily transfer census of four patients in the CICU that when added to the current census of six coronary patients totals ten. Even though the average census projections of the CCU and CICU are six and ten respectively, it is anticipated that the CICU may manage the less acute patients and that patients may overflow into the CICU from the CCU. The level of nursing skill in the CICU will be equal to the skill level in the CCU.

Patient Demographics

The MI patient origin is spread almost equally between patients admitting from within a 50-mile radius of the Medical Center and those admitting as referrals from the five counties in the region, which are 343 and 228, respectively. Table A-2 also shows that the majority of patients are men between the ages of 40 and 49 who are primarily insured by major commercial insurance carriers. If the same mix of patients is retained, the prospect of the strategic long-range plan could be lucrative for the Medical Center.

Exhibit A-1 Census Analysis

CCU Census	
Total patient days	= 3,854
Average length of stay	= 7 days
Annual admissions	= 551 patients
Projected days in unit	= 4 days
Projected CCU patient days	= 2,204
Projected census	= 6
CICU Census	
Annual CCU transfers	= 551
Projected days in unit	= 3
Transfer patient days	= 1,653
Transfer patient census	= 4.5
Current coronary patient days 4-W	= 2,180
Current patient census 4-W	= 6
Combined patient days	= 3,833
Combined census	= 10.5
Projected CICU census	= 10

Table A-2 Age Range, Gender, and Payer Source of MI Inpatients: Last Fiscal Year

Age Range	Male	Female	Commercial Carriers	Medicare	Medicaid	Self-Pay	Other
30–39	25		21		3	1	
40–49	370	5	315	3	11	5	41
50–59	82	9	85	2			4
60–64	30	15	30	10		2	3
65 and over	8	7	5	10			
Total	515	36	456	25	14	8	48

External Environmental Assessment

The external environmental assessment shows the market demand and growth potential of the MI inpatient population. These reinforcing data have been presented previously in more detail with the submission of the long-range facilities modernization proposal. The factors that are significant for the proposed CICU are presented here.

Competition

Historically, and because it is a designated trauma center, the Medical Center attracts approximately one third of its intensive care patients from the region. This is also the case with the MI population. Until the long-range facility modernization program is underway, the objective is to retain the current market share in an environment of slow growth. It is anticipated that the Medical Center will retain the market share from the regional referrals because of the cardiology marketing efforts there. The concern, at present, is to remain in a competitive position with nearby Sommerford General Hospital, which also admits MI patients from communities surrounding the two hospitals.

Although the market share data indicate that Sommerford General Hospital has a census of six coronary inpatients, the hospital claims 4 nondedicated coronary beds in a general 12-bed medical/surgical intensive care unit. Plans for a 20-bed intensive care unit with dedicated coronary beds are underway, and construction will begin within the next year. It is anticipated that Sommerford will begin regional marketing once the new unit is finished.

Table A-3 shows the five-year market share trends in coronary inpatient services of the Medical Center and Sommerford. The patient days at Sommerford have remained relatively stable over the past five years. However, the total available market and market shares have not. The data show that the total available market has increased and that the market share of the

Table A-3 Five-Year Coronary Care Unit Market Share Analysis

Year	Patient Days SGH*	Market Share (%)	Patient Days STMC**	Market Share (%)	Total Available Market
1	2,559	54	2,190	46	4,749
2	2,565	51	2,540	49	5,105
3	2,422	43	3,216	57	5,638
4	2,516	43	3,425	57	5,941
5	2,407	39	3,857	61	6,264

*Sommerford General Hospital.
**St. Theresa's Medical Center.

Medical Center has increased. This increase is due primarily to the number of regional referrals and the regional marketing of the cardiologists, which began in year 2.

Price Competition

The advertised per diem charge for the coronary intensive service at Sommerford is $950 in comparison with $1,200 per diem at the Medical Center. The charge difference reflects the fact that separate charges exist at Sommerford for a variety of specialized equipment. Therefore, the Medical Center is price competitive with the competing hospital.

Technology, Innovation, and Life Cycle

Although pharmacological advances, such as the clot-resolving enzymes Alteplace and streptokinase, have altered the course of MI, the course of hospitalization remains relatively unchanged. Patients receiving these pharmacotherapeutics will still be hospitalized for monitoring and observation. Additionally, not every patient is a candidate for the enzyme therapy. However, the impact of Alteplace and streptokinase may ultimately be a decrease in the number of bypass surgery procedures performed.

Although special interest groups continue to concentrate on public education to decrease the risks of heart attack, the fact remains that in 1986, the leading causes of death in the United States were major cardiovascular diseases and diseases of the heart, with ischemic heart disease and MI ranking first and second, respectively, within diseases of the heart.[1] Therefore, the life cycle of the CICU as well as the CCU in terms of total market is not expected to be affected by known technological and medical advances.

Implications of Environmental Assessments

The strengths of the Medical Center in establishing this proposed unit are

- an existing, well-established, reputable cardiology group who is loyal to the Medical Center
- an already established, technologically updated CCU
- a cardiovascular clinical nurse specialist
- a sufficient supply of nurses interested in cardiology
- excellent support services

Identified weaknesses include

- limited expansion potential in the CCU until the long-range plan is implemented
- a long-range modernization plan that is five years away
- potential inadequate supply of nurses in a nationwide shortage

Identified opportunities are

- to expand and retain the current census
- to develop a larger specialized cardiology team in preparation for the long-range plan
- to standardize the care given to cardiology patients, thus improving the service and its marketability and competitiveness

Threats include

- continued loss of patient days because of deferment to other centers
- fragmented care because of the continued use of the MICU for coronary patients
- loss of market share because of the new unit planned at Sommerford
- loss of market share because of credibility problems in the region

The threats and the potential losses magnify the need to implement this plan in the immediate future. The strengths of the Medical Center show the ease with which the program can be implemented, and the opportunities are lucrative enough to offset the few identified weaknesses.

MARKETING OBJECTIVES

As previously discussed, the objective is to establish a CICU in order

- to eliminate the use of the MICU for admitting MI patients
- to eliminate the diversion of patients to other centers
- to retain a market share by promoting the CICU as an improvement in services to the present user groups

Achievement of the objectives will be determined by monitoring and analyzing

- number of patients diverted to other hospitals
- census levels in the CCU and CICU
- patient population in the MICU
- market share data
- physician and patient satisfaction levels

Exhibit A-2 shows a time table for the implementation of the major ob-

Exhibit A-2 Timetable of Events

Event	Completion Date	Responsible Party
Approval of the plan	June	Board of Directors
Renovation begins	July	Medical Center Construction
Ordering of equipment	July	Purchasing
Hiring of nurse manager	August	VP Nursing
Development of unit policies and procedures	September	Nurse manager
Hiring of nursing staff	October	Nurse manager
Education of nursing staff	November December	Clinical nurse specialist
Promotion of unit	November December	Marketing, PR, and project team*
Development of unit standards	December	Nursing staff
Completion of renovation	January	Medical center construction
Opening of unit	February	Nursing staff

*Project team: VP Nursing, Director of Critical Care, Director of Cardiology, nurse managers (CCU, CICU), clinical specialist, marketing coordinator, planning coordinator, PR representative, and construction coordinator.

jective. The project team will develop detailed subobjectives with exact dates.

ORGANIZATION

The proposed unit will be under the medical direction of the Director of Cardiology, who reports to the Chief of Medicine. The nursing management will consist of a unit nurse manager, who reports to the Vice President of Nursing. Policies, procedures, standards of care, and education will be planned and implemented by nursing management and staff and the medical director. The clinical nurse specialist assigned to the unit, who reports to the Vice President of Nursing, will coordinate the education of staff and patients.

MARKETING PLAN

The patient population will consist of post-MI patients, patients with unstable angina, and patients with arrhythmias not diagnosed. Other patients will be admitted to the unit upon the recommendation of the medical director.

The benefit to patients is participation in a progressive stage of care in a monitored primary care environment that is family and wellness oriented. The benefit to the hospital is improved and upgraded care to this segment of the patient population.

The target market is patients of physicians on staff with the listed diagnoses in surrounding communities and the trauma region from which the Medical Center draws patients.

Consistent with the designation of *trauma center* and *regional referral center,* the positioning of the unit is that it is an expansion service for improved care in the already existing Heart Center, which is recognized as a leader in the specialty in the southern half of the state.

Promotion strategies will be directed to the source of referrals, which is the internists of the various hospitals within the region. Direct mail and personal contact by cardiologists here will be the methods of promotion.

The charge structure will be under that of the CCU and over that of the general unit. The benefit to the patient is having a more definite course of hospitalization and, therefore, a more predictable total charge.

FINANCIAL PROJECTIONS

Financial projections include start-up costs and pro forma statements for three years. Because census is not predicted to increase measurably in the next three years, increases in cost and charges represent consumer price index increases as well as area wage rate increases.

Start-Up Costs

The start-up costs include the cost of the equipment, the construction costs, and the operational costs. Exhibit A-3 shows these in detail. Totally, the start-up costs are projected at $412,531. This amount is easily recoverable in operating revenue considering the number of patients who were diverted to other hospitals in the last year as well as those who were transferred to the general units earlier than usual. Bedside monitors are requested in order to expand the CCU prior to the implementation of the long-range plan in the event that growth trends continue upward.

Staffing and Salary Projections

In Table A-4, the hours per patient day of 12 includes all staff except the nurse manager and the clinical specialists. The fixed staff are those who are least likely to be affected by the unit census. In other words, if the census declines, minimal staffing will still consist of a nurse manager,

Exhibit A-3 Start-Up Costs for CICU

Capital expenditures	
Central station monitoring equipment	$ 55,458
Bedside monitors (10)	122,088
Computer	120,000
Antenna	2,500
Total	$300,046
Operational expenditures	
Education program for nurses	$ 6,580
Biomedical education	2,500
Repair kits, parts, and diagnostic testing	9,233
Service contract (1 year)	10,172
Total	$28,485
Construction expenditures	
Nursing station and conference space	$ 80,000
Revision in patient call system	4,000
Total	$ 84,000
Grand Total	$412,531

Table A-4 Staffing and Salary Projections

Category	Number FTE	Salaries Year 1	Salaries Year 2	Salaries Year 3
Fixed				
Nurse manager	1	$ 38,000	$ 39,900	$ 41,895
Clinical specialist	1	34,000	35,700	37,485
Unit secretaries	2.8	46,592	48,223	49,911
RN	4.2	122,304	126,584	131,015
Total	9	240,896	250,407	260,306
Variable (RN)	14	407,680	421,948	436,717
Total	32	$648,576	$672,355	$697,023

HPPD = 12
Average RN salary = $29,120.
Average RN increases = 3.5%.
Average unit secretary salary = $16,640.
Average unit secretary increases = 3.5%.

a clinical specialist, unit secretaries, and one RN per shift. The 3.5 percent staff increases reflect turnover of the staff and different mixes of longevity rather than actual increases.

Revenue and Patient Days Projections

Table A-5 shows revenue and patient days projections for three years. The patient days are based on projections for modest increases in the next three years. Several alternatives are available if patient days exceed the projections

- extend the CCU into the CICU and the CICU into 4 West by including an additional semiprivate room
- revise the admission criteria of the CCU and CICU

Table A-5 Revenue and Patient Days Projections

Patient Days Revenue	Year 1	Year 2	Year 3
Patient days	3,833	3,900	3,924
Census	10.5	10.7	10.8
Gross revenue	$2,874,750	$3,012,750	$3,122,229
Per diem charge	$750.00	$772.50	$795.68

The revenue is based on a $750 per diem charge, which includes room and board, monitoring, arrhythmia detection, specialized nursing, and use of other equipment in the unit such as the automatic blood pressure monitoring device, intravenous medication titration pumps, blood glucose monitoring device, urine specific gravity monitoring device, and ultrasound auscultation device. The per diem rate is increased approximately 3 percent in each of the two remaining years. The per diem rate multiplied by the patient days provides the annual projected revenue.

Pro Forma Statement and Three-Year Projections

Projected income and expense are projected for three years in Table A-6. The medical specialists are physician fees for the medical direction of the CCU and CICU. These fees, representing a total increase over those budgeted for the CCU, are shared between the two units. Allowances for bad debts and discounts are estimated at 23 percent of the gross revenue; physical plant, 15 percent; and administration, 3 percent. Sufficient miscellaneous dollars are budgeted for the first year for unanticipated

Table A-6 Pro Forma Statement: Three-Year Projection for Proposed CICU

Item	Year 1	Year 2	Year 3
Patient Days	3,833	3,900	3,924
Revenue			
Gross Revenue	$2,874,750	$3,012,750	$3,122,229
Contractual agreements, allowances, bad debts	661,193	692,933	718,113
Gross Profit	$2,213,557	$2,319,817	$2,404,116
Expenses			
Fixed			
Plant operation	$431,212	$451,913	$468,334
Administrative	86,245	90,383	93,667
Salaries	240,896	250,407	260,306
Medical specialists	50,000	55,000	58,000
Depreciation	35,525	35,525	35,525
Total Fixed	$843,878	$883,228	$915,832
Variable			
Salaries	$407,680	$421,948	$436,717
Supplies	11,545	11,891	12,248
Tuition & Meeting Fees	6,500	4,500	3,500
Miscellaneous	4,500	1,255	500
Total Variable	$430,225	$439,594	$452,965
Total Expense	$1,274,103	$1,322,822	$1,368,797
Net Profit	$939,454	$996,995	$1,035,319

costs. The net profit for the three years shows positive figures, which can be used to fund long-range capital expenditures and other improvements. Marketing costs for the unit have been included in the budget of the Marketing Department. Physicians will be used for marketing the unit, and $8,000 has been appropriated for mail, telephone, and personal contact promotions.

SUMMARY AND RECOMMENDATIONS

Justifications for this plan are

- provision of one standard of care for the MI patient population
- improvement of care by providing appropriate skill levels of nursing and upgraded equipment
- improvement of the relationship of the Medical Center with regional referring physicians and hospitals
- improvement in reimbursement for care given
- improvement in the utilization of the MICU and CCU

The recommendation is approval of

- building and construction modifications
- equipment and supply purchases
- designation of the CICU
- time frame for development

EXECUTIVE SUMMARY

St. Theresa's Medical Center is recognized as a leader in care of the acutely ill primarily because of the traditional rapid response in adopting new technology and new innovations that represent improvements in services delivered. Additionally, the Medical Center is known for identifying its own limitations and responding in a timely fashion. This plan presents a limitation in services provided to the coronary patients, a limitation that results in a financial loss for the Medical Center and a loss in credibility, with regional systems referring coronary patients to the Medical Center. However, this plan also proposes a solution that will be viable until the implementation of the facilities modernization plan.

Specifically, the plan proposes the establishment of an intermediate care unit for coronary patients to provide specialty care to these patients in a more standardized and controlled environment. This plan will relieve the existing shortage of CCU beds and eliminate the diversion of patients from the region to other facilities.

Advantages are realized not only in care to patients, but in reimbursement for the Medical Center. This proposed unit shows a profitability margin of 42 percent in the first year.

The plan has received the full support of all constituents here. Upon obtaining signatures by the board, the renovation will begin.

NOTES

1. *World Almanac and Book of Facts, 1988* (New York: World Almanac, 1988), 810.

A Sample Business Plan for the Development of a Rheumatoid Arthritis Home Care Program

EXECUTIVE SUMMARY

This business plan presents an alternative to inpatient care for persons with arthritis and arthritis symptoms. This alternative, which is a one-cost, six-week home care program, is based on the need for a lower-cost option of quality equal to that of inpatient care for persons with rheumatoid arthritis. Also, as outlined in the plan, the benefits to the Medical Center are the following:

- reduction of the inpatient loss in cost and charges
- increase in the Home Health Service activity and revenue
- opportunity to be the first provider of a formal arthritis home care program
- opportunity to enter a potential high growth area

Because no competition exists at present for such an organized program, future strategies include the possibilities of contracting with other hospitals and seeking funding for the program as a demonstration model. The recommendation is to proceed with the design, development, implementation, and evaluation of the program.

INTRODUCTION

According to World Health Organization statistics for 1983, rheumatoid arthritis (RA), combined with other musculoskeletal connective tissue diseases, resulted in 6,035 deaths.[1] Compared with the 442,985 deaths from malignant neoplasm in the same year, RA does not constitute a major life-threatening force in the United States.[2] However, because arthritis categorically affects 27 million Americans and is the second most prevalent chronic condition in the United States, it is a major health care problem.[3] The problems are social and economic consequences to patients and the extensive health care costs associated with this progressively disabling disease.

Social and Economic Costs

Since continuous exacerbations and remissions are characteristic of RA, persons with the disease can anticipate a gradual decrease of mobility and possible disability and unemployment. Table B-1 shows the number and percentage of arthritic persons who were limited in activity in the United States between 1979 and 1981. Almost 20 percent of male arthritic persons and 21.4 percent of female arthritic persons were limited in major and outside activities. Another 16.3 percent of the men and 17.1 percent of the women were limited in their major activity.

In March 1988, Mitchell, Burkhauser, and Pincus[4] reported a study of the disability and working status of 9,859 symmetrical polyarthritic persons based on data from the 1978 Social Security Survey of Disability and Work. Some of the findings were:

- Fifty-one percent of the women and 47 percent of the men were severely disabled compared with 4.5 percent of women and 3.7 percent of men with no arthritis.
- Earnings of women with arthritis were 27 percent of the earnings of nonarthritic women.

Table B-1 Number, Percentage, and Activity Limitations in Arthritic Persons in the United States in 1979–80

	Men	*Women*
Number	9,540,000	17,418,000
Percentage	35.39%	64.61%
ALMOA*	19.7%	21.4%
ALMA**	16.3%	17.1%
1 physician visit	78.0%	82.6%

*Activity limitation in major and outside activity.
**Activity limitation in major activity.

Source: "Prevalence of Selected Chronic Conditions," *Vital and Health Statistics,* DHHS Publication No. (PHS) 86-1583, pp. 34–35, National Center for Health Statistics, July 1986.

- Earnings of men with arthritis were 48 percent of the earnings of nonarthritic men.
- Earnings lost because of arthritis averaged $6.5 billion annually.

These data emphasize the magnitude of the socioeconomic problems associated with arthritis. Disability often leads to loss of income, lowered economic status, increased difficulty accessing the health care system, and increased dependence on government funding.

Medical Costs

The total medical costs of RA in DRGs 240 and 241, which are connective tissue disorders with and without complication and comorbidity, respectively, at Rush–Presbyterian–St. Luke's Medical Center in fiscal year (FY) 1987 was $705,932 per person hospitalized.[5] Of the approximately 27 million persons in the United States with arthritis, 2.1 million have RA.[6] In a longitudinal study of 305 arthritic patients in Stanford, California, a hospitalization rate of 11.8 percent for one year was reported.[7] Based on these parameters, hospitalization costs for RA patients per year are projected at $1.8 billion. Since the government's share of health care expense is approximately 45 percent of the total, the cost to the American people in social security dollars is projected at $800,000 per year for care of the RA population. The objective of this plan is to reduce the personal and health care costs associated with RA.

OVERVIEW OF DISEASE

RA is an inflammatory disease of the joints that occurs most frequently in the fifth decade of life. The disease is characterized by joint swelling and pain. The results of the inflammatory process are often bone destruction, deformity, crippling, and disability. Although the cause of the disease is unknown, the most current hypothesis is that it is a disorder of the immune response system with a hereditary predisposition. Recent evidence shows that persons with RA have an increased incidence of the HLS antigen DR4, which determines immune responsiveness.[8]

Medical criteria for the diagnosis of RA are

1. morning stiffness
2. joint tenderness or pain on motion
3. synovial effusion or swelling of one joint

4. synovial effusion or swelling of a second joint (within three months)
5. synovial effusion or swelling of symmetrical joints (excludes distal interphalangeal joint)
6. subcutaneous nodules
7. X-ray joint erosion(s)
8. serum positive for rheumatoid factor[9]

If a patient has three or four of the eight points, the diagnosis is probable. With five or more points, the diagnosis is definite and is classical with seven or more points.

Although the cause of the disease is unknown and there is no preventative treatment, deformity and crippling can be prevented with appropriate care and patient compliance with the medical regimen. The aim of therapeutic treatment is to maintain mobility and functioning so that patients will remain contributing members of society.

INTERNAL ASSESSMENT

Part of the internal assessment conducted for the development of an arthritis home care program consisted of analyzing the demographics of the RA patients admitted FY 1987. Additionally, admitting physicians will be analyzed as well as the DRG cost, charges, and reimbursement.

Patient Demographics

The patient population of the Medical Center is the most available market for home care because of the proximity of the home care to the hospital and the well-established referral system presently in place. RA patients were analyzed according to specific demographics in order to identify market segments for home care. The demographic data included

- DRG
- number of patients
- age
- sex
- race
- source of referral
- payer mix
- physician service

- discharge disposition
- area of residence

DRGs

DRG 240 is connective tissue disease in patients over 70 years of age or patients with comorbidity or complications. DRG 241 is connective tissue disease in patients 70 years of age or under without comorbidity or complication.

The DRG system of allocating costs, which was adopted by the federal government as a mechanism to reduce costs, is based on a fixed reimbursement per discharge in 467 disease categories. Each DRG has a relative weight and an outlier day cutoff. The relative weight is a measure of severity of illness and intensity. The higher the weight, the higher the intensity and severity of illness. The day outlier is assigned to provide a proportion of reimbursement to hospitals (60 percent of the per diem rate) when the cutoff is exceeded by the patient's length of stay.[10] Additionally, hospitals may receive 1.5 times the DRG reimbursement or $1,200, whichever is higher, for cost outliers exceeding the assigned cost of the DRG.[11] Table B-2 shows the number and distribution of RA patients according to sex and age admitted to the Medical Center during FY 1987.

From this table the following facts can be identified:

- RA occurs more frequently in female than in male patients in both DRGs.
- The most frequent occurrence of RA in DRG 240 is within age range 65–80, followed by age range 25–39.
- The most frequent occurrence of RA in DRG 241 is within age range 55–64, followed by age range 24–39.

The Medical Center's RA distribution by sex is consistent with national data showing RA gender distribution to be 35 percent male and 63 percent female.[12]

National data on frequency by age groups are

- age group 17–44: 17 percent
- age group 45–64: 41.5 percent
- age group 65 and older: 40.9 percent[13]

Table B-2 shows a higher frequency of RA in younger age groups than do

Table B-2 DRGs 240 and 241: Frequency of RA by Age and Gender

	DRG 240				DRG 241			
Age Range	Men	Women	%	Age Range	Men	Women	%	Total %
1–14	4	1	8	1–14	2	4	12	10.0
15–24	0	5	8	15–24	1	1	4	7.0
25–39	1	17	29	25–39	2	11	26	26.0
40–54	0	7	11	40–54	1	10	22	16.0
55–64	1	5	9	55–64	4	10	28	18.0
65–80	2	20	35	65–69	1	3	8	23.0
Total	8	55	100		11	39	100	100.0
Total		63				50		

Total group: 113; men: 19 (17%); women: 90 (83%)

Source: Rush–Presbyterian–St. Luke's Medical Center Demographic Profile by Diagnosis Related Groups, Fiscal Year 1987.

national data. However, consideration must be given to the facts that the Medical Center data are broken into six groups and national data include only three groups. Additionally, national data are taken from the last survey by the federal government between 1979–81 and Medical Center data are from FY 1987.

Race

Although race is not a factor in the occurrence of RA, prevalance by race data assists in targeting specific market segments. Including both DRGs in the Medical Center data, the percentages of white and black occurrence in Cook County are 73 percent and 27 percent, respectively.[14] This approximates the percentages of white and black occurrence in Cook County, which are 65 percent and 35 percent, respectively.[15] Although the primary market segment by race is white, the percentage of afflicted blacks is significant enough to include both groups as the target market.

Payer Source

The payment source by DRG for the Medical Center is shown in Table B-3. The data show that Medicare is the primary payment source in DRG 240 and commercial carriers are the primary payment source in DRG 241. By definition, DRG 240 is comprised of admissions with ages greater than

Table B-3 Payment Source of Patients in DRG 240 and 241

Payment Source	DRG 240		DRG 241	
	Number	%	Number	%
Commercial	12	19	21	42
Blue Cross	8	13	9	18
Medicaid	9	14	1	2
Anchor	6	10	10	20
Medicare	26	41	9	18
Self-pay	1	1.5		
Undefined	1	1.5		
Total	63	100	50	100

Source: Rush–Presbyterian–St. Luke's Medical Center Demographic Profile by Diagnostic Related Groups, Fiscal Year 1987.

70 or comorbidity or complication. These qualifiers alone tend to skew the distribution toward Medicare recipients. However, Blue Cross and commercial carriers combined comprise 32 percent, marking these two carriers major customers of the arthritis program. Likewise, in DRG 241, the major carrier is commercial insurance, and the combined percentages of commercial and Blue Cross in this DRG confirm these two carriers as major forces in the reimbursement of arthritis health care delivery. However, the significance of Medicare reimbursement cannot be discounted. Medicare reimbursement is likely to be the prototypic reimbursement method adopted by private insurance carriers in the future.

Patient Origin

The patient origin of RA patients admitted to the Medical Center is primarily within Chicago proper and the Chicago metropolitan area. Distribution is as follows:

- Medical Center contiguous: 11 percent
- Chicago remainder: 49 percent
- metropolitan area: 37 percent
- out-of-state or unknown: 3 percent[16]

The Chicago metropolitan area includes Chicago and the counties of Cook, Lake, McHenry, Kane, Dupage, and Will.

Admitting Physicians

In both DRGs, six physicians were responsible for admitting the most patients under one physician to the Medical Center. All but one are rheumatologists, and they are listed by rank order:

1. physician A: 21 patients
2. physician B: 9 patients
3. physician C: 7 patients
4. physician D: 7 patients (nephrologist)
5. physician E: 6 patients

Exhibit B-1 shows the distribution of admissions by physician service. Rheumatology is the major admitting service, followed by general medicine.

Discharge Destination

The after care and discharge follow up of combined DRGs 240 and 241 are as follows:

1. routine home care: 89 patients
2. HMO follow up: 15 patients
3. Rush Home Health Service: 3 patients
4. other (acute or skilled care): 6 patients[17]

The data show that the majority of patients returned home without a follow-up program. Because of the nature of the disease, its recurrence, its complications, its subtle involvement of major systems, and its chronicity, a routine follow-up home care program emphasizing positive reinforcement, education, and prevention aimed at keeping the RA patient in the work force or active in society is indicated.

Cost, Charges, and Reimbursement

Hospital cost, charges, and reimbursement are significant issues in the assessment of the RA patient population. If hospitals are to plan, develop, and implement programs for the therapeutic benefit of the patients, hospitals must be reimbursed for these efforts in order to continue services.

Exhibit B-1 Rheumatoid Arthritis Admitting Physicians in FY 1987

Service	No. Patients
Infection control	2
General medicine	23
Rheumatology	54
Nephrology	12
Orthopedics	5
Pediatrics	9
Cardiology	3
Anesthesiology	1
Physical medicine and rehabilitation	1
Pulmonology	1
Family practice	1
Dermatology	1
Total	113

Source: Rush-Presbyterian–St. Luke's Medical Center Demographic Profile by Diagnosis Related Groups, Fiscal Year 1987.

On the other hand, third-party payers must be able to see the benefits of the program to patients in terms of returning patients to society as contributing members.

During the FY 1987, the reimbursement to the Medical Center for the care of arthritis patients did not cover cost or charges in DRG 240 or charges in DRG 241. Table B-4 shows the RA patient population average length of stay (ALOS) and financial data for FY 1987. The Medical Center ALOS is less than the assigned ALOS by 0.6 days in DRG 240 and 1.7 days in DRG 241. This could translate into a positive net gain over costs and charges for the Medicare segment. The Medical Center's profit margin (charges minus cost divided by charges) is 22 percent on DRG 240 and 13 percent on DRG 241. However, reimbursement, not charges, represents the true financial status of a DRG.

Tables B-5 and B-6 show gains and losses in cost and charges based on reimbursement for DRGs 240 and 241, respectively. Exhibit B-2 shows how the reimbursement was calculated for Tables B-5 and B-6. In DRG 240 (Table B-5), a net gain over cost is shown based on the reimbursement of commercial, Blue Cross, and an undefined area of reimbursement. A loss over charges is shown throughout except for commercial insurance carriers and represents a total loss of $163,298.

DRG 241 presents an improved financial picture with total gains over cost being $8,289, showing positive figures for all but Medicaid and Anchor

Table B-4 Financial Data: DRG 240 and 241 for FY 1987

Indicator	DRG 240	DRG 241
Patient days	566	323
Discharges	63	50
ALOS	8.9	6.4
Assigned DRG/ALOS	9.5	8.1
Outlier day cutoff	24	23
Total charges	$589,112	$282,349
Charge per discharge	$9,350	$5,646
Charge per patient day	$1,048	$8,764
Total cost	$460,577	$245,355
Cost per discharge	$7,310	$4,907
Cost per patient day	$813	$759

Source: Rush–Presbyterian–St. Luke's Medical Center Demographic Profile by Diagnosis Related Groups, Fiscal Year 1987.

HMO. Medicare reimbursement shows the greatest gain over net cost. Positive figures appear for all but Medicare and the HMO. Because Medicare pays a fixed amount per DRG on the basis of ALOS, the gain from Medicare could be due to the shorter ALOS. However, these positive figures are not enough to offset the loss on charges for the entire DRG. At present, the Medical Center

- is not meeting costs in DRG 240
- is barely meeting costs in DRG 241
- does not meet the costs of the combined DRGs

Exhibit B-2 Method of Reimbursement Calculations

1. Commercial insurance	90% of charges
2. Blue Cross/Blue Shield	90% of charges
3. Medicaid	Fixed amount of $541 per day × LOS
4. Medicare	Fixed amount per discharge × DRG weighted index × number of discharges. Example: $6849 × 0.9047 × 26 = $161,103.
5. HMO	$750 per day × the LOS × the number of discharges

Source: Rush–Presbyterian–St. Luke's Medical Center Area Reimbursement Schedule.

Table B-5 DRG 240 Reimbursement: Gain/Loss by Cost and Payer Mix*

Payer	No. Pts.	% Pts.	Share of Cost	Reimbursement	Gain/Loss Cost
Self-pay**	1	2	$6,907	$4,491	⟨$2,488⟩
Commercial	12	19	87,510	100,738	13,229
Blue Cross	8	13	59,875	68,926	9,051
Medicaid	9	14	64,481	43,334	⟨21,147⟩
HMO	6	10	46,058	40,050	⟨6,008⟩
Medicare	26	41	188,837	162,162	⟨26,675⟩
Undefined	1	2	6,907	7,070	163
Total	63	100	$460,575	$426,699	⟨$33,876⟩

*Numbers are rounded.
**Assumed one-half of charges are reimbursed.

Source: Figures calculated from raw data of Rush–Presbyterian–St. Luke's Medical Center Demographic Profile by Diagnosis Related Groups, Fiscal Year 1987.

From the perspective of the Medical Center, a home care program may be a viable solution.

PROFILE OF PATIENT POPULATION

In summary, the RA population of the Medical Center under DRG 240 and 241 is primarily

- female
- between the age groups of 65 and older or 25–39

Table B-6 DRG 241 Reimbursement: Gain/Loss by Cost and Payer Mix*

Payer	No. Pts.	% Pts.	Share of Cost	Reimbursement	Gain/Loss Cost
Commercial	21	42	$103,049	$106,728	$3,679
Blue Cross	9	18	44,164	45,740	1,577
Medicaid	1	2	4,907	3,462	⟨1,445⟩
HMO	10	20	49,071	48,000	⟨1,071⟩
Medicare	9	18	44,164	58,714	14,550
Total	50	100	$245,355	$262,644	$17,289

*Numbers are rounded.

Source: Figures calculated from raw data in Rush–Presbyterian–St. Luke's Medical Center Demographic Profile by Diagnosis Related Groups, Fiscal Year 1987.

- from the city of Chicago
- admitted by rheumatologists
- reimbursed by Medicare (DRG 240)
- reimbursed by Blue Cross (DRG 241)

EXTERNAL ASSESSMENT

The external assessment relative to the RA patient includes

1. prevalence rates
2. competition
3. Medicare regulations
4. legislation

Prevalence of RA

RA as a category is not delineated in national and local data. Table B-7 shows the prevalence rate of the total category of arthritis, excluding nonarticular arthritis. In all age groups, Chicago and the surrounding areas show a lower prevalence than does the nation. The difference is more dramatic in the higher age groups. The highest prevalence in the Chicago area is in the 45–64 age group. However, these rates are still lower than for the same age group nationwide.

Table B-7 Prevalence Rate of Arthritis (Excluding Nonarticular) per 1,000 Persons: United States and Chicago Area Counties

Age	United States 1979–81	Cook 1980	Dupage 1980	Will 1980	Lake 1980
All ages	122.8	131.8	109.4	103.9	109.9
Under 17 years	3.1	.6	.6	.7	.7
17–44	48.9	21.3	23.4	22.6	23.1
45–64	255.8	57.8	52.3	42.2	51.6
65 and older	458.4	52.0	32.9	35.3	34.6
Total cases	26,958,000	692,497	72,067	33,755	48,352

Sources: United States data from "Prevalence of Selected Chronic Conditions," *Vital and Health Statistics,* DHHS Publication No. (PHS) 86-1583, p. 33, National Center for Health Statistics, July 1986. Chicago county data calculated from Arthritis Foundation–Illinois Chapter Profile, Chicago Arthritis Foundation.

According to Susan Manfred, Vice President of Public Education, Arthritis Foundation, Atlanta, Georgia, there are 2.1 million persons with RA in the United States, and the prevalence rate is 9 per 1000 population.[18] Based on these figures, the number of persons and the prevalence rate in the Chicago area can be calculated. Table B-8 shows the results. The 0.9 prevalence rate is consistent with national data showing the prevalence rate for RA in the United States stable at 1 percent.[19]

Competition

There is presently no competition for an organized home care program specifically for arthritis patients. At Northwestern Medical Center in Chicago, hospitalized patients are referred for outpatient physical therapy. At Chicago Rehabilitation Institute, patients are referred to the home health department and receive whatever modality of care their treatment plan specifies.

The Chicago Arthritis Foundation sponsors a six-week self-help course for people with arthritis.[20] This course costs $25 and includes

- designing an exercise program
- managing pain
- using medications effectively
- coping with problems
- working with health care professionals

The course is not an alternative to hospitalization, nor does it combine therapies with the education given. According to Mary Long, Vice President of Government Affairs, Arthritis Foundation, Atlanta, Georgia, the

Table B-8 Number and Prevalence of Persons with RA in the Chicago Area

County	1984 Total Population	Number of Arthritic Persons	Prevalence Rate
Cook	5,270,411	47,434	0.9
Dupage	701,382	6,312	0.9
Will	332,511	2,993	0.9
Lake	460,798	4,147	0.9
Total	6,765,102	60,886	

Source: Data calculated from Arthritis Foundation–Illinois Chapter Profile, Chicago Arthritis Foundation.

lack of an organized, standardized, home care program for arthritis patients is a nationwide problem.[21] Because of this deficiency, there are reimbursement problems for arthritis care.

Medicare Regulations

In the Medical Center in 1987, Medicare insured 41 percent of the patients in DRG 240 and 18 percent of the patients in DRG 241 (see Table B-3). Because of the age-specific incidence of RA being primarily in the fifth decade of life, it can be anticipated that Medicare will continue to be a major insurer of medical care for arthritis patients. The Medicare regulation for home care of the arthritis patient is the same regulation that applies to home care in general. These regulations specify the conditions that are reimbursable in home care. Some of these are:

- The patient must be homebound. This is further defined as the inability to leave home without considerable effort.
- A treatment plan is specified by a physician who also certifies that the patient is homebound.
- Intermittent skilled services are needed as certified by the physician in the treatment plan. *Intermittent* is defined as one visit in a 60-day period or two or three visits in one week. Daily visits are approved for a short time only. Evaluative visits for admission to home care are considered administrative and are not covered unless during this visit the first skilled service is performed and is a part of the physician's orders for care.
- Recertification by a physician is required every two months. Continued care is evaluated for being reasonable and necessary rather than chronic and custodial. Continued training, observation, and teaching are rarely justified after the first two months.
- Nursing visits are usually rendered a few hours a day several times a week. Services directed toward prevention are usually not covered. Observation and evaluation are reimbursed if deemed necessary by the physician. Teaching and training are reimbursed for a limited time and include giving injections, teaching activities of daily living techniques, positioning, transfers, ambulation with special devices, and exercises.
- Physical therapy visits are approved for evaluations, teaching, supervision, testing, gait evaluation, and establishing a plan of treatment or changing the plan. The patient must have restorative potential.

Maintenance programs must be established along with the regular restorative visits and are reimbursed separately. Range of motion, gait training, and therapeutic exercises are covered only if loss or impairment has occurred as a result of a specific disease. Documentation must indicate the degree of motion and ambulation to be restored.

- Occupational therapy must be combined with one or more skilled services. Therapy must be restorative for a patient who has restorative potential and must result in improvements in the functioning of the patient. Designing and evaluating a maintenance program are covered, but carrying out a maintenance program is not. The following are covered: evaluation and re-evaluation of functioning by diagnostic testing, teaching of compensatory techniques, orthotic devices, and vocational assessment and training when related specifically to employment opportunities.
- Medical social service is covered only for problems impeding the patient's recovery and includes assessment of social and emotional factors related to the illness, the home situation, and financial and community resources available and counseling services to the patient. One or two visits are deemed appropriate.[22]

DESCRIPTION OF PROGRAM

The proposed arthritis program is a six-week program designed specifically for patients with newly diagnosed RA or acute exacerbations of the disease who are without complication or comorbidity. Although the program is designed as after-care posthospitalization for newly diagnosed patients and as an alternative to hospitalization for patients with acute exacerbations, other patients with arthritis symptoms will be accepted selectively.

The six-week program includes evaluation and treatment by a multidisciplinary team working in collaboration with the physician who refers patients into the program. Although patients can be referred to the program by self-request, discharge planners, social service, and in-house physical therapy, a physician's order will be obtained prior to initiating evaluation and treatment.

The program has four aspects of care:

1. evaluation
2. treatment
3. education
4. prevention

MISSION

The Mission of the program is to provide a structured, time-limited, and restorative home care program to RA patients in acute exacerbation, offering a lower-cost, yet efficient and effective, alternative to hospitalization. Additionally, the mission is to provide Medical Center physicians and other referral sources the same alternative for arthritis care. Further, the mission is to contribute to the cost-effectiveness and patient-care innovation of the Medical Center.

OBJECTIVES

The marketing objectives are:

1. Decrease inpatient costs in DRG 241 by $24,536 (the cost of five patients projected to utilize the home health service instead of the hospital) during the first year.
2. Increase home health visits by 300 in the first year (projected visits).
3. Increase home health revenue by 1.4 percent (total FY 1988 home health revenue based on a projected volume increase of ten patients and 300 visits over the total 41,773 visits).[23]

Although these are adequate planning figures, more specific figures will be included in the financial plan.

Subobjectives for implementation of the program are shown in Table B-9. The subobjective for the business plan includes the mission, objectives, marketing plan, organizational plan, financial plan, and evaluation methods.

MARKETING PLAN

The marketing plan for the arthritis program

- outlines the targeted markets
- presents initial research
- describes exchange relationships
- details the planned marketing mix

Differentiated marketing is used in the home health department for care of the arthritis patient. First, the service already established on a fee-for-

Table B-9 Arthritis Home Care Program Subobjectives

Subobjectives	Target Date for Completion	Responsible Person
Submit business plan to home health administrator	8/23/88	Project coordinator
Refine program content	8/23/88 to 10/1/88	Project coordinator with home health OT coordinator and other home health staff
Complete market research with physician groups	10/1/88 to 11/30/88	Project coordinator
Develop promotional materials	12/1/88 to 1/31/89	Project coordinator
Prepare proposal to fiscal intermediaries	2/1/89 to 3/31/89	Project coordinator
Present to intermediaries and selected third-party payers	4/1/89 to 5/31/89	Project coordinator
Test program	6/1/89 to 6/30/89	Project coordinator with home health staff
Revise program	7/1/89 to 7/14/89	Project coordinator and home health staff
Print program	7/15/89 to 7/31/89	Project coordinator
Educate staff	8/1/89 to 8/14/89	Project coordinator and selected home health staff
Implement program	8/15/89 to 8/31/89	Home health staff
Evaluate program by program objectives	9/1/89 to 12/1/89	Project coordinator

service basis continues to offer care to arthritis patients. Second, the structured six-week program will be offered to a selected market segment.

Market Segmentation

Broad market segments are identified within the available market for the arthritis program. Some of these are

- patients according to DRG, severity and intensity of illness, geographic location, physician, disease status, restorative potential, age, sex, race, reimbursement source, income, education level, attitude toward disease, motivation, and compliance levels
- physicians according to specialty, membership on hospital staffs, location in the city or county, number of arthritis patients, and receptiveness to the program
- hospital staff according to job title, job function, contact with arthritis patients, and degree of influence on targeted physicians and patients

- other health care facilities
- the arthritis population in the Chicago metropolitan area
- community agencies having an interest in arthritis health care

Initially, the home care program is planned to appeal to narrow market segments in order to meet the objectives, test the program appeal to the targeted markets, and refine the program to appeal to broader market segments.

Targeted Markets

The market segments selected for program appeal are based on the objectives to decrease inpatient cost in DRG 241 and to increase activity and revenue in the Home Health Service. Therefore, the targeted market is the available inpatient population of arthritis patients, physicians, and selected Medical Center staff. More specifically, the targeted markets are

- patients classified into DRG 241
- patients with acute RA exacerbation excluding those newly diagnosed
- patients with RA symptoms such as acute exacerbation in systemic lupus
- patients with restorative potential
- patients with acceptable compliance levels as demonstrated by compliance with medical regimen
- patients of physicians who are rheumatologists and internists on the Medical Center's professional staff
- staff who have the capability of referring targeted patients to the program
- medical center rheumatologists and internists

The purpose of targeting specific market segments for the program is not to restrict other segments from entering the program but to narrow and focus the market research and promotional appeal to those most likely to be attracted to the program. Therefore, the program is selectively open to other market segments.

Marketing Research

Some marketing research has been completed in the internal and external assessments. Additional marketing research includes medical record research to determine the feasibility of providing the care in the home and a survey of the physicians to determine receptivity.

Medical Record Research

The medical records of 25 inpatients hospitalized in 1988 and classified into DRG 241 were reviewed. The objective was to extract common tests and procedures performed in order to determine if these tests and procedures could be performed in the home. Common diagnostic tests were

- complete blood count
- hemoglobin electrophoresis
- sedimentation rate
- blood electrolytes
- glucose studies
- autoimmune studies
- routine admission radiology (chest X-ray etc.)
- joint X-rays
- bone scan (one patient only)

Common treatments and procedures were

- physical therapy
- occupational therapy
- nursing (pain management and assessment)
- steroid injections to joint
- synovial fluid aspiration and culture
- gold injection
- Naprosyn p.o.
- gold p.o.
- Prednisone p.o.

All patients were hospitalized for acute exacerbation of RA or articular symptoms associated with systemic lupus. It is clear that bone scans and joint X-rays cannot be performed in the home, and it is questionable whether joint aspirations and injections can be performed in the home. However, with an aggressive home care program including intense therapy and home making, patients may be mobile enough to make outpatient visits to the hospital or physician for such procedures.

Physician Marketing Research

Although referral into the program can be made from many sources, a physician's order is required to initiate the program. Therefore, physician acceptance of the program is essential. Prior to implementation, the program content will be distributed to key physicians for review and input. Additionally, a mail survey measuring physician receptivity to the concept will be conducted among physicians identified in the internal assessment marketing research as prominent caretakers of patients with RA. Further, marketing research will be conducted by telephone and personal interviews to third-party payers in an effort to determine program receptivity and the most favorable pricing options.

Appraising the Exchange Relationships

The environmental factors that are favorable to positive exchange relationships in the market segments targeted for the promotional appeal include

- the exorbitant cost of inpatient care to persons with arthritis both financially and socially
- the lack of a structured program in the area
- the abundance of nursing and medical resources in the rheumatology specialty at the Medical Center
- the well-established home health service now associated with the Medical Center
- the growth potential for the program in terms of the potential market
- the proximity of an active, well-established Arthritis Foundation in the city

Those parties who will benefit from the program are patients, in terms of lower cost and easier access; insurance companies, in terms of lower cost; physicians, in terms of more progressive alternatives; hospitals, in terms of more cost-efficient service; and society, in terms of social and financial costs.

Marketing Mix

The marketing mix consists of the product, program positioning, pricing, access, and promotion. The appropriate mix is determined by the program objective and the marketing research.

Positioning

The positioning is that the program is the first and, therefore, the leader in home care programing for the arthritis exacerbations. The name, "Rush Acute Arthritis Home Care," capitalizes on the reputation of the Medical Center. The theme, "first to serve you better in the home," symbolizes the leadership, quality, and efficiency of the program.

Product

The product or service offered is restoration of mobility and activities of daily living to persons with arthritis exacerbation. The characteristics are intense progressive therapies designed to effect efficient, rapid, and effective recovery in the home. The tangible features of the product are an individualized written maintenance program and a copy of *The Arthritis Helpbook* by Lorig and Fries given at the end of the six-week program.[24] Packaging includes nursing, physical therapy, occupational therapy, and social service into a standard one-time fee after the program is concluded.

Pricing

Pricing policies are based on program objectives to increase activity and revenue in home health and decrease the cost of inpatient care. Because there is no home care competition, pricing need only compete with hospital inpatient care. Pricing objectives are profit oriented to a short-run targeted return set annually to a fixed percentage above cost but below the cost of inpatient care.

Access

Access to the program is not an issue since the care is in the home. In fact, easy access is part of the positioning that makes the program attractive to arthritis patients suffering acute exacerbations. With the pain and the immobility of arthritis, home care is a welcome alternative that will be used in the promotion as a program attribute.

Promotion

Initially, promotional activities are limited to internal personal communications and publicity to the targeted market segments for the purpose of attracting referrals into the program from the available population. Personal communications consist of telephone conversations and in-house mailings to physicians, discharge planners, and social workers. Promotional materials include letters and brochures describing the new program. Patients will receive brochures through the in-house physical therapy and rehabilitation departments.

Publicity will include free public service announcements about the program and how to access it. After the first year, evaluation of the program and the promotion strategies will be completed with the objective of expanding to sales promotion and media advertisement through the Medical Center's marketing and public relations departments.

ORGANIZATIONAL PLAN

The Arthritis Home Care Program uses a project coordinator only for the development, implementation, and initial monitoring and evaluation. The program will be under the direction of the home health occupational therapist, who is the rehabilitation coordinator for Rush Home Health Service (RHHS). Although the program features a multidisciplinary team, it will not change the organization of RHHS. Interested staff will be selected and oriented to the program.

RHHS is a decentralized department under the direction of an administrator who reports to the Chairperson of the Department of Community Health. The Department of Community Health is under the Department of Nursing Affairs, which is directed by the Vice President of Nursing Affairs.

FINANCIAL PLAN

Baseline statistics from RHH data, FY 1988, are used for the budgetary projections of the program and are shown in Exhibit B-3. Activity is projected at ten patients by estimating that five inpatients will utilize the program as an alternative to hospitalization, three presently served in the home health will enter the program, and there will be two new patients.

Table B-10 shows the home health statistics, which also form the basis for financial projections. There will be ten patients, 30 visits each in the six-week program, with a total of 300 visits. With these statistics, the first year income and expense can be projected. Table B-11 shows the projected first year income and expense statement for the program. The table is divided into total income and expense for the ten patients, units per patient, and units per visit. The figures for revenue per patient are the charges. In comparison with the $5,646 charge per inpatient discharge, the charge per discharge in the home health program is only $4,441. This savings amounts to $1,205, or 21 percent variance under the charge for hospitalization. If all of the 53 patients in DRG 241 in FY 1988 were qualified to utilize the

Exhibit B-3 Home Health Statistics

Total visits	41,773
Total charges	$2,720,422
Charge/visit	$84
Discharged inpatients in DRG 241	50
Home Health RA patients served	3
Estimated RA patients from inpatient discharges	5
Estimated new RA patients	2
Total RA patients	10
Visits per patient	30
Increase in home health visits projected	0.7%
Increase in home health revenue projected	1.4%

Source: Figures and estimations from Rush Home Health Service Fiscal Year 1988 Patient Log, June 1988.

program, the total charges for home care would be $222,050 compared with total charges of $282,300 for hospitalizing the 50 patients. Further, decreased costs translate into decreased charges to patients.

Table B-10 Home Health Statistics for Arthritis Program Based on One Patient

	Registered Nurse Visit	Occupational Therapist Visit	Physical Therapist Visit	Social Services Visit	Mileage/Visit
Salary Cost	$20*	$40	$40	$40**	$3
Visit charge	$85	$80	$80	$80	
Program visits	5	10	13	2	
Program salary cost	$100	$400	$520	$160	
Program visit charge	$425	$840	$1,066	$160	

Visit-related program cost based on 10 patients and 300 visits

Salaries	$1,100
Mileage	90
Total Charges	$2,491

*Estimated including visits.
**Estimated without mileage.

Source: Figures and estimations from Rush Home Health statistics.

Pharmacy, laboratory, and supply revenue and expense were included in Table B-11 in order to obtain a better comparison of home health charges and expenses to inpatient charges and expenses. Miscellaneous expenses include nonbillable supplies and equipment.

Discounts and allowances are included at 10 percent of the gross revenue and are intended to allow for bad debts and discounts to third-party payers. Medicare reimbursement is not expected to affect the bottom line significantly because of the small percentage of Medicare patients in DRG 241 and the low probability that the Medicare/commercial payer mix will favor Medicare reimbursement.

Table B-12 shows a three-year projection for activity, revenue, and expenses. The increases are due to annual increases in volume and annual increases of 3 percent in salaries and expenses. The FY 1988 markup on

Table B-11 Projected First Year Income/Expense Statement for the Proposed Arthritis Home Care Program (300 Visits)

Item	Total	Unit/Patient	Unit/Visit
Revenue*			
Patient care	$24,910	$2,491	$83
Pharmacy	7,500	750	25
Supplies	4,500	450	15
Laboratory	7,500	750	25
Total gross revenue	44,410	4,441	148
Less discounts and allowances	4,410	441	15
Net revenue	$40,000	$4,000	$132
Expenses*			
Salaries	$11,080	$1,108	$37
Mileage	900	90	3
Supplies	3,000	300	10
Pharmacy	5,000	500	17
Laboratory	5,000	500	17
Books and paper	300	30	1
Promotional and printing	500	50	2
Postage	125	13	0
Miscellaneous	1,000	100	3
Indirect program share**	6,300	630	21
Total	$33,205	$3,321	$111
Net Gain/Loss	$6,795	$679	22

*Numbers are rounded.
**Estimated by 0.7 percent of Rush Home Health estimated indirect expenses.

Source: Estimations based on projected activity and current per visit costs and charges.

Table B-12 Three-Year Projection of Activity, Revenue, and Expenses for the Arthritis
Program

	FY 1988	FY 1989	FY 1990
Patients	10	15	20
Visits	300	450	600
Gross revenue*	$44,410	$68,618	$93,030
Net revenue**	$40,000	$61,756	$83,727
Direct expense***	$26,905	$40,148	$54,104
Indirect expenses***	$6,300	$9,270	$13,367
Total expenses	$33,205	$49,418	$67,471
Net gain loss	$6,795	$12,338	$16,256

*Gross revenue is based on a 3 percent increase in charges.
**Net revenue is figured after subtracting 10 percent for discounts and allowances.
***Direct expenses are based on a 3 percent increase in expenses.
****Indirect expenses are based on a 3 percent increase in expenses in 1989 and 1990 and a 1 percent and 1.4 percent increase in the percentage of Arthritis Program visits to total Home Health Service visits in 1989 and 1990, respectively.

Source: Projections are estimates based on figures taken from Rush Home Health data.

cost is 21 percent and 17 percent on gross revenue. In FY 1989, the markup
on cost is 25 percent and is 28 percent on gross revenue. Further, the
markup in FY 1990 is 24 percent on cost and 28 percent on gross revenues.
There is a profit margin of 16 percent in FY 1988, 20 percent in FY
1989, and 19 percent in FY 1990. Activity is projected to increase by five
patients in both years. These figures are based on a slow growth pattern
because of two factors: (1) the program involves changing physicians' practice patterns, and (2) sizable volume increases will come only through
external marketing because of the small volume of RA inpatients.
The one price of $4,441 for the program will be billed to third-party
payers of patients. The packaged and printed program outline and content
will be the breakdown of services used in presenting the program to third-
party payers for endorsement and reimbursement.

CONCLUSION

The implementation of the program will follow the dates and times
outlined in the subobjectives, with complete implementation spanning the
course of one year. Fugure expansion plans for the program include marketing to the community and contracting with other hospitals to provide
the same quality and innovative care.[25]

NOTES

1. *World Health Statistics Annual* (Geneva, Switzerland: World Health Organization, 1986), 256, 260.

2. Ibid.

3. "Prevalence of Selected Chronic Conditions, United States, 1979–81," in *Vital and Health Statistics* (Hyattsville, Md.: Department of Health and Human Services, July 1986), 2.

4. Jean M. Mitchell, Richard V. Burkhauser, and Theodore Pincus, "The Importance of Age, Education, and Comorbidity in the Substantial Earning Losses of Individuals with Symmetric Polyarthritis," *Arthritis and Rheumatism* 30, no. 3 (March 1988): 348.

5. *Demographic Profile by Diagnosis Related Groups, Fiscal Year 1987* (Chicago, Ill.: Rush–Presbyterian–St. Luke's Medical Center, 1988).

6. Telephone interview with Susan Manfred, Vice President of Public Education, Arthritis Foundation, Atlanta, Georgia, June 10, 1988.

7. Patricia W. Spitz, "The Medical, Personal, and Social Costs of Rheumatoid Arthritis," in *Nursing Clinics of North America,* ed. Donna Hawley (Philadelphia, Pa.: W.B. Saunders Co., 1984), 578.

8. Duncan Gordon, "Diagnosis and Assessment," in *Rheumatoid Arthritis,* ed. Duncan Gordon (New York, N.Y.: Elsevier Science Publishing Company, Inc., 1985), 22.

9. Ibid., 4.

10. Michael D. Lockshin, "DRG Legislation and Rheumatic Disease," *Bulletin on the Rheumatic Diseases* 34, no. 4 (1984): 2.

11. Ibid.

12. John S. Newberger and Geri Budesheim Neuberger, "Epidemiology of the Rheumatic Diseases," in *Nursing Clinics of North America,* ed. Donna Hawley (Philadelphia, Pa.: W.B. Saunders Co., 1984), 715.

13. "Prevalence of Selected Chronic Conditions, United States, 1979–81," in *Vital and Health Statistics* (Hyattsville, Md.: Department of Health and Human Services, July 1986), 11.

14. *Demographic Profile.*

15. *Illinois Chapter Profile, 1984* (Chicago, Ill.: Arthritis Foundation, 1988), 20–24.

16. *Demographic Profile.*

17. Ibid.

18. Telephone interview with Susan Manfred.

19. Newberger and Neuberger, 715.

20. *The Arthritis Self-Help Course* (Chicago, Ill.: Arthritis Foundation).

21. Telephone interview With Mary Long, Vice President of Government Affairs, Arthritis Foundation, Atlanta, Georgia, June 16, 1988.

22. *Home Health Coverage Provider Training Manual* (Washington, D.C.: Health Care Financing Administration, 1985), 7–18.

23. "Patient Log," in *Rush Home Health Statistics* (Chicago, Ill.: Rush Home Health Service, June 30, 1988).

24. Kate Lorig and James Fries, *The Arthritis Helpbook* (Beverly, Mass.: Addison-Wesley Publishing Co., Inc., 1986).

25. Details of the Arthritis Home Care Program can be obtained by written request to Vi Kunkle, Molly McLaughlin, and Marianne Lackey, Rush Home Health Service, Rush–Presbyterian–St. Luke's Medical Center, Chicago, Ill. 60612.

Index

About the Author

From 1981 to 1986, Vi Kunkle was Assistant Administrator of Patient Services at Saint Francis Medical Center in Peoria, an 832-bed tertiary and acute care hospital. In 1987, she was Associate Consultant with M.J. Bullock & Associates, Inc. (Chicago). At present she is teaching in Nursing Administration at Bradley University in Peoria, Illinois and is a clinical instructor for the College of Nursing at the University of Illinois at Chicago, Medical Surgical Department.

Date Due